PRAISE FOR

Balance Is a Crock, Sleep Is for the Weak

"A must-read for all those who struggle to manage the chaos of modern motherhood."

—AMY KEROES, founder and CEO,
mommytracked.com

"Like a bracing, affectionate talking-to from a (funnier and more experienced) dear friend, *Balance Is a Crock, Sleep Is for the Weak* is the perfect irreverent self-help manifesto for any working mom who struggles to keep it together. That is: just about all of us."

—KRISTIN VAN OGTROP, editor of *Real Simple*
and author of *Just Let Me Lie Down*

"Get ready to laugh out loud. *Balance Is a Crock* provides no-nonsense, tell-it-how-it-is advice and practical tips for any mom who is trying to navigate working motherhood. No matter what age or stage your kids are in, this book will remind you that one of the most invaluable assets you need to survive is your sense of humor."

—CATE COLBURN-SMITH and ANDREA SERRETTE,
authors of *The Milk Memos*

"You needn't be an office-dweller to benefit from their wisdom: *Balance Is a Crock, Sleep Is for the Weak* is for every mother who has felt she was juggling too many jobs to do any of them well, for every mother bedeviled by guilt and the endless hamster-wheel pursuit of perfection. In other words, for all of us."

—ALEXA STEVENSON, author of *Half Baked*
and creator of Flotsam (flotsamblog.com)

Balance Is a Crock, Sleep Is for the Weak

An Indispensable Guide to Surviving Working Motherhood

AMY ESCHLIMAN *and*

LEIGH OSHIRAK

AVERY
a member of Penguin Group (USA) Inc.
New York

Published by the Penguin Group
Penguin Group (USA) Inc., 375 Hudson Street, New York, New York 10014, USA ·
Penguin Group (Canada), 90 Eglinton Avenue East, Suite 700, Toronto, Ontario M4P 2Y3,
Canada (a division of Pearson Penguin Canada Inc.) · Penguin Books Ltd, 80 Strand, London
WC2R 0RL, England · Penguin Ireland, 25 St Stephen's Green, Dublin 2, Ireland
(a division of Penguin Books Ltd) · Penguin Group (Australia), 250 Camberwell Road, Camberwell,
Victoria 3124, Australia (a division of Pearson Australia Group Pty Ltd) · Penguin Books India Pvt Ltd,
11 Community Centre, Panchsheel Park, New Delhi–110 017, India · Penguin Group (NZ),
67 Apollo Drive, Rosedale, North Shore 0632, New Zealand (a division of Pearson
New Zealand Ltd) · Penguin Books (South Africa) (Pty) Ltd, 24 Sturdee Avenue,
Rosebank, Johannesburg 2196, South Africa

Penguin Books Ltd, Registered Offices: 80 Strand, London WC2R 0RL, England

Most Avery books are available at special quantity discounts for bulk purchase for sales promotions,
premiums, fund-raising, and educational needs. Special books or book excerpts also can be created to fit
specific needs. For details, write Penguin Group (USA) Inc. Special Markets, 375 Hudson Street, New
York, NY 10014.

Library of Congress Cataloging-in-Publication Data
Eschliman, Amy.
Balance is a crock, sleep is for the weak :
an indispensable guide to surviving working motherhood / Amy Eschliman and Leigh Oshirak.
p.   cm.
Includes index.
ISBN 978-1-58333-370-9
1. Working mothers.   2. Working mothers—Humor.   3. Motherhood.
4. Motherhood—Humor.   I. Oshirak, Leigh.   II. Title.
HQ759.48.E83   2010   2009051073
646.70085'2—dc22

Printed in the United States of America
1   3   5   7   9   10   8   6   4   2

BOOK DESIGN BY AMANDA DEWEY

To our husbands, Dwight and Jack,
and our kids, Harley, Theo, and Jack.
You matter most.

Contents

Part III. **The Crash**

Part IV. **Mommy Gets Her Mojo Back**

Part V. **We've Got Your Back**

The summer the twins were born, we considered our ability to hire a nanny. After a financial planner told us we were in a "slow bleed" financially with our monthly income, we decided to mortgage the house to pay for our wonderful nanny, Jenni. The following year, with finances even tighter because of all the diapers we're running through, we blew the bank on my retirement to keep Jenni around. Eventually the second mortgage on the house was paid off, and I would have lost everything in the retirement fund, anyway, when the market tanked. Not for a single moment do I regret spending that kind of money to keep Jenni—she was patient, kind, and totally in love with my boys. More important, she was a large part of the reason I didn't go completely mental the first two years after the twins were born.

—Cath, Mother of Three and Writer

Introduction

D o you recognize this woman? She's always screeching up late to the office carrying a stylish pleather briefcase, a computer bag, and a Venti nonfat latte, while wiping some offending organic material off her shoulder. By six a.m. she'd packed two lunches, flipped the laundry, negotiated a backup nanny for next week's business trip, refereed an argument over "orange bear," coordinated a service call with the cable company to coincide with a conference call to discuss the latest contract negotiation, AND found her husband's wallet.

So it's no wonder that when you greet her with a "Good morning," she either screams "Great!" or looks too spaced-out to hear you. In meetings she's the master of efficiency and laser-focused on wrapping up at 4:55 p.m. And last time the gang asked her to drinks after work, tears welled up in her eyes. Once the epitome of "tucked and belted," you could swear that's the third time this week you've seen her wear that skirt. She might not be "killing it" at work like she used to, but you can tell she's going to DIE trying.

Aaahhh. Now you recognize her. It's the working mom in the office . . . the one who either just returned from maternity leave or got hit with the brick that she's working a full-time job with a kid (or more) to raise, a household to run, and the dawning realization that she hasn't had a moment to herself for the last eighteen months. Your best friend? Your boss? Oh, it's you. You! You're the one with the Crazy Eyes. Welcome to the party! We've been waiting for you to arrive!

We placed bets on how long it would take you to lose your sh*t. We're not mean, just realistic. There is too much to juggle, too much to do, and too much to think about. It took Leigh six months after her first son, Jack. Amy lasted a little longer, but only because she was too busy to think or feel.

We know that we're not alone. Every conversation we've had, every survey we've collected suggests that working moms are in it deep. And there are a lot of us. In the United States, 24 million moms have either part-time or full-time jobs. And of those women, 35 percent have at least one kid under the age of six. Put it this way: That's six billion mornings a year where moms struggle to get the kids out the door and make it into work on time. Six billion lunches packed for the next day and dinners that have to be thrown together at the last second. Damn! It's no wonder that working moms everywhere are melting down.

We want to help. This book, the culmination of many painful conversations huddled in one office or the other, over lunch or at the wine bar, is meant to offer real guidance and hilarious stories of how to survive working motherhood with your sanity (and hopefully your marriage) intact. We cover the whole cycle, from the moment you figure out you're knocked up to the day you break down in tears because the school called and complained that you forgot to drop off Junior's permission slip for the field trip to the zoo and now he's the only one who can't go. We want you to know all the survival tricks—from scheduling pumping in Outlook to avoiding every time-sucking obligation you possibly can—including picking up your husband's socks and reminding him of his mom's birthday (yes, that sounds heartless, but you are a busy, busy woman with "actual" kids).

This book isn't about the injustice of it all. And it's certainly not about "taking it to the streets" and burning our double D nursing bras. This book is about SURVIVING, not whining. Just a quick nod to what sucks about life and then we want to light a fire under your arse in an attempt to keep you afloat.

So, why should you listen to us? Good question. We are women just like you: our whole lives we were told that we could have it all, and therefore we *expected* it all—marriage, career, child. Sound familiar? We are two women with full-time careers that we love. Women who actually need to make money and contribute to our family's financial well-being and take pride in doing so. We'd describe ourselves as confident, type-A borderline perfectionists who were surprised by our collective fall from grace, our inability to do it all, and our misguided attempts to nurture everyone but ourselves.

We don't have Ph.D.'s in women's psychology, and we aren't nutritionists, diet experts, beauticians, childhood development gurus, or life coaches, but our lives make us well versed in the subject of survival. We've got two husbands, three kids, and seventeen employees between us, and we are still standing. Actually we are finally smiling again. We've lived this book—every single word of it.

While writing this, we juggled work, kindergarten registration, karate lessons, soccer practice, swim lessons, speech therapy, child-care crises, doctor appointments, birthday parties, a gazillion play dates, family vacations, twenty business trips, and all the other stuff that life throws your way. Besides jobs and family, Amy sold a house, bought a house, and moved a family of four while writing this book. Leigh nursed her kid back to health after minor surgery, unexpectedly took on a ton more responsibility at work, and saw her career take a direction she didn't see coming. Many pounds were lost, gained, kind of lost, and really gained again. How could we possibly find time to write a book? Only a working mom could understand how we did it . . . in the cracks of time that pop up between work and home life. Commutes to work, ten-minute lunches, an hour or so past the bedtime routine, thirty minutes before the rest of the house wakes up, and meetings at the "office" (otherwise known as Wellington's, our favorite wine bar) on Tuesday nights.

We know what it's like to juggle and feel just one step away from completely losing your sanity. And even in the moments when we're totally overwhelmed, we've got our sense(s) of humor and a now much healthier sense of when to let go of perfection and just do what we can. We are mothers who aren't afraid of telling you OUR truth (and the truth of the hundreds of women we surveyed and talked to in order to make sure that we weren't the only ones!). And in that truth you will see that, YES, it is possible to have well-adjusted children and be a working mother and a wife. However:

Achieving Balance Is a Crock of Sh*t, and Sleep Is for the Weak . . .

Trust us (all of us): In the pursuit of perfection you'll lose your sanity. We've learned through experience, therapy, and many glasses of wine that you have to let go to stay afloat. We also know that you have almost no time to get yourself out of this mess. This book is here to help you, when you need it.

We've tried to keep the advice short, to the point, and practical. God knows you don't have time to read a lot of crapola. Frankly, we didn't have time to write it.

HOW TO USE THIS BOOK

We know you working moms have no time to waste. NO TIME. We get it. So we're going to help you sort through yet another to-do by helping you navigate this book in the most efficient, useful way possible.

First, we've organized it chronologically—from the very moment you discover you are knocked up all the way through those first months back at work, when you're leaking milk from your big old boobies while holding forth in front of a high-maintenance client who claims he can't find that e-mail you swore you sent. But that still doesn't tell you how to read this. Here's what you need to know:

- **If you just found out you're pregnant,** read the whole thing— from start to finish, every last word. Hell, we know you've got the time now, and it's going to set you up for Success (with a capital S).
- **If you're on maternity leave and thinking about your transition back to work,** start with Part II and read on from there. You've got some homework to do before you head back to the office!
- **If you're already back at work and yet another stressed-out working mom,** skip to Part III. We're going to give you some tricks to help you survive.

All that said, there are a few chapters that we'd suggest you bookmark and refer to again and again and again—either for the helpful tips or because you simply need a laugh and a reminder that you are not alone. Trying to figure out child care? Or just lost your nanny? Or think the day care is feeding your kid too many Cheetos? Earmark chapter 4 and keep it handy. You're going to need it again and again and again. Chapter 9 on Crazy Eyes is required reading, even if you think you're the sunniest person you know. We find we need a constant reminder of what to do in order to keep ourselves together.

If you've got life (temporarily) totally under control, read the whole book, just for sh*ts and giggles and BECAUSE YOU CAN. This book is, at the very least, a reminder of all you've accomplished (and may have to accomplish again if you have another kid).

Most important, we want you to know that we endorse any chapter skipping, skim reading, snoozing, note taking, revisiting, and out-of-order reading. You're a busy woman, and we're not going to stand in the way of anything that saves you time!

Part I

The Pollyanna Period

Congratulations. Now Where Do I Slot "Baby" in Outlook?

Delusions

- No one can hear me puking in this six-stall bathroom.
- This pashmina will hide my growing belly.
- I need to wait for my review before I announce I'm pregnant, despite the fact I'll be six months along.
- No one will notice that I'm not drinking tonight.

You're pregnant! Congratulations! The excitement, uncertainty, and joyfulness are like nothing you've ever felt before. You want to shout out to the world that you're pregnant, and you feel like everyone can tell just by looking at you. The glow or the green gills. Just pick one.

Not to rain on your parade and all, but at work there might be a more prudent approach than high-fiving everyone you see as you walk in the door.

SHUT YOUR PIE HOLE

You, your boss, and your team have plenty of time to sort out the implications of your ever-expanding belly (according to our quick math, thirty-six weeks or thereabouts). If you tell them the minute you find out, you're just freaking everyone out too early, before you've had a chance to think through your plans. Second, while you might tell your best girlfriend if something goes wrong with the pregnancy, chances are you're not going to want to share such painful moments with the receptionist, the IT department, the CFO, or anyone else you happened to tell on your way in the door that first day you found out.

Everyone knows the telltale signs that you're knocked up. The BGTs (Big Giant Tits), the mysterious weight gain, and the fact that you might be puking your way through the workday. To our surprise, these are a lot less noticeable than you think (unless you just went from an A cup to a D cup in a month . . . hello, stretch marks). Chances are that unless you work in a cube next to Uncle Pervy, no one is looking as closely at your boobs and waistline as you are. As for the morning sickness, we've noticed that very few people can spot it. You might be doing a great job of passing it off, or they truly don't care that much about you to notice. Either one works for us.

Green Gills (Your New Eating Disorder)

Nausea was the first true sign that we were pregnant. That and the veiny boobs. (The chest hair came later.) It's difficult to survive the day at your desk if you're struggling to keep the saltines down. There is also nothing as humbling as puking in the work bathroom. Humbling, and really, really depressing, not to mention disgusting.

There are a few key things about the green gills. You've got to know how to prevent and/or postpone the onslaught as much as possible. Then you have to figure out a way to deal with it in a discreet and efficient manner. Now, telling this to the pregnant woman who's about to recycle her lunch because the guy in the cube five rows away decided to go for a double dose of cologne today is a little like pouring salt into the wound. All we can say is, these days will pass for the majority of you. For the very few of you who puke all the way to the finish line, well . . . what can we say besides look on the bright side. You have less weight to lose than the rest of us.

First things first. You've got to know what to avoid and what to do if you find yourself in one of these horrific situations.

Key Hazards That Are Guaranteed to Make You Puke

Hazards	How to Deal
Cologne and/or perfume. Particularly in a closed-door meeting. Almost impossible when not pregnant. Cruel and inhumane when pregnant.	Sit near the door and escape when you must. Or tell them you're really warm and crack a door or window. Mention something about too much Diet Coke and excuse yourself temporarily.
Jobs with smells. Hospitals, schools, doctors' offices, food services, any job that requires travel off the North American continent, etc.	These are true hazards. Can you switch to the nonsmelly wing of the hospital? Not bloody likely, we know. Avoid travel? Or how about finding a happy smell? Paint it on your wrist and hold it to your face when necessary. Peppermint actually does the trick for doctors. We're not sure anyone will notice obsessive sleeve smelling but we are willing to risk it. Frankly, your best bet might just be to figure out your favorite place to puke.
Coffee breath. Gross all of the time, intolerable when pregnant.	You know who's got the coffee breath. Just stand back. Bring a pack of gum everywhere you go and offer to share.
Meetings that happen at "that time." There's always a time of the day that most of us wanted to recycle our meals.	Can you propose a new time? Can you double-book an "Important Meeting" when feeling at your worst? Outlook is your friend—schedule "one-on-ones" with yourself at the worst times of the day.
Smelly, dirty restrooms. Again, gross all of the time.	Our only advice on this one is to hold it. You heard us. Hold it! Otherwise it just might start coming out both ends.

Where to Puke at Work

The executive restroom. Particularly before the upper crust roll in, or after they go home, or especially when they are all on a trip. It's always nicer and kept in better condition.

The trash can under your desk. And then you just need to find a place to put the puke so it doesn't stink up your office.

A handy quart-size Ziploc bag. Should you ever meet the Ziploc brand manager, you might want to suggest this new marketing opportunity.

Tales from the Trenches
(i.e., the Bottom of a Wastebasket)

• •

I was nauseated for seventeen weeks. I used to tell my secretary to hold my calls, and then crawl under my desk and lie down. I kept Lemonheads in my purse, my desk drawer, my car glove box. After about three weeks of this, my boss noticed that my door was closed a lot more often and that I was coming in to work a bit later. She thought I had cancer or something. I think she would have been happier if that had been the truth, rather than finding out that I was pregnant!

Bethany, Mother of One and Attorney

I was sick for eight months straight. My car was in a garage under the building and my assistant would get me ginger ale and saltines for my "break." Every day at eleven a.m. I would go sit in my car and hide, trying not to vomit.

Nicole, Mother of Three and Communications Consultant

I was having terrible "all-day sickness," as in throwing up all day long. I was in trial and was not telling anyone I was pregnant yet but had to somehow tell the judge I was in front of that I might have to run off to throw up at any point in the trial. Well, I just flat-out told his clerk that I was sick and unable to control it and might run out. I was told that the judge would only let me leave with his permission and if I needed to take a break I would have to ask to approach the court and ask for a break or get a note to the clerk asking for the break. Good luck, pal, I was thinking. I'll be lucky if I make it to the trash can outside the courtroom. Luckily, there were no incidents during the trial, but what a nightmare! The trash can outside the courthouse was not so lucky.

Danielle, Mother of Two and Attorney

One time I faked morning sickness because I was sick of being in a meeting. I ran out holding my mouth as if I was going to throw up everywhere. It was awesome.

Katherine, Mother of One and Attorney

Coping Mechanisms

We've heard all of the tricks for staving off the barfs—saltines, frequent snacks, ginger, preggie pops, naps, etc. But the working mom-to-be doesn't really have the luxury of midday naps or casually snacking on saltines all day long. Pull out the saltines during one of those horrible all-day brainstorming sessions and you might as well pass around the double-pink-lined EPT stick to all in the room. A working woman has to be a bit more creative and perhaps more devious to get through this stage. We both spent a great deal of time first thing in the morning staring at the ceiling wondering how we were going to make it through the day when all we really wanted to do was stay home, remain in bed, and moan and moan and moan. So what can you do to get yourself through the horror?

- **Work around the nausea.** Sometimes it hits in the morning. Sometimes it hits in the afternoon. You know your body. Please don't be an idiot and try to do something important like cold-call some new sales contacts during these times. It will end poorly.

- **Know where to hide.** Under your cube, in the car in the back parking lot, in your office with the door closed, or if you can, go for a walk or sit on a bench somewhere until it passes. These are all viable hiding spots and should be used to your best advantage.

- **Know where to puke (and when).** We've both held our puke in our mouths until there was no one in the bathroom and then when we heard that door close, we let it fly. Gross! And then you taste it all day. Not recommended, but it works. You've got to know your happy places. And here's a trick we learned from our bulimic friend (not condoning it, just saying she had a useful tip and that's what we are here for). If you must puke in the bathroom, make sure your feet are facing in the right direction and puke between your legs as quietly as possible. If someone catches you, just mumble something about the Indian buffet and an upset stomach.

- **Take some sick days, for God's sake!** What are you trying to prove? If you feel that bad, get out of Dodge and lie around at home where you can moan and puke in peace (we hope).

- **Hide your snacks.** For heaven's sake, be discreet and have a secret stash of nuts and goodies in the back of your bottom drawer. Or come up with a damn good reason besides "I'm pregnant" to explain it. The "South Beach Saltine Diet" doesn't seem like it's going to cut it.

- **Have some damn good excuses.** (Just watch, these might come in handy at other times as well.) Add just enough detail to throw them off your scent.
  - "I've got this horrible flu that I just can't shake."
  - "I'll be at our downtown office for a meeting." (And then go lie down in the car or in a closet or under your cube.)
  - "I've got a sinus infection. I'm taking dry-up pills but I still feel awful."
  - "I forgot my wallet in the car. I'll be back in a few."

- "There's a package for me at the front desk. I'll be right back."
- "Ugh. Horrible case of food poisoning. Why does sushi taste so good?"
- "Had a hell of a night last night."
- "My bowels are in an uproar."

Events That Might Do You In

Forget the normal workday. Most of us have responsibilities that go far beyond the office door. An early morning breakfast to make a sales pitch and win a big deal. A work retreat that's held at some lame hotel with offensive "peaches and cream" scent diffusers stationed in every corner. We've been there, but somehow we got through it. Needless to say, the working pregnant woman MUST get through—you really don't have any other option. We found that there are ways to get around it without letting your colleagues in on your condition. True, some of them require deception and all-out lies, but here's the deal: All will be forgiven when you can finally share your fabulous news.

Danger Zones	How to Deal
Drinks after work	Order a drink. Make your way to the restroom, but do a quick detour at the bar. Ask the bartender to switch your drink out to a nonalcoholic version. "Vodka tonics" with a squeeze of lime are a good ruse, as are fake beers poured into a glass. The trick is intervening without being noticed by colleagues.
	If the night will be a long one, pull the waitress aside and explain your situation. Slip her some extra cash for her trouble. Your work friends don't know, but a perfect stranger does. Whatever.
	Say you're on "a cleanse." That will work ONE TIME ONLY.

Danger Zones	How to Deal
Business dinners, and especially business trips	Try to meet them for dinner, not drinks. Say you've got some work to do. You can nurse a glass of wine for HOURS. If you've already outed yourself as a hard-core drinker, you may have to bribe the waiter (see above).
	If traveling, for at least one night feign jet lag so that you can get some rest.
	Some brilliant women claimed they were training for a marathon. No late nights, long stretches of time to yourself—so what if no one has actually seen you in running gear.
Networking events	Easy to slip away for a moment and order a cranberry with tonic with the oh-so-important squeeze of lime.
	Be nimble and speed-date your way through the event. No one will be around you long enough to notice.
	Or skip them!

Dumb-ass Moves to Avoid

Boobs and barf may be hard to avoid. But there are some things that you can control. Or at least give it a world-class effort.

- **Never take a pregnancy test at work.** We can't believe we need to say this, but we've seen it happen several times! We know you feel that you can't wait because it's SOOOO important. Wait. Let this be your first test on learning maternal patience. There will be many, many opportunities, but this is your first. Seeing a colleague bound out of the loo with pee-stained pumps and a positive pregnancy test in hand is just gross.
- **Don't start scheduling lots of doctor's appointments in the middle of the day.** Go for the beginning of the day (when

doctors are generally on time) or at the end when you can minimize the interruptions. The trick is to not announce to all that you're going to yet another doctor's appointment. Get creative and don't be so obvious. Make up a home renovation project, a busted water main, or something, anything. "I'm going on a job interview" is almost better than yet another "doctor's appointment."

- **Don't fall asleep at work.** This can be difficult to avoid. You're so tired and sleepy and completely incapable of concentrating for more than just a few minutes in a row. If you have the luxury (read: no other kids), go to bed as soon as you get home from work and sleep through the weekends during these early weeks.

- **Try not to let the hormones get the best of you while at work.** It's hard to maintain your professionalism when you're bawling over the fact that you forgot to print in color. Ladies, hold it together. There is never an occasion to cry at the office. Unless someone has died, we just can't sanction it.

Abducted by Hormones

The true sign that I was abducted by hormones was when I started crying while watching My Big Fat Greek Wedding. *I did not start crying during one of the emotional parts. No! That would have been too logical. I started crying when the guy pretends to walk downstairs while she's sitting in her office watching him through the window. Remember that part? Of course you don't because it was NOT emotional or moving in any way. I was sobbing uncontrollably! It was the beginning of the end for me. I was an emotional wreck the entire pregnancy. I learned to leave the room or tune out from the discussion so as to not repeat the experience at work.*

—Amy

● ●

Pregnancy stupidity was a huge problem. I have many examples (sadly) but my favorite is the time when I was leaving for work in the morning and needed to take the garbage out. When I arrived at the office I looked at the passenger seat where my purse should be, only to find a large kitchen Hefty bag. I had thrown my purse down the apartment garbage chute and had taken the trash to work with me! My brain has never fully recovered—can't believe someone actually hired me.

Alex, Mother of Three, and Event and Marketing Director

● ●

Wardrobe Trickery (i.e., "Nice Shawl")

Every pregnancy book has a section on wardrobe—what not to buy, what key pieces are worth the investment and on and on. We are not attempting to give you fashion advice—just trying to save you from yourself. We've seen so many women foolishly think that the poncho they wore for the fourth time in a week is hiding their bellies that we feel we must intervene. The truth is that it's hard to hide a pregnancy—especially after week 10. And it's almost impossible the second time around. Hell, both of us got caught before we wanted to share our news, so we're really just hoping that you have better luck than we do.

So let's get to it. Some of us are blessed with bodies that don't POP a belly until the eighth month, and some of us look pregnant when we wake up the morning after. If you're trying to hide it between weeks 12 through 20, you'll need some wardrobe trickery. We all know that woman who tried in vain to mask her belly well past the day it made sense. And then there are the examples of those savvy women who finally announce that they are six months pregnant and the office jaws drop to the floor in shock and awe. What separates the fools from the foolees? Do not change up your wardrobe and switch the style and content too quickly. And do not pick two favorite pieces and wear them ALL THE TIME. If you've never worn a scarf before and suddenly a pashmina becomes a key part of your ensemble, you're asking for trouble. Build up gradually. Start with those blousy pieces well before you start to show. Pretend you're trying to be fashion-forward.

If you need to be tucked and belted each day, you're hosed. Time to invest in some scarves and blazers. Or buy a few key blouses or a pair of pants or two in a size larger than you normally wear or a forgiving dress you can wear with a jacket or cardigan to cover your belly. You'll wear these clothes on the other side of your pregnancy as "transition" clothes. Do your best. We're rooting for you.

Key Wardrobe Pieces That Might Just Help You Out

- Untucked blouses, particularly those of the loose-fitting variety
- Loose sweaters/cardigans
- Dresses without waists
- Unbuttoned blazers
- Cute shoes. Distracts from the thickening middle section
- Lots of black with fabulous accessories

Key Wardrobe Pieces That You Should Never Wear

(If people don't think you're pregnant, they'll just think you have a fat ass.)
- Muumuus
- Pants with elastic waistbands
- Sweater "jackets" (the ones that are like a bathrobe)
- Wide belts (especially the ones that hit you right above the waist)
- Anything with an empire waist. You can pull those out once you announce your pregnancy.

Three Sweaters and a Scarf

My early pregnancy was complicated, so I just wasn't comfortable sharing my news. I didn't want to have to "unshare it" if things didn't work out. Unfortunately I stopped fitting into my pants around week 10 and went for the belly band (you know the tube top thing that you wear around your waist so you can leave your pants unbuttoned?). Sadly, it only extended the life of my pants for about two more weeks. Then baby got back (and thighs) and none of my clothes fit. Convinced my secret was still safe, I decided it was time for some maternity tops that were not too obvious. I picked up a basic cable-knit sweater in three colors and alternated each day with accessories in a futile attempt to draw attention away from my ENORMOUS boobs and growing belly. The real clincher was the scarf. Each day I would throw around my neck a thin scarf equivalent to a four-foot piece of toilet paper. I kept up this pathetic practice until 22 weeks, when I confidently announced, "I'm pregnant!" to my team. They all burst into laughter, given that they'd figured it out a good three months before and gossiped about it freely. Three and a half years later I'm still getting ribbed about my UGLY cable-knit sweaters and my sad little scarf.

—Leigh

DROPPING THE BOMB

OK. It's finally time to share the good news with your boss. Either you finally exceeded the constraints of the belly band, the test results came in OK, or your boss has finally stopped freaking out about that big report that you turned in last week. Obviously, your boss can't hear the news from Suzy in accounting before she hears it from you. That's a hell of a bomb to hear through the grapevine and you'll NEVER be forgiven for that transgression. It's your job to make sure your boss hears it from you first. If she doesn't hear it from you, it's guaranteed to make her feel like she can't trust you, even if you swear on a Bible that you'll be back after leave.

As for the message, it should be as straightforward as possible. No need to hem and haw. We don't care how nice your boss is or how many kids she has . . . Despite the fact that she's said, "Congratulations" and "That's the best news ever!" your boss is also thinking, "OMG, now I've got to deal with this?!" By the time you've blabbed on about how you're at this certain stage in life and you've long been feeling that there's something missing blah, blah, blah, your boss has got it figured out and is already prepping questions that you may or may not be prepared to answer.

So how and when do you tell your boss that you are with child and will therefore be going to more doctor's appointments than you ever thought possible and then be GONE for anywhere from six weeks to six months? Put yourself in your boss's shoes. Don't do it when she is liable to FREAK out. Potential freak-out times include particularly stressful periods of work or when someone else just quit. You know your work situation and your boss. You've got to be able to pick your moment.

Now, there's a school of thought that says you should never announce a pregnancy right before reviews or bonuses. Your boss will assume that you don't (or won't) have it all together and end up either docking you on performance or docking you on cold, hard cash. No matter how insensitive or boorish your boss is, never fear, it's illegal for your employer to discriminate (i.e., you won't be fired or have your pay docked just because you're asking for maternity leave). If you are fired, well, call your lawyer and start planning for a windfall. If you're talking goals, it might be a fabulous time to tell your boss that the annual sales goal might have to change since you won't be there for a good portion of the year.

If you are getting a bonus payment with your review, some words of wisdom . . . Those bonus payments are often not only for a job well done, but a "Hey, thanks, and we really want to keep you around." If your boss even suspects for a moment that you might not be coming back after you have the kid, you might be forgoing the "And we'd like to keep you around" portion of the payout. That's no good. And it's not illegal. You might want to wait until after you have the bonus check in hand, locked down the promotion, or made partner before you spread the good news. Sounds cynical but unless you're into charity work, we're sure you'd rather have your raise and bonus, thank you very much.

So what do you actually say? Find time when you and your boss won't be interrupted—schedule an appointment if you have to, or close the door. Keep it simple. Keep it honest. Keep it short.

"I have some news. I'm pregnant."

"Guess what? I'm pregnant."

"I don't know if you've noticed that my boobs are huge. That's because I'm currently growing a human (ha ha). You know, I'm pregnant!" (We're kidding—don't say this!)

"As you might have suspected, I'm expecting a baby. Don't worry. I'll be working on a transition plan. We've got plenty of time to hash it out. You know how much I value my career, and I want to make sure that you're all teed up for success."

No need to discuss your maternity leave in detail just yet. Chances are you both know it's coming (unless you plan on bringing the baby to work the day after you get out of the hospital). We'll cover this in detail in chapter 2.

What You'll Likely Hear Back from Your "Supportive" Boss, and How to Translate

The Question Asked	And What the Boss Really Wants to Know
"When are you due?"	When will you be going out on leave?
"You must be so excited."	Really, how excited? So excited that you won't be coming back?

The Question Asked	And What the Boss Really Wants to Know
"Do you know yet if it's a boy or a girl?"	How long do you think you'll be out on maternity leave?
"Thought of any names?"	When you come back are you going to be full-time?
"Have you registered anywhere yet?"	Uh-oh. Are you going to ask to work from home?

Blessed with a Belly

I am cursed with a body my family fondly calls "the tomato on toothpicks." I can be at my skinniest and I'll still have the dreaded pooch in my belly. Well, when pregnant, that pooch grew instantly. I tried the best I could to adapt a wardrobe that properly masked my gut. As it turned out, I didn't do too well. A senior executive saw me in the cafeteria (at 2.5 months) and said, "So, you're pregnant, huh?" I was floored. How could I lie to the man and say no? I am a terrible liar to begin with, but I especially couldn't lie to the man who doled out my bonus each year. So I said yes, and then had to literally run down and tell my boss before he did. Their offices were next to each other and I was CONFIDENT he would not be keeping this news a secret. It wasn't the graceful delivery I'd hoped for.

—Amy

Bob and Weave

There are a few questions that have only one answer and others you should not answer because you don't know the answer. You might think you know the answer, but you don't. And committing now only backs you into a corner from which you may desperately want to claw your way out of later. Think about your answers. We've both regretted some things we committed to prior to realizing how much we would value our time with our kids.

Are you coming back? Your answer? "That's the plan." This is not a lie. It is your plan, or it might be your plan, or when you finally sit down and think about a plan, this could be part of the plan. All bets are off until you actually hold the baby or leave the kid in someone else's arms while you take off for work. But there's no point in saying that you're thinking about not coming back. That's telling your boss, "I'm going to be checking out so please don't count on me, don't give me any cool new projects, and I'm kissing off any hope of career progression until I've been back at least a few months and finally regained your trust." Why say that now unless you are 10,000 percent sure that you won't be back? Plus, why would you say you're not coming back now when you just might be able to collect some disability or sick time before really making up your mind?

How long will you be on leave? Your answer to this is "I'm going to schedule an appointment with HR to understand the options." Even when you're thinking, "As long as I can!" There's no need to figure this out until you're closer to the finish line. You're going to need to do some research and some personal soul searching before you say a thing. Every state has different rules and regulations, and you might find that your financial situation (i.e., your spouse either got laid off or won the lottery), your desire to spend time with your kid (you're losing your mind or you cannot bear to leave your precious darling), or your child-care situation (e.g., the fact that you can't find a nanny) dictates either an earlier or later return than you thought. As long as you have the talk about six weeks before you plan on leaving work, you should be good.

Are you still interested in submitting your name for that promotion? The only answer on this one is "Hell, yes." Why do we think that? Because what's the downside at this point? Keep your name in the game and commit only when you need to. Why doom yourself?

THOSE DREADED WORDS: BED REST

We've said it before, but we'll say it again. It's illegal to discriminate and just because you've got a huge belly and fell asleep in the middle of a meeting, they can't fire you. It's important for you to know the rules about how your status in the company is protected, because sometimes the sh*t hits the fan.

Like, let's say your doctor says you can't move a muscle for the next six months if you have any hope in hell of having this kid. Frozen in fear, you won't leave your bed for the duration. But do not worry about your job. You've got every right to sit on the sofa if that's what the doctor has ordered. Although we were never on bed rest, we know that it's HELL. Sitting still and stressing about the health of your unborn baby is horrible enough. Add daytime soap operas on top of it, and you've got the recipe for a total mental breakdown. It's not the smooth exit that you anticipated, but the first priority is your health and the health of your child. Every HR department worth its salt is going to back you up on this one, despite the fact that your boss is freaking out. The Americans with Disabilities Act is your friend here. When you're experiencing a complicated pregnancy, you're officially disabled.

If you really are feeling fine and your doctor will approve it, you can ease the concerns of your boss, stop your brain from atrophying, and keep the vacation and sick time accruing by doing e-mail and conference calls from the comfort of your sofa. You, your doctor, and your boss will all want to make sure that you've got the medical OK (in writing) to do this.

WHILE YOU'RE SURFING
THE WORLD WIDE INTERCOM

We know your secret. When you've got a few minutes at work, you're tracking every embryonic milestone on the Web. Better yet, you've signed up for the daily e-mail from BabyCenter and all that heart-warming commentary about your little almond. (Oh, now it's the size of a plum, and now it's an apple, and now it's an eggplant! Really? How fascinating.) Although titillating, we're going to give you a few things to do that might save your butt later.

Start researching child care. You heard us. Start now. See the chapter on child care for everything you're going to need to figure out. It's overwhelming, so maybe have a nonalcoholic beer first. You can pretend that it's taking the edge off.

Get your supplies ready. This is your opportunity to stock up on all of the paraphernalia that no one tells you you're going to need . . . The maxi-pads that don't look like Depends, the gazillion baby supplies that aren't cute enough for a registry, and on and on. Start your online shopping now. For a working mom there is no such thing as "It's too early" or "I'll have time for that later."

Be self-indulgent. This is it, the last moments where you actually come first. You're huge, your husband should be answering to your every beck and call, and you've got no other obligation than to percolate that kid. So take care of yourself and demand that someone get you some cookies.

Whether You Like It or Not, These First Few Months Set the Tone for the Rest of Your Life!

Ladies, you are about to become working mothers. If you can announce your pregnancy on your own terms and establish the precedent that balances your family needs with your career, you're headed for success. Dropping bombs or overworking yourself to the point of exhaustion does not bode well for the future. Getting you out of that mess is going to take a lot of hard work, and honestly, we're really busy so bailing you out is not a top priority. Listen up NOW and we'll all be in fat city.

CU Wouldn't Want 2BU /

Will You Miss Me When I'm Gone?

Delusions
• The last two weeks of work will be a cakewalk. • I will find time to prepare for the baby despite the fifty-hour-a-week work schedule. • My boss and team are completely ready for life without me. • If my water were to break at work, I'm sure it would be in my office. • Despite the fact that I weigh more than my husband and my belly and ass are as big as a house, I'm comfortable in this TINY desk chair.

Before you know it, you're going to start the countdown to your last day. Despite the fact that you're as big as a whale, believe it or not, it's possible to let your last day sneak up on you. Don't let it. You've got to know when and how to slow down, extract yourself gracefully, and GET THE HELL OUT.

So what do you need to do to leave on your own terms (or the terms of your baby, as the case may be)? We'll admit, like most things, it's going to take some legwork and drive to get yourself teed up for success—both when you leave and when you come back.

YOU ARE NOW OFFICIALLY "DISABLED"

Maternity leave is a complex thing. Why would anything about being a working mom be easy? Each state has its own rules and regulations, and they are always changing, and never for the simpler. It's almost impossible to keep up, but you've got to try. Consider it your part-time job to figure this out while you work your full-time job. Fun stuff.

Know the Rules

Filling out documents in triplicate and working through vacation, sick time, and unpaid leave calculations sound about as fun as a Pap smear. But suck it up. You're about to dive headfirst into the morass of rules that IS maternity leave. When it officially starts, how long it lasts, how you're paid while out, if you get health care coverage, and the transition back to work are all on the table. You need to know about all of these, and it's a pain in the ass.

Here's the most important thing we can tell you about all of these rules: Do not offload responsibility for knowing your rights and your options to someone else. Misinformation can cost you money or time with your child. Don't let your boss research this for you. Do not assume that you already know the rules (even the second time around); they can and do change. Don't trust your girlfriend who just came back from leave. The stakes are too high. Would you assume that your taxes are the same this year as last year? Probably not. The same approach applies here. You need to know the rules so you can assess your options. You've never seen so much paperwork in your life . . . really.

So what's the starting point? What's the bare minimum amount of time you could have with your baby? Well, have you noticed that we don't live in one of those countries where everyone rides bikes and gets a year off for "bonding" with their babies? No. We live in the U.S. of A. where the good news is that under the federal Family Medical Leave Act (FMLA) you are protected for twelve weeks of UNPAID leave for the birth (or adoption) and care of your new baby. That's right: twelve weeks of unpaid leave and you will LOVE it. Of course, there's a ton of fine print like you're only eligible if you've been at the same company for a year and worked at least 1,250 hours. And your employer must employ fifty or more people within seventy-five miles of the work site. That may leave a lot of you in the lurch. The Americans with Disabilities Act can affect your time on leave as well. If you are having complications, you might have the right to extend your leave. You probably never knew that. Well, neither did we. See? You've got to ask a lot of questions. No one will be volunteering this information.

But did you notice that we said UNPAID? You'll enjoy those fabulous twelve weeks ONLY if you can afford it. For many women what's affordable is only what's allowed under Short Term Disability. Even though we all refer to this time as "maternity leave," your HR department and the law consider you disabled. Roll with it. It means you get paid disability by your company's insurance—a whopping six weeks for a "natural" birth (i.e., the baby came out of your va-jayjay) and eight weeks for a c-section. Honestly, can anyone even sit down comfortably at six weeks? Let alone try to slog it out back at work?

Now, each state has its own rules in addition to the federal rules and regulations. Rather than trying to help you out by listing each state, we're going to make you figure that out on your own. Why? Because each state is different and it's going to drive all of us crazy! California (the blue states do offer some benefits, ladies) is particularly generous. Others, not so much. It's up to you to figure out what kind of state you live in. Once you figure this out, we bet that you start to think differently about socialism. Or at least you'll consider moving to Sweden or one of those other places that offers at least a year of paid maternity leave.

And remember how we said maternity leave is UNPAID? Well, some companies actually pay you for leave, but more typically, you're going to cobble together a paycheck with some combination of short-term disability, sick time, and vacation time. State rules kick in here as well. Some states offer disability and bonding time and some don't. Sometimes you get it through your employer. Sometimes it's a combination of both. Whew. It's confusing. And we haven't even started talking about health care coverage. That can be an entirely different story, and it also depends greatly on where you live and for whom you work.

Finally, there's the transition back to work. Some companies have these fabulous programs where you can gradually creep your way back in. And they actually encourage you to take advantage and swear on a Bible that it's not going to affect your career trajectory. Others make you go cold turkey. Again, you have to think about what you can afford. We all would love to work a twenty-hour workweek, but sometimes you still need that forty-hour paycheck. There are creative options if you are asked to come back full-time. Can your company support a four-day week with a ten-hour-a-day schedule? Can they give you every other Friday off if you make up the hours on the other days? This is going to depend on your company, its official policies, if/when/how they've been flexible before, the overall corporate culture, and if your boss wants to stick his or her neck out for you.

You're going to need to do some homework. We know that it sucks, but it's important. Don't you want to spend as much time with your kid as you can? Or at least as much as you can afford? And do you want to be able to take advantage of any rules that let you ease back into it once you're ready to return (without killing your career)? If you don't know the answer to that question, take our advice: The answer is a resounding YES to all of the above.

It should be clear to you by now that we're no experts. We're simply know-it-alls, and it can be dangerous to take anything we say without a grain of salt. So where are you going to go for all of this insanely important yet mind-numbingly dull information?

1. Talk to HR and figure out what they have to say. Yes, they are paid to know the rules mostly to protect the company from getting sued to death, but the side benefit is that it also helps you, the employee, out. They'll know the official policies. Don't ask them to bend the rules, as they are paid to NEVER BEND THE RULES. Save that for your boss when you're working out the timing of your leave.

2. Check in with the state employment office—a bureaucratic mess. But they will help you. Check the website. Or call. If you must call, make sure you have specific questions. Don't just call and ask to hear about maternity leave. That's a waste of everyone's time—mostly yours since you're not paid by the hour to hang out on the phone!

Now that you know the official rules, it's time to do your underground research. You are going to go deep within your own company to understand what roads were paved before you. We can't answer these questions for you, because everything depends on the company and the secret subculture of working moms. Find out who just came back from leave. Ask them what they did, how long they were out before they had their babies. What scams can be scammed? How long were they on leave? Was the leave paid? Unpaid? Did they use sick time? Vacation time? Did they come back full-time? Part-time? Was there an official transition plan? Grill them.

Often you'll find that a rule was bent somewhere along the way. Now remember, you are not trying to rat out the clever ladies who figured out how to work the system. You're trying to figure out what you can ask for. But to set your expectations, let's be honest. There aren't that many secrets and it's unlikely you'll get anyone to sign up for an extra six months of paid leave. We're talking about negotiating a week of unpaid leave to stretch it out from December 24 through January 1. Or you might be able to work things out with your boss that you can work from home one day. Small victories, but victories nonetheless.

Sneaky Little Tricks About Maternity Leave

- Save some sick time for your return. The baby will get sick, especially if he or she is at day care. Or the nanny will flake out. Or the water heater will suddenly start leaking and threaten to flood your garage. Something will happen, believe us.

- Save some vacation time for day-care holidays. Often, day-care centers follow a school calendar. Make sure you're prepared for "ski week," even if your child is four months old.

- Look at holidays. If your maternity leave officially ends on December 13, what's really going to happen before January 2? Will anyone be desperate to have you back December 14 to December 23? (All bets are off if you work in retail.) See if you can stretch it out.

- Think about your transition back. As with everything in life, no one size fits all. Does your first week need to be all five days? Can you work four days a week in the office, one day a week from home? Can it be four days a week for four months instead of three days a week for three months?

Negotiating 101

So, by this time, you've got your ideal plan in your mind. You know when you want to go out, when you want to come back, how you want to come back, and how you want to get paid while all that's going on. Depending on the company, you'll find that your ability to get all of that accomplished has a great deal to do with your direct supervisor—and your negotiation skills. If you don't ask for it, you're not going to get it. Have a clear view of what you'd like, and what you'd settle for. Remember, you want them to be happy to have you back, so be nice.

How do you negotiate leave? A few tips:

1. Know the rules better than anyone. No one can question your authority on the subject if you can talk intelligently about what you know you have coming by law.

2. Know the precedents. Remember all of those girlfriends you spoke to? And all of the leaves that have happened before you? Again, you're not ratting anyone out or mentioning first and last names. But you are going to be able to say, "I'm aware that others in the company have worked four days a week when they returned." This lets your boss know that he might be able to fight for you, or that he is going to need a damn good excuse why you can't do the same.

3. Know what you want to prioritize. If coming back after the Fourth of July is more important to you than working four days a week for a few months, make sure that you push for that first.

4. Don't get defensive or angry. You are going to have to work for this person when you return. Make sure that you're not burning any bridges.

5. And for God's sake, please make sure you have a leg to stand on! If you're the number one office flake or your performance sucks or you've been saying since month three that you can't do anything because you're pregnant, it is UNLIKELY that you'll get anything you ask for. Know that, and make sure you smell like a rose before you drop the stink bomb that you'd like to come back on a part-time schedule. Duh.

Lightning Can in Fact Strike Twice

Desperate to ensure that I had plenty of money still coming my way during maternity leave, I cashed out as much as I could in sick and vacation time. I thought I was being smart—I saved two days. I was all set to go to work the first full week that my older son was in day care, and what do you know, he starts puking. Given that I was a new mom and somewhat naïve (and in denial), I thought it was just major spit-up (never mind the fact that it completely drenched the blanket he was on). I brushed it off. But then he did it again, and I could not deny that the kid had the stomach flu. I quickly went through my emergency sick time and then began relying on the kindness of my mother to step in. Second time around, I thought I played my cards right and I saved a full week of sick time. Of course, my second child also ended up with the stomach flu right when I went back to work. (Something about exposing those kids to day-care germs . . .) Puked for ten days (that's right, ten days) straight. His pediatrician had our phone number memorized.

—Amy

Hand Over the Cash!

With all of the various state rules, company rules, and sick time, vacation time, and short-term disability combinations out there, it's almost impossible to keep on top of how much money you are owed, and how much each person has paid. We don't think of ourselves as rocket scientists, but we're not a couple of dumb-asses, either. It took all of our mental energy and brainpower to try to figure out what we had coming to us and if the people paying us got it right. We caught the big things, but probably missed a bunch of small things. We know some enterprising ladies who set up spreadsheets and did all sorts of advance calculations. They couldn't figure it out to the penny either. There's a business opportunity out there somewhere . . .

GET THE HELL OUT!

So how do you gracefully extract yourself from work? The trick is to know how to get as much mileage as possible out of that belly without being a total flake. There is a certain period of time, too, when people start to just assume that you're going to be gone soon, so they'll automatically cut you some slack. The glory days.

It's okay to do the following during the last few weeks of work:

- **Pass the torch.** Go to meetings as a participant and trainer—not as the meeting leader. Let others walk through the presentations rather than doing them yourself. You can add a running color commentary on the sidelines (thus becoming highly annoying). You need to start teaching people how to function without you. Inform your clients/accounts/customers/contacts that you will be on leave, for how long, and who will be handling your work while you're gone.
- **Miss some meetings.** Skip the third meeting in a series of twelve that will continue on well after the birth of your child. Seriously. Work will continue without you. You do not need to sit there and endure the torture any longer. Time to find a surrogate, so to speak.
- **Stop taking incoming fire.** Transition the projects and problems that typically head your way. Who should be able to handle them besides you? Because they are going to need to handle them once you're gone! Here's their chance to practice.

- **As you try to extract yourself, tie up the loose ends.** Spend time answering those long, lingering e-mails that you never had time to get to, including those horribly complex and yet unimportant e-mails that have been clogging up your in-box for weeks. God, it feels good to get rid of those. Or pass them off to some poor, unsuspecting sucker who fills in for you while you're gone.
- **Get yourself set up for your return.** Start researching child care as you slow yourself down (OK, don't freak out, but it's actually too late if you're within a month or three of your due date). Or schedule all of your appointments that you'll never get done once the kid comes—pedicures, haircut and color, dentist, doctors (not the kind who are now looking at you every week), etc.

It's NOT OK to do the following:

- **Sleep at your desk.** We don't care how tired and pregnant you are. Don't start snoozing where everyone can see you. Hide!
- **Ignore any e-mails or voice mails.** You aren't gone yet. Although you can claim pregnancy stupidity, you can't just blatantly act as though you don't care anymore. Keep that under wraps! We get it, but pretend.
- **Gloat.** Don't say things like "Not my problem" or "Good luck to you" in a smug voice. Try to act as though you care for your colleagues and give them some moral support as you gleefully skip out the door.
- **Check out too soon.** You'll be able to check out eventually, but trying to pull that off when you're only seven months pregnant is not okay. Too many women have kicked ass to thirty-nine weeks before you were even thinking of having a kid. Precedent is set, and you're on the wrong side if you think you can take it easy even before you can feel that baby kicking.
- **Waddle.** A slow waddle down the hall while hanging on to the wall for balance is not a good look and starts to make people

nervous. Can you please try to tuck in the knees? Or at least stop sighing?

Here's the key: They are still paying you. Presumably, you'll be asking them to pay you when you return. Remember that when you start picking out baby announcements when you should be doing the budget. Save the baby announcements for when they're asking you to help prep the temp who will be taking your place.

> *We've been on a few maternity leaves ourselves, and then managed through a few employee leaves. Having been on both sides of the bump, we've uncovered two indisputable facts: (1) It sucks to have to work to the bitter end; and (2) Sometimes it just doesn't matter because there's a whole lot of work to do, regardless. All you can hope for is a sympathetic boss and a team that can help pull together and get all of the work done. In our current economic state, chances are there are fewer people doing the same amount of work and you don't have the luxury of coasting up to your last day.*
>
> —*Amy and Leigh*

Teed Up for Success

No matter how insecure you are, or how flaky you get during those last few weeks, you want to tee up your team for success. If it's a colossal failure when you're out, it can and will be used against you.

When you're about to leave have some heart and set up your peeps for success. Tie up the loose ends and make sure that your critical responsibilities are covered. Is there a temp coming in to replace you? Can you train the temp before you leave? Have you assigned your tasks to others? Have you sat down with them and walked them through your responsibilities? Can they shadow you for a few meetings? Make sure that it's clear how your job will get done. You might be on your way out the door, but if they are going to be in constant crisis and cleanup mode during the next three months, you will not be doing yourself any favors on your way back.

Don't Talk Smack About Me When I'm Gone

My first maternity leave, I did something crazy. I was in the middle of building my team and I ended up hiring two direct reports and my temp replacement all in the three weeks leading up to my leave. And two of the three started AFTER I went out on leave. To set them up, I had to do some serious legwork. I wrote down everything I did, when I did it, and whom I talked to in order to get it done. It had to be good, because it was the only link to me while I was out. I handed it over, wished them well, and waltzed out the door. They did well. But that said, I didn't exactly call in to see how they were doing . . .

—Amy

Don't Try Too Hard

Now you're all wondering if you can do too good a job of transitioning your work. You expect us to say, "Of course not! Give it your all!" Um, no. You can do too good a job. Remember, your goal is to tee them up to live without you, not succeed beyond their wildest dreams, forget your name, and realize that they really don't need you. They should miss you and be really happy when you come back.

• •

Be careful what you delegate (keep some special responsibilities to yourself). I transitioned my entire job to three different people and did such a good job with the transition (pat on the back) that my boss chose to leave those responsibilities with their new owners when I returned. That left me searching for new responsibilities and feeling somewhat lost and ineffective.

Kelly, Mother of Two and Marketing Manager

• •

Are You Crazy?

You've all heard the stories of those über-women who work to the bitter end: gave birth on a conference call, broke her water in the elevator, sent e-mails from her BlackBerry while getting her epidural, and on and on and on. If you aspire to that, or if you've done it, kudos to you! You are truly amazing and your commitment to work is admirable (and we not so secretly think you're CRAZY, though we're working hard to be nonjudgmental and totally politically correct so as not to offend you, you nut roll).

But a few words of warning: Did they appreciate it as much as you think they should? And is work still creeping into your home life? If you can't take the time to relax for a few days before the planned due date, you need to have a serious "Come to Jesus" moment with yourself. Is that behavior going to continue when you've still got the job and a kid or three in tow? If so, you'd best start planning to shore it up with some serious outsourced help, a good therapist, and a few glasses of wine each night.

Of course, there are the situations where you have no choice. Either you need the cash (did we mention that leave is UNPAID?) or work is such that you feel you must, under the most daunting of circumstances, stay. Or sometimes those little buggers end up coming out before you fully expect them. Be prepared to share a good story if any of those situations happen to you.

● ●

When I was almost ten months pregnant with my second (and was due in three days), my VP boss put me in charge of our plant site for the week (think 2,000 people and multiple manufacturing operations). He was on vacation. On day one of this assignment, my water broke in my office while I was in a meeting. Felt a gusher and soaked my office chair. I had to sign a critical document about a half-hour after that, so I greeted the guy who brought the document to me (while leaking) and I was doubled over. I made him justify the document to me, and then, while almost passing out, I signed it, and got to the hospital and had the baby shortly thereafter. That guy had a good story to tell his wife that night, and luckily I've never seen him again.

—Laura, Mother of Two and Director of Manufacturing

● ●

Working to the Bitter End

I often get asked when I went out on my maternity leave. When I answer, "The day my son was born," I can always tell it leaves inquirers a little befuddled. They often rebound with "Oh my god, you are incredible" or "How did you do it?" The answer to those questions is "NO, I'm not incredible." I'm more nuts than anything, and I don't know how the hell I did it. At that point in my pregnancy, I was literally putting one foot in front of the next, hoping each step would get me closer to getting the baby out.

While I was pregnant, work was chaotic at best and apparently I didn't take enough time to look into the rules and regulations of maternity leave because I foolishly thought if I worked up until the end I would get more leave on the other side. DUH! If I'd only asked a few more questions I would have figured out that once your doctor writes you a "stay off your feet" note, you can get two to three weeks of leave BEFORE the birth of your child in addition to the time that comes after the baby's arrival.

Looking back, I feel like a big, fat idiot. I learned that there is no shame in taking some time for yourself prior to the arrival of your child. No one will think less of you and there really is no good reason to work until the end unless you work for yourself. Having a baby is stressful enough. You don't need to add your water breaking at the office.

Not to gross you out, but the only thing that pried me from my desk was a telltale biological and somewhat disgusting sign that the birth was imminent (two words: rhymes with "pucus mug"). Needless to say, after a trip to the ladies' room I was on high alert that it was time to get out of the building before I soaked my socks!

My commitment to work until the last minute turned out to be a colossal failure. My coworkers were nervous about me even being in the office (they kept asking what they should do if I went into labor), and I inadvertently set an unrealistic expectation about my work ethic post-baby.

—Leigh

And All of Your Plans Fall to Pieces

So what happens when you've got the countdown all planned out and the baby decides to show up early? There's not much you can do. Make sure that someone has your husband's number so he has a fighting chance to meet you at the hospital of the ambulance driver's choice. As for work, you can let it go for a few days. We're convinced that no one is actually going to call you given how insignificant a job can look in the face of a woman going into unplanned labor.

• •

Both times I was pregnant, I was really looking forward to the two-week "vacation" before the babies were born (exactly on their due dates, of course). Call it Murphy's Law or my life, but both of my kids came super-early, so I never got to enjoy that "me time" of taking leisurely walks and hikes, prenatal yoga, reading all the books that I was supposed to read before the baby came, washing and ironing all the baby clothes, etc. In fact, with my first child, I went to the doctor's office (on my lunch break) for a routine checkup and she realized my water had broken. She immediately sent me to the hospital to deliver the baby. I literally had to call my coworker and be like, "Um, can you turn off my computer and let everyone know I'm not coming back, I'm having a baby right now?" I was supposed to train my temp replacement that night and everything, but somehow everything works out and life (and work) goes on. I guess they both had a master plan for me. In the end, I wouldn't have changed it for the world.

Jenny, Mother of Two and Sales Office Manager

• •

VACATION . . . NOT!

Hooooraaay! You are officially on your way out the door. It's shockingly easy to leave. Shockingly! Give your hugs, make some empty promises about stopping by with the new baby and make sure you've got the e-mail address of whoever is going to be spreading the news. And, for the love of God, please make sure that your husband does not e-mail the picture of you in the hospital with the baby sucking on your enormous breast. Uncomfortable for all involved. Really.

On Leave: Vacation or Hell?

You Make the Call

Only on the other side of maternity leave, do you realize that you have some (OK, a lot) of control over determining whether maternity leave is a vacation or a living hell. Now, we realize that this is hard news to hear if you've just spent three months nursing a colicky baby and suffering through horrific post-partum depression. But here's the deal. If you're lucky, you'll get four months with the baby and no work. If you're not so lucky, six to eight weeks. Either way, you can't waste this precious time being miserable. Clear? It's all you've got, so you better enjoy it! There's no other opportunity. You must proactively take control. Feeling slightly crazy? Call the doctor NOW and get some happy pills. Kid crying, despite all of your best tricks (and tricks from your doctor, your mom, your mother-in-law, your best girlfriends, and not-so-good friends, strangers, mailman, etc.)? Get some earplugs AND let the kid cry it out in the other room. You gave it your all.

You've got to take control of this situation. You do not have the luxury of time to nut it up and convince yourself and others that the crazies will pass with time and that all moms deserve to go through this misery. These thoughts are a WASTE of your precious TIME. Watch out or you're going to end up going back to work burned-out, stressed-out, and sleep-deprived . . . Why are we being such bitches about this? Because we know (and try not to freak out) that it's not going to get any easier once you go back to work. In fact, brace yourself, it could get worse. If you want even a fifty-fifty shot of surviving working motherhood, you need maternity leave to set you up for success and, at the very least, be less stressful than your job.

SAY A FEW *OMS*

So, what's the key to vacation rather than hell on earth? Relax. That's right. Relax. It's going to be okay. As long as the kid is safe and thriving, you're doing great. Stop wigging out that your baby is screaming in the grocery store or that you might be flashing some boobie when you breastfeed while out to lunch with your girlfriends. The child is not as loud as you think, and if you just had that kid two months ago, chances are you're not back to hottie status (just yet). No one cares that they saw a flash of your ginormous boobs and pancake-sized nipples. In five years we can guarantee that you will NOT be embarrassed when you think back on the day your boobs flew out at Starbucks. In fact, you will be laughing your ass off when you tell the story.

Easy for us to say, right? Well, we both had vacations for maternity leaves—Leigh because she never passes up an opportunity to have a good time, and Amy because she learned from her miserable first experience the second time around.

Amy's Maternity Leaves in Chart Form

	The First Time Around	The Second Time Around
Nursing	Always at home or in a familiar spot with the Boppy buckled around my waist. Freaked out that someone might see my nipples. Obsessed about feeding kiddo only every three hours. Would walk around the yard for thirty minutes in a desperate attempt to stave him off.	Where didn't I breastfeed? And who didn't see my nipples? Inadvertently flashed them everywhere I went. Fed the kid when he seemed hungry. Sometimes every two hours, sometimes every three. Wondered why I stressed so much the first time.
Grocery store	Tried to go only after a feeding or without the kid. Kept three binkies in my pocket for fear the kid might start screaming.	Went whenever—even when kiddo was screaming at the top of his lungs. I needed Häagen-Dazs (and milk)!
Contact with the outside world	Forced friends to come to me for fear I might have to nurse at a "stranger's" house without the beloved Boppy. Trips out of the house were timed on three-hour feeding increments.	Lunched with all friends living within a hundred-mile radius. When else was I going to see them?
TV viewing	Decided that TV would rot kiddo's young brain. Would only watch baseball games while nursing, and only with the sound off.	Daytime TV was my friend. Discovered I got a quick letdown while watching *Ellen*. I think it allowed me to forget that there was a kid latched on to my boob.

	The First Time Around	The Second Time Around
Sleeping schedule	Never allowed kiddo to sleep outside his crib. Always made sure that we were near his crib within thirty minutes of the napping window.	What "napping window"? Let kiddo sleep wherever he could (car seat, stroller, bassinet, Pack 'n Play, etc.). No possible way to limit sleep to the crib while chasing a two-year-old around town. No permanent damage observed as yet.
Checking back in with work	Called a few times to make sure that all was going well. Came back a few weeks early to get us through the three-year plan. Man, that was painful!	Waltzed in only when absolutely required, and all my leave was used up. Called two weeks prior to returning to confirm my return date.
Child care	Checked him into the fancy gym day care and ran down to see him every twenty minutes.	Canceled fancy gym membership and checked kiddo into the nasty local dive gym day care. Asked them not to touch him. Made sure that he was drunk on mother's milk prior to arriving so that he NEVER woke up.
Postpartum depression	Mild, but told myself to nut it up and suffer through it. Wasted a month or two wigging out more than I should have.	Mild, but with two kids, so what! Didn't really have time to notice. Plus, was too busy watching *Ellen*, a natural antidepressant, to get too bummed.

WHAT IN THE WORLD DO YOU DO WITH ALL THIS TIME?

When leave first starts, it seems to stretch into eternity. Especially those first few weeks when it's a fog of nursing, catnapping, not sleeping, burping, diapering, etc. And, at the same time, it seems to all go so quickly. Blink, and you've missed maternity leave and the first year of the kiddo's life to boot. Knowing you working mom types, we'll bet that you are not going to sit on your ass for three to four months. We know that you're going to keep busy—or risk being checked in for OCD sometime around month two. Because we're bossy know-it-alls, we're going to insist that you get a few things done during this "vacation."

Like Clockwork, Baby

There are a few schools of thought on sleeping and feeding schedules for babies. Being control freaks, we're big fans of having a schedule. Why? Because when you head back to work, you need some predictability and routine. And this routine must function in the real world—the world in which you'll be working a freaking job and trying to take care of your kid at the same time. Imagine trying to get it together for an eight a.m. meeting if you're regularly nursing the kid every two hours on the half-hour. That's not working for anyone— especially you.

So here's your chance. Four months to give it your best shot and create a schedule that works once you return to work. A word of caution—it is possible to go too crazy about sticking to schedules. Those moms who are so super-rigid about their baby's nap schedule can be annoying. We know this because Amy was one of those crazies the first time around and annoyed even her own mother with rules and regulations. And then she chilled out for kid number two. Flexibility is your friend. Remember that.

THE SCHEDULES YOU SHOULD REALLY FIGURE OUT

- **Sleeping through the night—or at least minimizing the wake-ups.** We're not softies about this. Our husbands are much bigger softies than we are, so we had to get their buy-in first. Or in Leigh's case, wait till he was on an extended out-of-town trip. We let those darling, precious, sweet little things CRY IT OUT. For several nights in a row. But by the time we got back to work, it was one thing we didn't have to worry about, and we promise it didn't cause any permanent damage.

- **Dinner at six p.m., or whenever you get home.** We didn't see this one coming, but the chilling effect of sending your baby to day care is that chances are you are going to need to race home to feed that kid before a full-scale meltdown ensues. If you can, start stretching the feedings so that the last one comes at that perfect time when you can leisurely roll up, put on some comfortable sweats, and feed that kid on your own terms.

- **Waking up when it's time to go to school.** There's nothing as sad as waking up your sleeping baby only to throw him in the car seat and drive him to day care. And just fast-forward a few years, and there is nothing as annoying as trying to bribe a three-year-old into getting dressed in time to go to preschool. Running late in the morning is a buzzkill for the entire day. And it's an element of stress that you don't need. You've got enough.

For baby number two (or three, or even four), the story changes a lot. Yes, you need to get him to sleep through the night. But here's the deal. That kid is along for the ride. You're too busy chasing around town with the first kid to freak out if the newest addition is more comfortable in his crib than he is in the car seat. We bet that without even trying (for kid two, three, or more), you've got bedtime, wake-ups, feedings, and burpings down to a well-tuned science.

It Takes Some Practice

What's the one biggest panic about maternity leave? Who's going to take care of the kid once you get back to work and how it's all going to go down. The uncertainty is basically a guarantee that you are not as relaxed as you should be given that you're about to head back into the frying pan of work. You've got to get the routine down before you dive in whole hog.

How much practice time do you need? Well, what can you afford? Sacrifice might be involved but we'd argue it's worth it. In fact, we say beg, borrow, or steal, if that's what it takes. We recommend two weeks—time enough to work alongside the caregiver you've chosen to make sure that he or she knows exactly how your darling must be treated, fed, looked at, held, etc. More than two weeks is really only necessary if you can afford it and trust no one but yourself to care for your kid and want to hover and annoy the crap out of this hired gun. (If that's the case, you've got bigger problems than we can handle here.) If you can pass up enough takeout meals, new clothes, and organic milk to spring for four weeks of practice child care, you can schedule fun, fun, fun in order to get your last moments of completely hedonistic "me time."

This is also an excellent opportunity to get your darling hubby involved in the plan. Sending kiddo to day care? Have your spouse drop off the kid on these practice days. This spares you the trauma of letting your darling child go, and it gets the routine down. Once you've got him dropping off the kid, it's going to be more difficult for him to say he "just can't do it" on a regular basis. He proved he could! You were there and you're going to hold him to it.

The practice drop-offs help you get your sh*t together prior to going to work. We're not going to lie to you—this can be traumatic. You need to get the sobbing out of the way before your first day back at work. (We mean you, not the baby. The baby will be fine.) It's JUST PAINFUL to leave an infant in the care of anyone else. It's OK if you feel sad and conflicted, and if you told us you had NO worries, we'd call you a liar.

Sweating to the Oldies

Let us ask you a personal question, and unless you're a supermodel, we think we know the answer. Did you gain some extra pounds during your pregnancy? Did your old work clothes not fit like they used to? Guess what, neither did ours. But here's the kicker. Look ahead a few months and tell us when you think you're going to find the time for a daily workout and the discipline to care about what you're throwing into your mouth. You want the truth? Once you head back to work and have a job and one or more children, working out and eating healthy will be a luxury that you must force yourself to fit in. Chances are the pile of laundry, the e-mails, and the chance to relax in front of *American Idol* with a glass of wine are going to win out over exercise.

We're going to tell it to you in as direct a manner as possible. If you don't spend your maternity leave at least trying to lose the baby weight, it's going to take much, much, much longer than it otherwise might. Or it just might never come off. We're not saying starve yourself. We're saying eat healthy, take the time to exercise, and at least give yourself a fighting chance of returning to work feeling good about yourself.

I Worked My ASS Off

I'm admittedly neurotic. And none of my friends, my family, or my poor husband would challenge that. When I get fixated on something, I'm a bit OCD. After my first kid, it took a while to get the weight off, but I didn't stress too much. I was bigger than my old size when I headed back to work, but I figured the pounds would continue to slowly fall off. WRONG. The stress of work, the lack of time to exercise, and the fact that I was no longer nursing all added up to a significant delay in reaching my desired (okay, acceptable) weight.

When I got pregnant with kid number two, I was in horrible shape and still a few pounds too chunky at the starting line. And I stayed chunky and got chunkier and chunkier until he shot out like a cannonball nine months later. The minute I had enough bladder control to make it around the block, I started walking everywhere. I'd put him in the car seat, set it in the Snap-N-Go and go and go and go. I did laps around the hills in our neighborhood. And when he hit six weeks, I found a month-to-month gym with day care and religiously checked him in for an hour, every day of the week. I was obsessive about exercise and diet. Sure enough, the pounds came off. (I worked my ass off!) I was in shape and looking good by the time I entered the doors of my office. I knew without a shadow of a doubt that it was going to be a long downhill slide from that point forward. Until the kids were old enough to function without me, I'd rarely be working out—and I'd be eating their cheesy leftovers.

If people ask if it was easy to lose the baby weight, I look them straight in the eye and say, "Hell, NO!" It was hard. Really hard. It was time-consuming. It was how I spent my maternity leave. Here's another tip: Anyone who tells you that the baby weight just melted off is not only a liar, but mean to boot.

—Amy

Enjoy Yourself—Now!

You're going to be busy with all that we've loaded on you already. Schedules, weight loss, happy pills, etc. But there's something else that you must do . . . Enjoy yourself! Here's the cruel reality of the situation: You are busy with this kid and we're confident that you're filling up your days, but at this point you do not have the additional COLOSSAL obligation of work loaded atop your plate. This, our friends, is it until you're able to steal a few minutes here and there from work, family obligations, and all of the other to-do's that fill the day of a working mom.

We're not asking you to spend weeks and weeks escaping the house in order to find yourself and meditate on what it is to be you. Nor are we saying that you should find a nanny on day six and take it easy for the rest of your maternity leave. You now have a kid, and if you somehow think that this new baby is not your first priority, you're in deep denial (and we might need to call Child Protective Services). But don't panic. You are allowed to take the baby with you on a few adventures (errands) and then find some time to do basic "you maintenance."

- **Live your (new) life!** Although it took us some time to figure this out, those babies are amazingly portable. You can throw them in Snap-N-Go's, slings, strap-ons, whatever! If you want to take a walk in a new part of town, go for it and take the kid on the road. The first time you try, it's typically a disaster. All of the gear, spare outfits, and stressing about napping and feeding is enough to make you want to quit. But this is good practice for real life. Eventually you'll get so good at it, you'll be able to get a stroller out of the trunk and unfold it with one hand, holding the baby and a bag of groceries in the other, while your right foot reaches around and slams the passenger door shut. Most important, getting out of the house makes you feel like you have some control over this new crazy situation in which you find yourself.

  Here's the other thing—it took us a while to figure out that we did not have to stare at our four-week-olds and play with their toes EVERY hour that they were awake. Granted, we wanted to spend as much time as possible looking at every detail of their faces and kissing their adorable round shoulders (Amy has a thing for baby shoulders!), but you have permission to glance at *Us Weekly*. Or check in with your friends, or try a new recipe!

The funny thing that Amy realized the second time was that this is a luxury that comes only with the first child. Other than fleeting glances at kid number two, you're likely too busy chasing down the first child to have time to kiss those precious baby shoulders.

- **See your friends (and family).** That's right! Go and meet your friends for lunch or for coffee. Get over your flashing fears and take those boobs on the road! When works starts up again, the amount of time you spend with your friends and family diminishes. It's true that spending time with friends is the first thing to go. So here's your chance. If they're good friends, they'll understand that babies cry and boobs hang out, and you need to get out of the house because with *Ellen* on summer hiatus there is no possible way you could stay home without going absolutely bonkers.

And yes, that's right, we did tell you to visit family because now you can do it on your own terms. The cruel reality is that once you go back to work, every one of these familial visits counts as VACATION TIME, even when it's clear that you'd rather be spending your vacation on the beach, drinking margaritas, and catching up on all of those back issues of *People* you've been missing. Yes, it can be a pain in the ass to travel with a baby or two. ("Yard Sale" aptly describes watching our families try to stuff in the shuttle bus from the airport parking lot to the terminal. Not pretty.) But if you wait for a holiday break you're asking for it. Trying to travel with one or more kids during the Thanksgiving break gives new meaning to "living hell," especially when the Salt Lake City airport is closed for a storm and you missed your connection and you're trying to figure out if that family of five that's also stuck would be willing to share a room with you at the horribly overbooked Motel 6.

- **Find some time for basic maintenance.** What's basic maintenance? A pedicure once in a while. A haircut and covering up those brown or gray roots that you might be growing. No offense, but you're probably feeling like a fat schlub—especially that first month or two. Why compound the misery with crappy hair and ratty toes? Here's your husband's chance to step it up and take care of the kid for a while.

    The definition of "basic maintenance" is flexible. It can include anything you require to maintain sanity and feel good about yourself. We've seen definitions range from fake trips to the gym to a full day at the spa. Whatever floats your boat. Just make sure that you go back to work feeling like you've got "you" under control.

THE SEVEN DEADLY SINS
OF MATERNITY LEAVE

We're not going to lie to you. You can mess up maternity leave so badly that it's going to take you months to recover. You've got six weeks to six months to set yourself up for a successful reentry into the world in which you have a kid, a job, and presumably a marriage to keep afloat. Don't make these mistakes.

Isolate yourself. The mere thought sends shivers down our spines. We know how horrible this can be, and we want desperately for you to avoid this. You've got to get some help if the only people you see each day are your kid and your spouse when he comes home from work. This is a disaster waiting to happen, and it's a pretty good sign that you're either deep in the depths of postpartum depression or headed there within a few milliseconds. If any of the following sounds familiar, it's time to call for professional help:

- You haven't been out of the house for days . . . it's just too much effort.

- The baby is two months old and hasn't been outside.
- You can't remember if you spoke to someone other than your husband in the last week.
- You've been wearing the same pair of pajama bottoms for a few days now and see no reason to change out of them.

Pretend you're June Cleaver. Were you the perfect domestic diva prior to having kids? No? Then why are you trying now? Redirect all of that energy that you're spending on keeping the laundry under control, the house spotless, and dinner ready to go by the time hubby comes home. You need to relax a bit (see above) if you want to emerge from this leave feeling like you actually had one. The horrible side effect of being June-like is training your husband and family into believing that they can expect dinner on the table and a clean house. Sad news for all . . . Once work starts again, there is no possible way it's going to continue.

Start taking on all of the household responsibilities. Yes, it's true. You are technically "at home" while your husband is "at work." But pretty soon you will not be "at home" anymore and you're all going to have to "share" some of these chores with your better half. If you take on all of the appliance repairs, car maintenance, grocery shopping, prescription picking-up, laundry, housecleaning, Costco runs, etc., it's going to be tough to shed them when it's time to go back to work. Share the grunt work. See if you can score yourself some free time while your spouse heads to the grocery and the baby sleeps. And then you've just set precedent. It's all about precedent.

Set the kid up to be dependent on only you. Yes, we get it. You're the one with the boobs, and therefore the most important person in your child's life. But beyond feeding, the list of things that your child needs is long. Very long. Time to make sure that you're getting that little darling used to others. Make sure that you're not the only one giving baths, putting the kid to sleep, changing diapers, etc. If you don't, before you know it your two-year-old is screaming that Mommy is the only person who can make bubble bath. That might happen anyway, but then at least you'll be able to tell yourself that the child is delusional. Or just your typical two-year-old.

Let the kid rule your world. There are basic functions that cannot be avoided—eating, sleeping, etc. We've already told you that setting up a schedule is important to your success. But it is possible to take it too far. Taking it too far suggests that you aren't leaving the house and you've become annoying to all of your friends. Especially the friends who already have kids and KNOW that you're taking it too far. It's okay to leave the house and feed the kid in a spot other than the gliding rocker. You can occasionally allow the child to sleep somewhere other than his or her crib. This gives you the ability to hit the road and see friends. How do we know this to be true? Second kids. The world is full of second and third kids who have had to bend to the ongoing schedule in the house. They seem fine, don't they?

Try to save money and eliminate child care for the older kid during maternity leave. If there's a deadliest sin, this is it. The absolute chaos that results from changing up child care is beyond your ability to fathom. Yes, it will require sacrifices. But did we mention there will be a sh*tstorm if you pull the oldest kid out of her routine?

Do not pull your oldest kid out of day care, preschool, or whatever child-care situation she is in for the duration of your leave. That kid is on a schedule and is presumably happy in the routine and you're happy with the care that she receives. Changing that could jeopardize your spot, but it also upsets the routine to such a degree that going back to work will be almost impossible. You're already going to transition kid number two into a child-care situation. Why are you creating drama with the first kid? Can you get a part-time child-care schedule for those few months and save some cash in the process? Or send kid number one for three days a week instead of five days and still get your five days back at the end of leave?

Do not let the nanny go and hope that you'll find one who works out just as well. If you are happy with your nanny, you do not want to go through the hell of finding a new one. And we're guessing that your first kid is happy with the nanny as well—otherwise you wouldn't be either. It can be tricky to have two caregivers in the house at the same time, but let's think about the advantages: two people to sort through the household responsibilities together, someone to take the older kid to the park while you and the baby nap, and someone to take both kids for a stroll while you take the shower you've been meaning to have for the last few days. To cut down on the expense, consider asking the nanny to take her vacation while you're on leave—rather than a few weeks after you head back to work. Again it's what you can afford, and who needs a vacation when what you really want is to keep your nanny!

We want to be clear. We do not advocate that you sit on your ass while someone else takes care of your kids. We do believe that there are significant advantages to keeping the child-care routine somewhat intact while you're on leave. Everyone will be happier in the end.

Friday Adventures

I kept my older kid in day care when kid number two came around. But I totally changed up the schedule. I'd drop him off at 9:00 a.m. instead of 7:30 and I'd pick him up right after nap time (3:00 p.m. instead of 6:00 p.m.). I got to spend more time with him and in reality he was only spending four waking hours at child care. This gave me the time to hang out and bond with our second baby, time to exercise, and time to get a few things prepped for dinner. And every Friday we'd all go on an adventure. I'd take the kids to visit with friends or go to the zoo or the park. It was great and I loved those Fridays.

I paid a fortune in child care that I didn't use. But in the end it was worth it. The transition back to work was easy and we had an amazing summer of relaxing days and Friday adventures.

—Amy

Check in with work. We can't believe that we have to tell you this, but apparently we do. You need to let it go and try to disengage. There will be a time when you should check back in with work, but repeated calls to the office will only get you involved before you should be and leave you wondering if you even had a leave to begin with. Yes, this can be hard to tell the woman who just made partner at the firm. But unless they can take it away from you, relax. The right time to call is four weeks before you return—and not to ask what you can do. The call is to remind everyone of the plan and make sure that there are no surprises.

Now, this deadly sin does have a giant caveat. We have a lot of friends who work at companies where you can easily find yourself with a target on your back upon return. It's been a while since they've seen you, and others have been gunning for your position. If this is you, then do what you must to keep your job. We don't want to hear, and neither do you, that your job has been given to someone else and you've been assigned "a similar role at an equal level." That's code for "You've been replaced, and since we didn't see you the last few months, we're not sure if you're even any good." You might have been fantastic, but in some corporations, memories are short. Have fun in your role as the company's new Sarbanes-Oxley compliance manager.

• •

The first time I went on maternity leave, it was only six months after I started my job. I felt guilty for being away from work, so I told my boss I would come back after three months, which seemed reasonable to me. But once the time came, I realized I shouldn't have spoken so soon. So two years later when I was having my second child, I decided to maximize the time I had—after all, it was probably going to be the last time I had this much time off work in a long while and I wanted to make sure to get the most out of it! So I gave everyone a vague timeline for my return and then booked a two-week cruise to the Mediterranean three months after my due date (with the in-laws, to help with the kids!), just to force myself to take all the time that was allotted to me. After all, if you have the benefits, use them!

Jen, Mother of Two and Marketing Director

PREPARE FOR REENTRY

Eventually the day will come when you need to go back to work. It's like a feeling of dread that hangs over you for the last two weeks. You'll be having a good time, and you'll suddenly realize that this time is soon coming to an end, and it hits you like a brick. Or you'll wake up in the morning wondering why you feel like something bad just happened, and it will dawn on you that it's just the fact that the days are dwindling. Or the kid is still not sleeping through the night, and you don't know how you'll get through a full workday without your afternoon nap. Time seems to be moving at hyper-speed, and chances are the day before you head back, the kid does something amazing and makes your heart break for leaving. We know. But you're going back to work—because you enjoy working and you're good at it. Or you need the money. Or some combination, and this is the way maternity leave works in this country. So how do you head back? There are rules of engagement that must be followed to ensure you're prepared, work is prepared, and everyone is set up for success.

About four weeks before leave officially ends, you're going to need to give your boss a call. This can just be a message, but it's preferable if you can speak live. What do you need to say? Just a simple reminder of all that you signed up for before leaving:

"Hi, ____! It's _____. I hope you're doing well! I wanted to call to check in. I'll be back on ____, about four weeks from now! As we discussed, I'm planning on coming in Monday, Wednesday, and Friday for the first few weeks and then will go to full-time on _____. I've got the child-care situation all nailed down so I'm confident the transition will go well. Please give me a call if you've got the chance. I'd love to hear what's going on at work. If you don't have time to call me back, no problem. I'll plan on calling in a few weeks to see if I can get the full download of what's been going on. I'll work with _____ to schedule some time. Thanks!"

No one needs to know that making that phone call created a gigantic pit at the bottom of your stomach and you were PRAYING that your boss wouldn't pick up the phone. It's our secret. Failure to call and check in pretty much guarantees that they think you're not coming back and they are in the process of mentally writing you off and working through the game plan of hiring your replacement. Resumes might already be on your boss's desk. Hard to hear but true. It's difficult to recover from that, especially when you're already swimming in quicksand and need every ounce of energy just to fake your way through the day.

Two weeks out, it's time to finally figure out what they've all been doing for the last four months. You don't have to care deeply about what's going on at work or memorize the updates in the employee handbook. You just have to get yourself familiar with the landscape so that you can walk in without the deer-in-the-headlights look. You know the one.

If you can, schedule a coffee or an hour chat with your boss. Use this time to hear what's been happening, what the challenges are at work (who's about to quit, the imminent reorg, who's out to railroad your pet project), and where you'll be focusing your attentions when you return (best to learn now that the company has completely changed its strategic direction, rather than in your first meeting with your boss's boss). There's nothing worse than uncertainty and you'll be full up trying to get out the door without boogers on your shoulder that first day back. No point in coming in blind.

If you're fully dedicated, it's time to place a few more phone calls as well. Call your friends at work, call an employee or two, and just check in to chat. No need to go deep, just get a sense of what you're up against when you return. You can save the gossip for your first few weeks back. Adds a little spice to those first few foggy, exhausting weeks.

Let the Countdown Begin: The Last Four Weeks

Countdown	What to Do
Four weeks out	Call child-care provider. • Confirm the official start date. • Confirm "practice days" start date. • Go through expectations (what you need to provide day care, or job expectations for the nanny, etc.) Get your feeding routine down (This is no small task! See chapter 5 on breastfeeding.) Call and leave a message for your boss. • Confirm start date. • Confirm work schedule. • Set up time to talk in a few weeks.
Three weeks out	Visit family and friends—last chance! • Make sure everyone has seen the baby who demands to see the baby. • Make sure that everyone you want to show the baby has seen the baby.
Two weeks out	Practice child care. • For day care, have your husband do a few drop-offs and do some early pick-ups. • For nanny, have her come a few days a week, or on some other abbreviated schedule. Get used to each other. • Go out and enjoy yourself while the kid chills with the child-care provider!

Countdown	What to Do
Two weeks out (continued)	Meet your boss for coffee. • Check in on the last few months. What projects are going on? • Any new additions to the team? Forthcoming departures? What are the coming challenges? • Are you clear on your expected work schedule and workload? Call your friends at work. What's the real scoop?
One week out	Do something fun! • Meet your husband for lunch. • Go out to dinner on a "date night." • Spend a day with your friends. • Go shopping! At least feel good about your outfit that first day back at work. Do the basic maintenance. • Get your teeth cleaned. • Get any doctor's appointments and prescriptions out of the way. • Go get your hair cut/colored.

WORK THAT LEAVE

We hope that the message is getting through . . . This is your chance to set yourself up for success as a working mom. When you go back, you're going to feel differently, act differently and care differently. And you'll have more to do and care about than you ever thought humanly possible.

Make maternity leave a vacation. It might be the only one you get for a while.

Part II

The Bitch Is Back

Child Care: It'll Make You

or Break You

Delusions

- The kids will not call the nanny "Mommy."
- I chose day care because I wanted the kiddo to build up a strong immune system.
- I am not threatened by the gorgeous twenty-one-year-old Swedish au pair.
- Day care is the only option we can afford.
- My mom will love caring for my children each day. She's retired and bored.

We're friends now right? Good—so you'll forgive us when we forget to immediately congratulate you when you announce in the office hallway that you are pregnant. As much as we'd like to fling our arms around you and get a little misty we are, unfortunately, already thinking, worrying, obsessing about your child-care situation. You think we're kidding but, sadly, we're not. Choosing child care is a biggie even more important than those mandatory childbirthing classes you attend with your husband. Our advice: skip the childbirth classes. The baby is going to come out whether you take the class or not. Child care, on the other hand, will not happen spontaneously. There are only three things you should NEVER do while pregnant: ask anyone if you look fat (YEAH, you do!), watch all those Discovery Health Channel and Lifetime Channel shows on childbirth (e.g., how much can go wrong and, boy, does it look like it's going to hurt), and neglect the child-care issue.

We know what you're probably thinking: "Geez—chill out, you freaks, I just want to spend my first trimester bragging, glowing, and eating." Well, lucky for you, and you WILL thank us later, we've made it our job to kick your ass into high gear. So listen up, there's an elephant in the room and it's on a deadline!

Finding the right child-care solution for your family is probably one of the more important decisions you will make in early parenthood. Want a happy marriage? Invest in good child care and use it. Your choice is critical to the success and well-being of your child AND your family, and should not be based on price alone. If your husband's a cheapskate, this is gonna be a tough sell, but if he ever wants sex again, he will suck it up and get onboard. What you don't realize as a new parent is that your child-care provider becomes an integral part of your family. There's God, your family, and your child-care provider all vying for the number-one slot, and if you ask us, depending on the day, it's a tight race. For heaven's sake, these people are helping you raise your children, and what could be more important than that? A round of golf? Don't do the math, and see chapter 10 on guilt, but your children really do spend more waking hours with your child-care provider than they do with you.

The hard part, especially for first-timers, is you can't possibly anticipate all the ways this decision will impact you, your marriage, your job, and your child until you've done it and, in our case, done it wrong. Our goal is to share our screw-ups with you so you can make an informed choice, in plenty of time to help the family adapt to this new stranger in your midst. It's also to get you comfortable with the fact that your choice is dynamic, and the solution that's best for your family will likely change as your family does. The ultimate success story is that you've got enough time to select the option that is right for you, you've put your plan in place, and if you can afford it, you've built in time for a one- to two-week trial run to your return to work.

So if you've read this and sense your blood pressure going up, do a few downward-facing dogs and get over it. You have no time to waste.

WHERE DO YOU START?

We think the best way to get the ball rolling is a conversation with your spouse. We don't want to add further stress, but this little chat needs to happen about 7.3 seconds after you've peed on the stick and received double-line confirmation that you are knocked up. If you procrastinate, you will find that you might have screwed the pooch and are too late for some options. And here's why you absolutely need to involve your spouse: he likely has an opinion—ours did—and you never want to hear the phrase "Well, you picked the place." Or "She was never my first choice." This is too important to do alone, so have your spouse get some skin in the game. Then it's a joint decision and both of you are invested in the success of your child-care choice and neither of you has to hear "I told you so."

During your initial chat with your spouse, be realistic, be honest, and talk about what you THINK your life will look like after you have children AND work two freaking jobs. Now take that post-baby work-life scenario you've imagined and double it. You are now getting close to what real life will look like. If you are a first-timer, use the list of questions below to help guide your child-care conversation.

CARE CHART

Care Options	Cost ($–$$$$)	Safety	The Sick Time Factor	The Underwear Factor	Flexibility / Scheduling
Licensed Day Care	$$$	CPR training and state-licensed.	Greater exposure to (and this is not a complete list): rotavirus, influenza, pinkeye, hand-foot-and-mouth disease, ringworm, lice, slap cheek, etc. You and your child spend time out sick as a result!	They shouldn't but they did! Thanks to a bad case of static cling, Leigh's Hanky Pankys ended up on display on her son's napping blanket. Lucky for her, day care returned them in a baggie in an effort to maximize humiliation.	Set hours (e.g., M–F from 7 a.m. to 6 p.m.). You'll get kicked out if you're screeching up at 6:05 p.m. too often. Plan on "ski week" even if your kid is six months old. Day care closed? You're on your own. Discover Canadian Turkey Day is celebrated in some parts of NYC.
In-Home Day Care	$$	Ask. If they are worth their weight in salt, they are CPR-trained. Ask if they are licensed.	See list of ailments above. However, chances are diminished with smaller population of kids.	Pretty safe no one will be seeing your britches!	Rules above apply. However, get ready for two weeks at Christmas, summer, family weddings, family illnesses, etc. The owner needs a vacation too!

Guilt (sad to happy face)	Reliability	Impact on Child	Hidden Inconveniences
Kiddo has a longer day than you. ☹	Very reliable. If a teacher calls in sick, day care remains open and just calls a substitute.	Get ready to wake kiddo up in order to make it to work on time. Kiddo has more best buddies and party invitations than you've had since college! Kiddo is going to learn the ABCs and you won't be the one to teach him.	Packing lunches. Schlepping supplies (bedding, diapers, wipes, milk, etc.). Getting "benched" for 24 hours or more when your child has a fever. Did we mention lice?
Medium to high. You get a false sense of security thinking they are "at home," coupled with panic that since there is a lower ratio of providers, your child might get hit and no one would see it. ☺ ☹	If provider falls ill you could be left in the lurch. If child-care provider has one more baby, she is likely to shut down and take care of her own kids! She could pull a Marie Osmond and split if she's had it!	See above. It's not that much different. But if the teacher never learned her ABCs, there's no one to correct her when she continuously skips the letter E.	Same as above. If the day care is closed for two weeks, it could eat up all of your vacation time and add undue stress on your marriage. They could close up shop with little to no notice and you'd be screwed.

Child-Care Options	Cost ($–$$$$)	Safety	The Sick Time Factor	The Underwear Factor	Flexibility / Scheduling
At Work/ On-Site Day Care	$$$	Typically CPR-trained and state-licensed, but do your homework.	See list above, and the downside is you'll be getting and giving the germs to your bosses' kids, too!	Same as above!	Would typically follow the company holiday schedule, which is a big perk!
Nanny	$$$$	Screen for CPR-trained nannies. Check references like you work for the FBI.	Kiddo won't get too sick until he heads to preschool; he then becomes the bubble boy!	She'll see 'em. Time to get new bras and panties!	To be negotiated before she starts: hours, vacation, sick time. Be clear if you need some flexibility to come home late sometimes. See if overnights are a possibility, as they may be needed on occasion.

Guilt (sad to happy face)	Reliability	Impact on Child	Hidden Inconveniences
Medium. You get to see them at work and can run right to them when the day is over. Seeing performances, reading stories is that much easier since kiddo is on site! ☺	Very reliable. If a teacher calls in sick, day care remains open and just calls a substitute.	Kiddo gets to drive to and from work with you. However, he will likely need to be woken to get there on time.	Same as day care. PLUS Your kid could be spilling the beans to your colleagues' kids about your personal business. Might be awkward when your kid bites a colleague's kid. Play date circle could look like another day at the office, which sounds so NOT fun. You don't get that commute time to roll calls or just enjoy some peace and quiet.
Low as it can go. You are paying someone BIG BUCKS to make your child the center of her universe for 50 hours a week. ☺☺☺	Check references and discuss ramifications if she calls in sick, comes late, or suddenly goes MIA.	Your kid gets one-on-one attention ALL DAY.	Your kid might like the nanny more than you. No joke. Your kid might not have any age-appropriate friends. Your child speaks poorly in two languages. You have all of your eggs in one basket. When nanny gets a nasty bout of flu, you are screwed for a week solid!

| | st
–$$$$) | Safety | The Sick Time Factor | The Underwear Factor | Flexibility / Scheduling |
|---|---|---|---|---|---|
| **Live-in Au Pair** | $$$

Low hourly pay, but get ready for agency placement fee, application fee, extra car, cell phone, car insurance, higher food bill, and the drama that comes with the age. | Contingent on experience. However, you could screen candidates for CPR training. | As long as the au pair doesn't have herpes or the clap, you should be okay. | Face it, if she's living in your home, she is going to see you in your underwear at one time or another. Just make sure it's you and NOT your husband! | Usually 40–45 hours per week at your beck and call.

Can't work overnight.

Can't work 24 hours a day.

Plan two weeks for her trip back to see the family in Sweden. |
| **Nanny-Share** | $$$ | Same as for nanny. | Exposure to illness will be extended to an additional family and their child(ren). | You've reduced the likelihood by 50%, but only because half the time she'll be at the other family's house! | Set a schedule, but don't change it. Remember, there's another working mom involved . . . |

Guilt (sad to happy face)	Reliability	Impact on Child	Hidden Inconveniences
Medium. You feel good about hanging out with a hip 21-year-old whose sole job it is to take care of YOUR kids . . . ☺☺☺	Depends on how good you are at interviewing. Can you be a judge of reliability in a one-hour phone screening?	Infants and toddlers can wake on their own schedule and remain in their home. More one-on-one time.	There's a hot 21-year-old from Sweden LIVING in your home. You now have another kid on your hands—especially if she is homesick. You're tapped for "cultural enrichment," whatever that means. Driving in the U.S.A. can often be "new," thus leaving you uncomfortable with au pair driving your kids (a major part of the job description). Uncomfortable conversations once au pair has tapped into the Brazilian au pair club and constantly parties all weekend long!
Medium to low. Your kid has built-in playmates and lots of attention. ☺	Just as with nanny, but they are screwing two families at the same time when they up and quit!	Child will have set play dates, but who's hosting will always be up in the air.	You will likely know too much about the other family, and vice versa. Going back and forth means more cleaning and wear and tear on the house. Constant coordination. Two families both vying for Saturday night babysitting.

Child Care Options	Cost ($–$$$$)	Safety	The Sick Time Factor	The Underwear Factor	Flexibility / Scheduling
Relatives	No $, but much blood.	Your mom raised you, right? Do you trust her?	Your mom / mother-in-law will probably be on the losing end of this equation.	Yep, done deal!	Per her availability. Does your mom have a weekly quilting bee? And does she summer in Florida?
The Wolves	Free.	Worked for Romulus and Remus, right?	Rabies are a significant risk.	Hmmmm.	24/7. Packs are always recruiting.

Guilt (sad to happy face)	Reliability	Impact on Child	Hidden Inconveniences
Almost none. With emphasis on ALMOST. Does your mom know the going rate for nanny work? Don't tell her. If she doesn't support you working in the first place, be aware of passive-aggressive behavior and regular guilt trips. ☺☹	ÜBER-reliable. Rock solid. Consider it done. Check. Etc.	Your kid is going to grow up the exact same way that you (or your husband) did. Lucky him.	Temptation to abuse privilege. Your parents will know more about your marriage than you'd rather. They earn the right to a strong, vocal opinion on how you raise your kid. Even though you're a lapsed Catholic, your mom is NOT. If she's sitting on Sunday, church is on the program!
Medium. Wouldn't you like them to work on their verbal communication skills? ☺	"Lone wolf" says it all.	This could impact his ability to get along well with others.	The elements. The smell.

1. How many hours do you really need? Discuss and run through some mock weekly schedules. If you are considering day care, can both parents do drop-offs and pick-ups? If the answer is no, day care is NOT a sustainable option. The parent who is required to do all drop-offs and pick-ups will go mad by month seven and start foaming at the mouth.

2. What kind of baggage are you bringing and what's the damage? Did mummy and a governess raise your hubby while you were making your way as a latchkey kid? Don't tell us, you're in therapy, too?

3. What are your goals for child care? Do you simply want somewhere to park your kids for the day, or do you have visions of them becoming fluent in Cantonese, mastering the harp, or studying under Buddhist monks?

4. What are your work hours? Are you expected in the office from eight a.m. to six p.m. every day? If you are already freaking out that you'll have a hard time screeching up to day care's door by six p.m., it's only going to get worse. Bail and consider something else.

5. What about sick kids? Will Mommy stay home on some days and Daddy on others? If it's always going to be Mommy, think about how this will impact your career, your stress level, and your propensity for resentment. And how much sick and vacation time do you have racked up? Remember that epic diarrhea can last two weeks! (Brutal on so many levels.)

6. Who's traveling, and why? How will business travel impact the spouse remaining at home? Now that there are kids in the equation, we no longer give a rip about all the miles you are racking up on business trips! Who's going to pull the weight when you're gone?

7. Are your children vaccinated? Most child-care facilities require proof.

8. What are your deal-breakers when it comes to child care? Cheerios on the floor or dirty fingernails on the child-care

provider? Everyone has individual issues, but you might just have to look the other way when you see your kid sharing a pacifier with someone else's kid. Can you do that?

9. Will one parent be more responsible than the other parent for child care? If so, he or she gets veto power, assuming that his/her preference is affordable.

10. What can you afford? Are you willing to forgo those handbags and facials or, more realistically, organic milk and the occasional dinner at a nice restaurant? Knowing what we know now, we'd say your money is better spent on the right amount of child care. Otherwise you'll look great but be a psycho headed for divorce court!

11. What are two or three of your similarly situated friends doing and why? Buy them a few glasses of wine and get them talking. If they are still acting like everything is perfect, move on to the hard liquor. That always gets them talking. Listen with both ears and heed their advice.

When Should I Start Looking for Child Care?

Day care. As soon as that little sperm is swimming upstream. OK, maybe not that soon. Once you have confirmed your pregnancy for sure. Many day-care facilities have long waiting lists. If you get on the waiting list early, you maintain your options. Procrastinating could squash your chance for a spot, thus making you feel like you are already a bad working mother. Get ready to pony up some cash because a deposit is typically required to hold your slot!

Au pair. Most agencies encourage you to begin the process sixteen weeks before you expect to have an au pair in your home. This includes time to fill out the application, match with an au pair, and actually have them in your home ready to work. To play it safe, if you are going the au pair route, start the process when you are seven to eight months pregnant.

Nanny. Six to eight weeks before you need the nanny to start. Nannies (the good ones) are in high demand and get snatched up quickly. When you find the one you like and you agree to go forward, nannies expect to begin work almost immediately (within two weeks). Six to eight weeks gives you adequate time to execute your search and check references. And if your nanny is working for another family, it gives her time to rock their world with the "I'm quitting" speech.

So you've had the talk and you're totally overwhelmed but ready to get going. Congratulations. At least you are at the starting line, which has got to bring you a little relief. Do not despair if you are a little behind. Just get going now and stop feeling sorry for yourself. If you are really behind, put your networking skills to work and start calling in favors. The bottom line: do whatever it takes. You got it? Poorly planned child care WILL be the catalyst for a working mom meltdown.

Day Care 101

We'll assume everyone knows what day care is, and if you don't, we're worried about you.

If you are considering day care, keep in mind, as with most child-related decisions, there are many choices of varying degrees of quality. There are three common types of day care: day-care center (usually pretty big and many go up to pre-K), in-home day care (typically smaller with one to two teachers at any time), and at work/on-site day-care center (sometimes funded by your employer and usually conveniently close to work!).

Each state has different laws, so get familiar with the laws in your state by doing your research online and at the day care you are considering. Day-care licensing is overseen by the Department of Social Services. Sounds important and official, but don't let that fool you. It's just the government and when's the last time you've given our government an A in anything? In California the rules and regulations fill more than twenty pages, so you can imagine why we won't try and interpret them for you here. Read up on the pros and cons of each type of day care and determine which, if any, might be right for your perfect little savant of a child.

In our opinion, parents often get so spun up about the vast myriad of parental decisions, when really you just need to use common sense and your gut instincts. Here are the things we think you should consider and do when evaluating a day-care facility.

1. What did you think of the director of the facility when you took the tour? Was she friendly or a prison warden? Did she answer your questions with real answers or the coy "That's a good question" response? What was her body language like? Could you sense her sphincter clenching when you asked about safety? Did you notice any teachers rolling their eyes when she walked in the classroom? Pay attention to what's NOT being said.

2. Observe the children at the center. Are their green boogers actually hard-crusted and obstructing their nostrils? If so, grab a Kleenex and wipe their noses and see what kind of reaction you get. Really, how hard is it to wipe a nose? WE HATE BOOGER-ENCRUSTED FACES! If they won't wipe a booger, do you really think they'll change your kid the minute she poops her pants? What are the kids doing? Are they engaged in an activity or eating Goldfish off the floor?

3. What did you think of the facility? Was it clean? Did it smell? Did you immediately get depressed upon seeing it? Did you notice any safety hazards? Can you imagine your child in this room all day long, from eight a.m. to six p.m.? If you burst into tears upon seeing the joint, let that be a sign, unless your hormones are still way out of whack.

4. Ask questions about medical emergencies, natural disasters, evacuation plans, etc. Don't you want to know what the protocol

is if your kid falls down and splits his head open? What do you do if there is a natural disaster and you can't get to your kid? We want to know, as we live in the middle of earthquake central. If you are not comfortable with the answer, then hightail it out of there. We can assure you that you will not be able to focus on your job/career if you are concerned about the basic safety of your child.

5. Talk to the teacher. Ask how long she has been teaching at the center. Does she have children at the center? Why did she choose to work there? Try to determine if you're going to be comfortable having those awkward conversations about your kid. You know, things like biting, saying naughty words, pulling down his pants, and the dreaded "Is everything OK at home—your kiddo is really acting up" speech. If you can't imagine having these conversations with her, you might want to move on.

6. Do your diligence. Just because they are licensed doesn't mean they're good. A license isn't a guarantee of quality; it just demonstrates that the facility has met the requirements set forth by the state and can fill out some basic paperwork. Ask to see the license and make sure it's current. Then ask all of your gossipy friends about the rumors. Basically we're encouraging you to snoop as you would if you thought your husband was cheating. This is important stuff, right?

Congratulations, You're on the Waiting List

When I found out I was pregnant, I had a million thoughts going through my head, one of which was child care. Instead of reinventing the wheel, I approached several colleagues who were at the same level as me (read: we could likely afford a similar situation), who lived by me, and who didn't seem like total nut jobs. I guess I didn't see the need to initiate the research as some pretty intelligent women had already done it with kids who were six to twelve months older than mine. What I really wanted to know was: what were the top three child-care facilities in my county? With that information I would schedule a tour with all three facilities and decide from there—which is exactly what I did. This still took a considerable amount of time filling out paperwork, touring facilities, and crossing my fingers I'd get my top pick. In the end, it kind of worked out. My application was accepted, but I was put on a waiting list. It was kind of like that Seinfeld episode where Jerry has a rental car reservation but arrives and they can't honor the reservation. I was "accepted," I just didn't have a guaranteed schedule. Whatever that meant.

Then came the best part. I had a chat with my husband and told him I just couldn't imagine taking our sweet little bundle to day care that first week as it would positively induce hysteria about leaving the baby and get me off on a bad foot at work. What a ruse, and I knew it. But it was the best chance I had at getting my husband involved early and it worked! Now we have established that when my husband's schedule allows, he will do the drop-offs and I'll handle the pick-ups. The added benefit is our son is so proud because "not a lot of 'papas' do the drop-offs" and our son thinks he's special!

—Leigh

Nanny 101

If you are considering a nanny, it's probably because your job requires more flexibility, you really want your child to remain in your home with more one-on-one attention, you have twins, or perhaps you are rolling in cash. That's OK—we are happy for you and, we'll admit, mildly jealous. Whatever the case, a nanny is the equivalent of hitting the child-care lottery. However, all this fabulosity comes at a price. It costs more, as you are typically paying for fifty hours a week and working around forty (don't forget commute and transition time), you have someone in your home most of the week, and it is one more person to manage and an important one at that. So let's jump right in. How does one begin to find a nanny?

Where Can I Find a Nanny?

- Professional child-care placement agency
- Through your new mommy network
- Newborn centers typically affiliated with hospitals (often have great bulletin boards)
- Jewish community centers (often have great bulletin boards)
- Craigslist (search under "child care")
- Ask around at the playground, at the children's museum, at Gymboree, and elsewhere
- Classifieds in daily, weekly, or specialty papers such as *Parents' Press*

• •

Finding a nanny takes creativity and determination. Our friends helped us poach our live-in nanny from another family. I'm convinced I'm going to hell for taking her, but it was a risk I was willing to take. It was a little bit like that episode from Desperate Housewives *where Lynette goes to the park to poach nannies. We literally had our friends talk to her at the park and convince her to work for us by telling her how great we'd be as employers. Too bad they didn't warn her that I'd be an overdemanding control freak.*

Andrea, Mother of Two and Business Owner

• •

How can you find a nanny whom you love? Our best advice is to undertake this task as if you are recruiting for a new employee at your job. What do you do when you are looking to fill an important role?

1. Phone-screen first. Weed out the psychos and the ones who say MORONIC things such as, "I just got my license back."
2. Conduct in-person interviews. Do you like 'em, and are they qualified?
3. Check references. Don't offload; do this yourself and check three or four—it's hard to have four phony references.
4. Arrange for the candidates to meet the kid(s). Observe their interaction but remember this is a blind date and we can't expect immediate chemistry.

Kicking Off the Search for a Nanny

Now is the time to create a job description and be as detailed as possible. Neither one of you wants surprises once the first day of work rolls around. Nannies aren't clairvoyant, and they don't know whether you require light housework unless you tell them. Outline all of the job responsibilities and add as much information as you'd like without looking like a total control freak. Diapering responsibilities, for instance, can include detail such as "Please apply a barrier cream at each change due to extremely sensitive skin. Kiddo screams like a banshee when his tushy is even slightly irritated." Information like this is helpful and appropriate and establishes your expectations. Save time and avoid repeating yourself by including an overview of your family within the job description and whom the caregiver can expect to see on a daily basis. This includes basic information on the family, the children who will be under supervision, names, ages, favorite things to do, personality traits, favorite foods (okay, overkill for babies, but you get the picture).

The last thing you need to do before you are ready to initiate your search is create a list of interview questions. Come up with five to ten questions for your first phone screen to weed out the misfits and then ten to fifteen questions for the in-person inquisition. During this process, try to set your emotions aside (we said "try") so you aren't blinded to inappropriate candidates. Many moms are so focused on finding the perfect nanny that they make the search process a living nightmare by interviewing twenty nannies in person for a marathon all-day session. Really? Would you do that at work? Hell, no, we'd rather have a colonoscopy; at least it'd be over in an hour. On the basis of the phone and in-person interviews, determine which of the candidates is worthy enough to come and meet the children.

Phone-Screen Questions

Question	What You Really Want to Know
Can you send me your resume?	Is this person serious enough to create one?
What draws you to the child-care profession?	Can you convince me you love caring for children?
Are you legally able to work in this country?	What are my options here? Am I aiding and abetting? Just need to know what I'm getting into.
Do you have a car?	Are you going to be reliable or am I going to fall victim to the bus schedule or the generosity of your family members? If you do have a car, is it death on wheels or fairly safe?
Are you working with a family now? If so, why are you considering leaving your position?	How quickly can you start? If you ARE working with a family, what's wrong with them that would make you want to leave, because it might be "wrong" with us, too?
Are you able to work 50 hours per week, which is the requirement of my position?	Have you READ the job description? Do you know what you are signing up for? This ain't a boondoggle.

In-Person Questions
(Follow up on any of the above plus all the qualitative stuff.)

Question	What You really Want to Know
Do you have any questions or concerns about the job description?	Have you read it? If so, speak up now or forever hold your peace!
What do you need to be successful? Name three to five key factors.	Are we in sync? How demanding are you?
Are you available for occasional overnights if both parents are away on business trips? If so, what do you expect to be paid?	Are you flexible? Will you be able to shift on a dime or are you Miss Hospital Corners?
What do you find to be the hardest thing about working with children all day?	Will you 'fess up that it's HARD work?
Do you have children of your own, and if so, what is your approach to discipline?	Will you forgive me on occasion when I completely lose it? Do you spank?
Are you prepared for an emergency? Have you handled one in the past? If so, please describe. This can include a nasty fall, choking, a flat tire on the highway, etc.	Some good "I averted disaster stories" with happy endings will make me feel really comfortable leaving my child with you.
How would you describe your personality traits?	Would I want to be your employer . . . your friend?
I will be checking your references and your driving record. Are you comfortable with that?	If you have anything to tell me, NOW would be the time. Really . . . I'm checking ALL references.
Can you tell me a little about your last child-care position and why it ended?	Did you quit or were you fired?
Describe some challenges you've experienced in your role as a child-care provider. What have you done to meet those challenges?	What do you consider a challenge— dirty dishes or the terrible twos? Do you have any problem-solving skills?

Question	What You really Want to Know
Can you tell me a little more about yourself and your family? Where were you raised, and where have you lived?	Do you talk to your family? What kind of baggage do you bring to the party?
How do you handle temper tantrums and potty training?	Do you have a secret method that I need to know, because mine aren't working!
How do you handle a crying baby?	Have you heard of shaken baby syndrome? DO NOT SHAKE MY BABY!
What indoor/outdoor activities could you suggest? Are you willing to take kids to play group, karate, soccer, etc.?	Are you creative? Will you charge me extra for getting my child to and from karate class?
Are you comfortable reviewing and/or assisting with homework?	Are you any better at math than me? Lord knows I can barely help with homework, as it's been a good 25 years since high school.

Obviously this is just a partial list, but you get the picture. The more thorough you are on the front end, the fewer surprises you will have down the road. Remember this mantra: Working mothers don't like surprises. Do the hard work now and you'll reap the rewards later.

Now you are in a position to evaluate your choices and select a nanny. But whatever you decide, sign a contract. It can be on a napkin for all we care; just make it official. Spell out the expectations about wages, schedule, responsibilities, vacation, sick time, first review, holidays, bonuses, etc. Again this protects both parties and minimizes surprises, as in: "Oh, I didn't know you went on a family vacation for the month of December." Now what?

There are many sample contracts on the Web. Simply type in "nanny contract" on Google and hit "search." Use that as your base and adjust as you see fit. Now you have no excuses.

Au Pair 101

Au pairs are those lovely young adults between the ages of eighteen and twenty-six who come to the United States and live as an extended member of their host family. Au pairs provide up to forty-five hours per week of child care in exchange for room, board, a small weekly stipend, and up to $500 toward six credits at an accredited educational institution. Think indentured servant. It can be amazing according to many of our friends, but it can also be a craptacular failure if you aren't a skilled interviewer. Many professional women we know utilize au pairs because they provide maximum flexibility. However be aware of all the costs. While the weekly stipend might seem low, you have to remember the application fee, the agency fee, the plane tickets, the extra car, car insurance, cell phones, one more mouth to feed, etc. Remember, you'll have another young adult living with you and taking care of your children, but on occasion it can feel like having another child.

There are many au pair agencies that you can work with if you want to go the au pair route. Check out the placement agencies on the Web by executing a Google search. If that seems like a pain in the ass, you can also treat your colleagues with an au pair to a quick coffee and have them fill you in on the good, the bad, and the ugly. If you are still interested, chances are you can reach out to the agency they used (assuming they are satisfied) and save yourself time on research.

How It Works

- An au pair comes to the United States on a J-1 visa typically for one year. Au pairs can be extended six, nine, or twelve months if mutually agreed upon. So if you find a good one, you can potentially have them for two years.

- The au pair lives with you as an extension of your family. You are responsible for room and board and cultural enrichment. (You know, teach them about the pilgrims, the Fourth of July, *Jon & Kate Plus Eight*, obesity, and all the other charms of American culture.)
- The au pair works up to forty-five hours a week on child care and child-related responsibilities (packing lunches, driving to sports practice, light cooking, laundry). (No, you shouldn't fire your housekeeper now that you have an au pair; they're child-care providers, NOT maids.)
- You pay them on average $176 per week. That's right, about FOUR BUCKS an hour.
- The au pair learns about U.S. culture and learns English, and can get up to six credits at an accredited educational institution.

What Questions Should You Ask?

Check with the agency you are using as they typically provide assistance with the nuances of interviewing international au pairs. However, here is a list of questions that can be used as a guide. Many of these questions would get you in trouble with an HR department, but remember that those rules don't apply here. You're interviewing someone to come live with you, and you are going to have to dig a little deeper. (You can supplement with some of the questions from the nanny list a few pages back, too.)

Question	What You Really Want to Know
Have you ever been out of the country before?	Are you going to have a period of culture shock? If so, how bad is it going to be?
Have you ever been away from your family for a while?	How bad is the phone bill going to be?

Question	What You Really Want to Know
Do you have a boyfriend?	Is it love or are you just getting a leg over? If it's love, it's going to be trouble!
Have you been an au pair before?	How did it go? Were you extended or fired?
What interests you in au pair work?	How good are you at selling me?
Do you have any friends or family near our home?	How dependent are you going to be on us—for everything?
Do you have an international driver's license?	Can you drive? Does SUV mean anything to you? There's a big difference between an Escalade and a Fiat!
What are your hobbies?	Are discos and clubs two of them?
What are your plans for the holidays?	Are you committed to the Christmas trip to Grandma's house?
Are you comfortable with the age of our children and their developmental needs?	Have you ever worked with toddlers?
How long have you studied English?	Can you speak it, read it, and write it? How hard is it going to be for us to communicate?
What techniques do you use for discipline?	Don't lock my kid in the basement. That dungeon scares even me.
Are you comfortable handling matters over the phone?	Can you speak basic English and schedule basic appointments?

How Long Does It Take to Get an Au Pair?

This is not a quick process. Something about trying to make sure that you're not in the business of sex trafficking or trying to set up a mail-order-bride service or some such thing. After you've filled out an extensive application and it's been accepted, you review dossiers, interview potential candidates (over the phone, mind you), find a match (the mutual acceptance and agreement between host family and au pair can go forward), and select your au pair. Once the au pair gets her J-1 visa from her home country (ENTIRELY her responsibility), travel arrangements can be made. Once in the United States, au pairs typically have a four-day stay in New York City for U.S. State Department mandatory training. Then, and only then, can the au pair make her way to you to begin work in your home. Most au pair agencies recommend that you allow at least sixteen weeks for this process, and if you're neurotic, perhaps a little more. We're neurotic.

GREAT—YOU'VE FOUND THE CHILD-CARE SOLUTION FOR YOUR FAMILY!

All your hard work has paid off, and you have finally landed on your child-care solution. Celebrate a little; this is a big freaking deal and with any luck you won't have to do it again for at least a year. Now, our last piece of advice: DON'T SCREW IT UP! Realize that this is essentially a business partnership with your child in the middle. Be reasonable, consider one another's intentions, and never, ever, ever skimp over a few dollars as it creates bad will and ends up costing you dearly in the long run.

Trial Runs

We are big believers in the trial-run period. Figure out what you can afford—even a day is better than nothing—and build the trial-run period into the budget and schedule. Many day cares like a week or two of drop-offs to get the child eased into the program and to see how they adapt. Nannies often like two weeks to a month part-time before you head back to work so they can shadow you and learn their way around your routine. Remember, this is a critical part of a successful child-care plan. You and the family get a sneak peek at your post-maternity-leave life (drop-offs/pick-ups at day care, nanny's daily schedule, or au pair's cooking prowess). It's as much emotional as it is logistical—don't kid yourself. Do you really want to drop off the kiddo for the FIRST time your first day back to work? Trial runs can bring to light issues that require troubleshooting, help you gain confidence that all will be OK, and in a worst-case scenario shake loose some losers before you head back to work. Skip the trial run and you're guaranteeing a few unwelcome surprises.

Treat Your Child-Care Providers Well— They Will See You at Your Worst!

If both parents work and you don't live near immediate family, you are going to be very reliant on your child-care provider; TREAT THAT PERSON WELL AND WITH RESPECT AND YOU WILL NEVER REGRET IT. You are all working in partnership (we hope) in a joint effort to make sure that the children are safe and cared for in a loving manner. On days when it doesn't go perfectly, recall how hard it was, when you were on leave, to keep the baby clean and fed, to clean the house, do the laundry, cook the meals, and so on. Taking care of children all day is hard work. Relationships with child-care providers, no matter the type, are complicated. It's going to require, on many occasions, that you set aside your personal issues and really think about what's best for your child. We are not talking about excusing matters related to safety, ever. We are talking about dirty clothes, skipping naps, stuff like that. Remember, no one likes a crazy lady, so save that tirade for your husband. At least he's used to it.

How Bad Can It Get?

• •

I ended up at the grocery store on a Tuesday night at nine after the kids were asleep and my husband was home. I hate the grocery store, but this is one of the few times I can go alone. Unfortunately, I ran into my daughter's day-care teacher in the freezer aisle and sobbed on her shoulder. It had been a long month of sick kids, new jobs, etc. She was so comforting, and I slept so peacefully that night. I was a bit sheepish at drop-off the next morning—the drop-off walk of shame!

Julie, *Mother of Two and Finance Manager*

After the birth of my twins (naturally, I must add) I was sooo consti-pated and very anxious about that first poop. On my third day home from the hospital, I finally went, crying the whole time. Well, the toilet overflowed and there was poop everywhere. I was hysterical, upset, and crying, and my nanny helped mop it up. All I could say through my tears of exhaustion and humiliation was: "I know this is NOT in your job description."

Nicole, *Mother of Three and Communications Consultant*

I once cursed at my husband; my daughter started explaining to our nanny (who was there when it happened) that I had called him an ass, and how that wasn't nice that I did it. And our nanny, God bless her, explained that sometimes mommies get angry.

Debbie, *Mother of Two and Marketing Executive*

My child-care provider has definitely seen some stuff I'd rather she had not. Let's just say she loved to organize things and one time ran across some of my bachelorette party gifts. Neither one of us ever said a word about it.

Miki, *Mother of One and Recruiter*

My nanny knows I don't shower until four p.m., if at all (and now you do, too)! She also has seen me sicker than sick, and dealing with family drama of epic proportions. Oh, and did I mention she has passed me rolls of toilet paper on more than one occasion. Not even my husband does that!

Nada, *Mother of Three, and Author and Small Business Consultant*

When my twins were babies, I said something like, "I don't think I can do this" and I looked at Jenni, my nanny, and she looked me right in the eyes and said, "It's a little late for that, don't you think?"

Catherine, Mother of Three and Writer

* *

Show Them the Love

Let us repeat: DO NOT SCREW IT UP ONCE CHILD CARE IS IN PLACE! You know that, right? Once you've got the day care sorted out or the nanny fully integrated and it's all humming along, you need to do everything in your power to shore it up. Lose your pride and start kissing some serious child-care provider ASS.

We've heard such amazing stories from our children about what teachers at day care or nannies have done, all in a day's work, and it's heartwarming. It's above and beyond, and they deserve our recognition and a few extra bucks, thank you very much. Spare them the regifting, it's soooo obvious, and give them cash for the holidays. If you can't afford cash, give something else. Cookies, clothes for her kids, drawings from the kids. It's the thought. There is a lot you can do; you just have to get creative.

The (Second) Most Important Person in My Life

* *

Like all of us, nannies need praise and soak it up! My closet is my nanny's best friend; I commit to quarterly purge parties and she leaves with shoes, handbags, hats, and what she calls "goodies." P.S. My daughter also tells me she wears my Manolo Blahnik stilettos around the house. I don't care—if it makes her feel good, it's fine with me!

Kate, Mother of One and Retail Executive

The nanny makes out much better at Christmastime than my husband. She received a $500 bonus, while he got a sweater.

JoAnn, *Mother of Two and Human Capital Manager*

I have given her extra days/time off without my husband knowing. I figure, "Hey, she is taking care of our son so she needs a break every once in a while." Not sure my husband would agree. I also give her little "bonuses" here and there to show my appreciation (movie tickets, a gift card for a manicure). They don't cost much, but they go a long way.

Heather, *Mother of One and Brand Strategist*

I've taken her on vacations, flown her home on her time off, given her gifts she really wants for Christmas—oh, and run cover for her "friend" who is not her husband.

Dawn, *Mother of Two and Advertising Executive*

The family we got her from tried to win her back. They called her non-stop and offered a lot. Luckily, she was too invested with my kids at that point. I buy this woman and her son the NICEST presents (better than I give my own family). She is so much more important than my husband, not even a contest!

Elisabeth, *Mother of Two and Television Marketing Professional*

After 9/11, both my nanny and my secretary wanted to leave New York City. The secretary I could live without, but we took the nanny and her husband out to dinner and put a $5,000 STAY bonus on the table. Stay for two more school years, and it was theirs. They stayed, and the money helped with the down payment on their first house.

Amy, *Mother of Two and Executive, Urban Public School System*

• •

WHAT TO DO WHEN IT ALL FALLS TO PIECES

Face it: a good thing cannot last forever. At some point your child-care relationship is going to unravel and leave you completely and totally panic-stricken. "ARGGHHHHHHH! How am I going to . . . ?" "You've got to leave the country when? But I've got a blankety-blank all that week!" Day care might lose its lease or your nanny will up and quit on you. Now what? You are going to have to deal. Instead of just using up all of your sick time and vacation time, we'd recommend you think ahead and plan for this very occasion, because it's going to happen.

Tips for Troubleshooting:
- **Demand some attempt at professionalism.** If the nanny quits or in-home day care suddenly closes, try to insist that they honor two weeks' notice. If not, start planning your revenge.
- **Use guilt to your advantage.** Ask your nanny or day-care provider whom she recommends. Often she has someone in mind, and her guilt at totally screwing you over will persuade her to help.
- **Call Parents in a Pinch or Rent-a-Parent or Mommy for Hire.** Get them lined up immediately for three days while you start the all-out search. It will be very expensive. Don't go nuts about the few extra dollars unless it will truly prevent you from feeding your family. Losing your job would be worse.
- **Call your mommy.** What grandma wouldn't want to come racing to the rescue (loaded question)? Beg your mom or your mother-in-law to help. Then shell out for the flight and suck it up as they become a permanent resident for the next three weeks.

Obviously, you're starting from scratch. Go right back to the beginning of the chapter, grab a glass of wine, and commence the do-over.

Nanny Bombs and Other Loaded Weapons!
You Know You're in Trouble When . . .

- You get a text message saying, "We need to talk."
- Your nanny calls from her vacation saying her flight has been "delayed" . . . indefinitely.
- Day care calls and says that there are some "behavioral issues" that you need to discuss.
- The au pair starts to cry and says that she misses her boyfriend.
- The child-care provider ruins your day with an armchair diagnosis of ADD/speech impediment/learning disability/you name it.
- The nanny says, "I've just met the nicest family at the playground . . ."
- Your nanny's eyes start to glaze over when you talk about the next six months. Clearly she doesn't plan on being around.
- You notice that her Internet history includes recent perusals of the nanny listings on Craigslist.

YOU THINK IT'S PERFECT, BUT THE TIMES ARE A-CHANGING

We must warn you, there is no perfect solution and no one size fits all. Child care is dynamic, and your needs will change as your child grows and goes from one stage to the next. There's a huge difference in dealing with spit-up and dealing with math homework and taking multiple children to soccer practice. What might have been a great solution—notice we didn't say perfect—when the kiddo was six months old may render them bored to tears when they are two and a half and catatonic when they're seven. So let go of seeking the "perfect child-care solution" and focus on finding the right age-appropriate child-care solution for your family at this moment.

When it all falls apart, don't worry. There is another solution behind that one and you are going to be that much better at finding it the second time around.

What We Do

Fair question. Our children are now preschool age, and we found we could not thrive, OK, survive, with our kids in day care five days a week. Had nothing to do with the quality of our day-care centers; it had to do with the demands of our jobs and even more important our sanity. The pressure was too much and left us both feeling stressed out every day. No matter how hard we tried, we were always late to work, and when the clock struck five, we hit the ground running like the building was on fire. We literally felt like we were living the movie *Groundhog Day*. Every day was the same marathon, with a pathetic little break on the weekends during which we were supposed to relax, bond with our families, and complete a week's worth of housework. This just wasn't working so we both decided to get part-time helpers. Two days a week with a nanny, three with day care. Voilà. It took the pressure off just enough and allowed us to focus a little time on ourselves, our husbands, our careers, and anything else we had been neglecting (exercise, friendships, etc.). That said, with Amy's older son starting kindergarten, it all ended up in flux again, with a few months devoted to finding the new "perfect" child-care fix.

So we share this with you only to demonstrate that the best child-care solution is often somewhere in the middle. It's not as simple as black or white; in our case we discovered the beauty of gray.

5

The Breastraunt Is Open for Business:

It's Official—You Are a DAIRY QUEEN

Delusions

- I'll be comfortable pumping in the women's restroom, especially when I can see my boss's shoes in the stall next to me.
- No one will hear that *sh-sh-sh*ing noise if my office door is closed.
- My kiddo will go to Harvard if I breastfeed; formula will turn my child into the devil.
- I am sure that I can make it until this meeting is over before I start to leak.
- This black pleather faux briefcase is so realistic that none of my male colleagues will know what it is.
- I'm sure there will be a nice private place at the office to pump. It'll be a welcome break.

N eedless to say, if you are weaning your baby before you go back to work or choose not to breastfeed, then skip this chapter. You've just saved yourself ten minutes of reading and a fighting chance at perky tits well into your forties.

If you haven't weaned or even thought about it for more than a fleeting second, it's time to deal. The decision to continue breastfeeding after you return to work is not one that should be entered into without some serious consideration. We are not going to get all "breast is best" on you; we'll leave that to La Leche League. But we are going to insist that if the Breastraunt is to remain open, you have a solid plan, a commitment to the cause, and an extra blouse or two for the occasional BLOWOUT.

CONGRATULATIONS, YOU'RE IN, SUPERBOOBS

The fact that you are still reading tells us you are in. Great—good for you! You are a regular superwoman, and your kid is going to be a genius given this decision. That IS what you want to hear, right?

Now come the reality checks: What are your goals for nursing and how long are you planning to keep it up? How the hell are you going to pull this off, and are you being realistic? Are you hell-bent on breast-feeding the kiddo exclusively for a year or are you willing to supplement with formula? All of these questions are important, and your response will impact your daily schedule (i.e., RULE YOUR LIFE) once you are back to work.

So when should you make your decision? Here's a tip. NOT the week before you are expected back at work, unless you really want to self-combust. We'd recommend that you commit to your feeding plan about a month prior to going back to work. If you are going to transition your baby to 50 percent breast milk and 50 percent formula, you need to give both you and your child the time to get a grip. You might find that they start pooping up a storm after you introduce formula or that they reject the fake nipple. And who could blame them given how lovely and supple yours are? Give yourself time to figure all of this out, do some trial runs, and most important troubleshoot. What could be more stressful than going back to work only to realize that this very important detail (i.e., how you will actually feed your kid) didn't get the attention it deserved. You won't be able to focus at work because you're freaking out that your kid won't take formula; you will be running to day care over lunch to give her the boob; or worse, you'll be having the nanny bring the kid to work in order to nurse while trying to keep this hidden from your boss. Can you blame your boss for being PISSED OFF that you didn't plan better? To say that this is a one-way ticket to meltdown city is the understatement of the century.

Making the commitment to pump on the job is an undertaking, and honestly it really isn't that fun. There is no baby staring up at you thanking you with loving glances for providing her with the nectar of the gods. Really, all you get is saggy tits, sore nipples, and a lot more stuff to clean. Recognize that, pat yourself on the back, and try not to place too much pressure on how long you want to continue this masochism. This coming from someone who did it for 365 days.

Look at your pumping goals in six-week increments when you go back to work. Who knows, your kid may lose interest, go on a titty strike, or you just might run out of milk. Point being it's not totally up to you. Some women stop pumping during the day and only nurse their children in the mornings and evenings. Boy, is that a model of civility! It can be overwhelming to even think about trying to pump for the next six months, or even the next nine. It seems like forever, and it is. It boils down to 360 times that you'll hook up to the milking machine and pump, pump, pump. And that's not even taking into consideration the fact that the sound of the dreaded pump is already annoying the hell out of you and it's only week one. Start with six weeks and see how it goes. Then try another six weeks, each time assessing what is working and what is not working. And only then make a decision to either continue or stop. This procrastination technique works well. Why decide today what you can put off until tomorrow? Before you know it, you will have a few months under your belt! Our lives are in constant flux; the more we learn to just lose the bra and relax, the better off we'll be.

Now for all the ladies who find themselves in one of those jobs (teacher, doctor, nurse, etc.) where you get one fifteen-minute break at best and have to choose between eating a banana, going potty, or pumping. It's your call, but we'd recommend you take the bio-break.

The pumping takes a backseat to certain biological needs. Some jobs make it almost impossible to pump. Cut yourself some slack; see what works and what doesn't work. Remember . . . six-week increments.

• •

I didn't have time to pump before back-to-school night, and the crying babies who accompanied the parents made me leak through my nursing pads! Good thing I could hold a clipboard up!

Jennifer, Mother of Three and Teacher

• •

Mixing Business with Breastfeeding? What to Do One Month Before Returning to Work

- Communicate your decision to your spouse and ask for the help and support you will need to be successful (e.g., "Honey, get your ass off the sofa and HELP me with the baby, DON'T stress me out, and for God's sakes when you see me fumbling with this damn pump, can you at least plug the motherf*cker in the wall?").
- Begin pumping and bottle-feeding your infant one to two times per day. (Check with your pediatrician to ascertain the right time to introduce a bottle. Don't trust us with that one.)
- Phone a fellow working mom at your office and ask for advice. She'll point out the potential land mines.
- Start getting in one extra pumping session a day to build a supply of breast milk that can carry you for a week if you run into problems. Trust us; there will be problems, missed pumping sessions, ungodly stress, clogged ducts, you name it. With a backup supply of milk at least your kid can survive all of this chaos. Can't guarantee the same for you.
- Get double the parts you'll need to pump so you have one set at home and one set at work. Flanges, tubing, extra bottles, breast pads, and don't forget the nipple cream . . . aaaahhhhh, nipple cream.

One thing you should not forget is that you are not the first woman to go through this transition. Reach out to another new mom; you know the one you met in the bathroom when you both were pregnant and peeing more than you were working? Call her and ask her how the pumping is going and if she has any advice. Chances are she will have lots of information and you will benefit from it.

As to whether you should tell your boss that you'll be pumping, that's a tricky question. We don't know your boss, but that being said, if your boss is a man, we really don't think he wants to hear about you milking yourself nor does he need that visual of you tits-in-the-wind somewhere in the office building. If you ever want to see a man's face turn beet red, especially a man who is not yet a father or had children in the days before the breast pump was invented, start explaining what it means to pump your breasts. In our opinion pumping is on a need-to-know basis, and almost NO ONE needs to know. Go about your business and unless someone has the nerve to ask where you are for those fifteen-minute intervals, keep it to yourself and maintain professionalism. Before having kids you didn't discuss your breasts in mixed company, so why do it now?

One thing we'd recommend you NOT do is use your boss as your mommy confidant. Remember that he or she is your boss. We know it's tempting if your boss is a mom with three kids to use her as a resource, but stop right there. You need to find someone else, a peer, a true friend, or anyone, for that matter, who has a pulse. You are a mommy, but you are also a professional and you need to draw the line and respect professional boundaries. Discussing your cracked nipples with your boss may seem like the fastest way to get invited to her Christmas dinner but it's not.

So what did we do? We found ourselves in different camps on our decision to continue breastfeeding, but careful planning allowed both of us to succeed and be confident with our choices.

Leigh's Plan: Pump or Die

I decided that I wanted to breastfeed my son until he was one year old. I don't know why I was fixated on 365 days, but something told me with that 365th day I would produce a brilliant child, and the doors of Harvard, Stanford, and Yale would fly open to welcome him. I know . . . sounds silly but have you not picked up that I'm a little bit OCD? Not even my husband understood, much less my mother-in-law, who saw me struggling and repeatedly said, "I don't know why you don't just give that child a bottle. He's hungry!" Which was always followed up by, "In my day [she had her first child in the '50s] they just bound us up and gave us a shot to dry up the milk." I allowed her to sound off, and her funny advice only fueled my desire more. So with my mind made up, I set my plan in action to find a way to nurse my son until his first birthday.

—Leigh

Amy's Plan: Pump = Death

I knew from the moment I found out I was pregnant that I would do everything in my power NOT to pump once I returned to work. I knew myself and I knew the situation to which I was returning, and there were three factors that were going to make it impossible for me to succeed. (1) I'm a prude and I don't like to have my boobs exposed to the world. (2) I'm impatient and cannot wait the fifteen to thirty minutes to pump. (3) I don't relax well, and I had recurring visions of me in the pumping room while I could hear people walking down the hall asking what the hell that weird noise was. There was NO way that pumping at work would be productive for me.

I had my plan in place before the kids were born. I had bottles, formula, a breast pump, and all the related paraphernalia. The pediatrician had my back and coached me through a time line. At three weeks old, I gave my son a bottle of 100 percent pure formula. Fortunately, he took it and my plan worked. Every other day at the five p.m. feeding, I would give him a bottle of formula. And as soon as he passed out, I started pumping. I realize that I got so incredibly lucky. Neither of my sons complained about the bottle or formula. About one month prior to returning to work (when they both were about three and a half months old), I started the weaning process. By the time my first day of work arrived, I was done nursing and welcomed the freedom from that dreadful milking machine. It never once dawned on me to feel guilty about it. Having the unwavering support of our pediatrician helped.

—Amy

Know Your Rights

Since you've chosen to continue breastfeeding, you should be pleased to know that the law is typically on your side. Go to the following Web address for a summary of breastfeeding/lactation laws that are in place in the United States and the United States Territories (Puerto Rico and the Virgin Islands), and be ready to recite them if any misogynistic asshole challenges you: www.ncsl.org/programs/health/breast50.htm.

If you are unclear in any way what your rights are, it's important to ask your human resources representative or your immediate supervisor. Make sure to get the information and all of the answers in writing. Especially when it comes to your paycheck, nobody likes a surprise.

• •

When I returned to work after my second baby, I was in an important meeting at which we were to discuss a brewing crisis. The VP—"Mr. Prim and Proper"—running the meeting told all attendees that he needed four hours of our undivided attention, and no one, NO ONE, could use BlackBerrys or leave the room. I had no choice but to tap him on the shoulder and ask if it would be okay if I left for twenty minutes to pump my breasts. I felt better about taking his arrogance down a few notches, and I'm sure he'll never issue that edict again.

—Laura, Mother of Two and Director of Manufacturing

• •

Milking Supplies (i.e., Your Feed and Tack)

So let's jump right in. Pumping at work is going to require some supplies. That's right, we said it: SUPPLIES. We recommend some dedicated items that stay at your office. This eliminates the hassle of having to tote them to and fro every day and reduces the chances that you'll forget some critical parts, and you will forget things. If this isn't affordable, then by all means schlep them but make a list and cross-check yourself daily. One forgotten part is all it takes to render the pump useless. As far as the pump itself goes, that is likely the only piece you'll need to take to and from your home. If this is a big pain in your ass—you ride a bus, subway, train, ferry—see if you can buy a pump on Craigslist for fifty bucks or ask a friend if you can use hers, using your own parts, of course, so that you can just leave it at your office and have another pump at home. This is such a convenience—the holy grail of pumping—and the easier you make it for yourself, the more likely it will be that you continue.

Supplies

- **Double electric breast pump.** DO NOT SKIMP. It ain't worth it. We loved the Medela Pump in Style in either briefcase or backpack. Doesn't matter how you try to disguise it—people still know.

- **Extra parts.** One DEDICATED set of bottles, flanges, tubing, and parts specifically for your office. It is insane to try to remember all of the parts every day when you can't even remember your name. It won't happen and forgetting a crucial part will throw you into a hormonal tizzy!

- **Milk storage bags.** We loved the Lansinoh bags, as they froze well and never leaked upon thawing.

- **Disposable nursing bra pads.** Have a box just for the office and use them until you are absolutely positive you will not leak. ABSOLUTELY POSITIVE, GOT IT?

- **Lanolin cream.** Otherwise known as nipple cream. Ladies, your boobies have never seen this much action. The double pump can turn your nipples into Silly Putty and unfortunately the end result is some chafing, some bleeding, and some cracking. This miracle salve will return them to such a condition that your husband will actually want to touch them again. There is a difference between a baby nursing and a machine. The babies are nicer to Mommy. The machine—not so nice.

- **Quick Clean Micro-Steam bags.** Trying to clean your stuff in the lavatory is awkward and gross, and running the dishwasher every night is a nightmare. Use the microwave steam bags at the end of your day at the office and start the next day with clean equipment. This ingenious invention will save you lots of time, and the added bonus is it works for steaming veggies once you've dumped the pump.

- **An insulated lunch bag with ice packs.** Needed only if your pump bag doesn't include insulated storage. This will be used for transporting the milk from office to home.

- **Three to five good maternity bras or maternity camisoles.** Ask friends for recommendations. All maternity bras are not created equal and these titty slings are not cheap. Leigh spent $250 before she found a keeper. In the end she loved Glamour Mom camisoles.

- **Hands-free pumping.** Get a bra, bustier, or hands-free kit that will allow for hands-free pumping. Remember, it takes fifteen to thirty minutes two to three times a day. Don't waste that time holding flanges to your breasts dreaming of your baby. Make calls, do e-mails, eat your lunch, or read a trashy magazine, for all we care, but go HANDS-FREE! Favorite hands-free solutions are:
  - Easy Expression hands-free bustier
  - Easy Expression hands-free halter
  - Pumpin' Pal hands-free pumping strap
  - Hands-free nursing bras
- **Pumping-friendly blouses.** Button-up blouses are ideal. T-shirts are not. Remember, this process is messy, so if you don't want it splattered with mommy's milk don't wear it. And for God's sake, bring an extra. You can explain why you changed shirts later.
- **Brown paper lunch bags and a black Sharpie.** Use these for storing and labeling your milk in the company fridge
- **A nursing cover or Hooter Hider.** Didn't some trendy friend give you one at one of your nine showers? Just take it to work and leave it there. Now when the janitor keys in to empty the office trash, at least all he will see is your Hooter Hider and not your hooters. It saves you and it saves them. When a man sees a woman hooked up to "the milking machine," it becomes etched on his memory and he'll never be the same.

Productive Pumping at Work

- **Find your happy place at work.** The mother's room, the ladies' room, a vacant office, wherever. Just make sure there is a designated place.
- **Get some privacy.** Make sure you feel like you've got some privacy, no matter where you are. Even a sheet to divide you from the other pumping moms. If you are going to pump in your office, pull down the blinds and lock the door. No blinds? If

you've got some serious clout, ask to have the windows frosted! Nothing kills a letdown like the risk that someone is going to bust in on you during one of your most vulnerable moments.

- **Find a fridge/freezer.** Find a place to store your milk. It takes a ton of work to milk yourself. Don't waste it because you couldn't keep it cold. If you will be utilizing a shared refrigerator/freezer, place your milk inside a brown paper lunch bag with your name on it. You really don't want a male colleague asking "What's that?" and mistaking mother's milk for frozen yogurt. AWKWARD and GROSS!

- **Block off the time.** Schedule your pumping sessions as thirty-minute meetings in Outlook. If you don't, the time will be taken by some exceedingly boring session on tax credits or proper accounting practices. If other colleagues have the ability to *see* your schedule and you're worried that the "pumping" meeting might require further explanation, simply label these meetings as a "special project update" or "none of your stinking business!" If and when they ask what the special project is, tell them it's an exciting new project you are working on and it will continue for months but it's strictly CONFIDENTIAL. They really don't need the visual.

- **Keep your records straight.** For the first month or so, jot down your yield from each pumping session with the date. Then when you panic that your supply is going down DRAMATICALLY because of stress, you will actually have some data. Alpha females like data. If you want, you can now plot a graph to confirm your dwindling and pathetic milk supply.

TROUBLESHOOTING (DOORS WITH NO LOCKS, BURSTING BOOBS, AND DWINDLING MILK SUPPLIES)

Keeping up with the demands of work, pumping, and home life can be challenging (the understatement of the year). Not only do you have to juggle all that paraphernalia, but you also can easily find yourself leaking breast milk into your belly button while the rest of the crew in the five-hour meeting looks on. To top it off, so to speak, the stress can decrease your milk supply, thus stressing you out even more and defeating the purpose of this noble endeavor.

So what can you do to weave your way through this mess? A few tips for your tits . . .

- **Extra stuff.** Doesn't matter if it's an extra blouse, extra nursing pads, or extra pump parts. Planning ahead will save your other end—your ass.
- **An out.** Don't be afraid to excuse yourself from those interminably long meetings. If your boss knows what you're up to, just get some balls and tell him you need to excuse yourself. This is a noble cause, and in desperate times, it's not a bad thing to watch the big muckety-muck who's forcing you to sit for that long turn a brilliant shade of bright red.
- **A ready response.** You can bet on it. Someone is going to be busting in on your party. We already mentioned the Hooter Hider, now use it. And come up with something other than "AAAAAAAAAAAAAAHHHHH!"

And when the milk supply threatens to dry up . . .

- **Fenugreek.** Follow the directions—it works. The only downside is you smell like curry.
- **Water.** Put a pitcher on your desk with sixty-four ounces of water and drink all day until it's gone. You can't make milk without water. You'll be peeing all day but that's the price of making the milk.
- **Pump it up.** If you find that the rigors of your schedule are decreasing your supply, add in one more pumping session to kick it up. Day or night, your choice.
- **Lactation consultant.** Make an appointment to confirm what's going on. Nothing like a lactation lady to kick your tits into high gear.

- **All of the above.** Leigh got so low on milk she had to do all of the above, but here's the good news . . . it worked!

The Pump Room

• •

Well, since I had to pump in the cleaning lady's closet, I had frequent surprise visits from her.

Mendy, Mother of Two and CPA

The firm I was working for did not have a pumping room when I returned to work after my first child. So I was offered an empty office on the twenty-second floor of a building in which I didn't have my office. I would have to leave my building and go to an adjacent building three times a day. Yeah, right. So instead of doing that, I decided to use the desktop testing lab across from my cubicle. It had a lock, so I thought it would be fine. One day I was happily pumping and browsing my e-mail when I heard the door being unlocked and opened. I called out, "I'm in here!" The woman proceeded to enter and sat down next to me to do some testing. I said, "Oh, um, OK, well . . ." She said, "Oh, I don't mind. I'm a mom too." Well, her child was my age! I sighed and said, "OK, as long as you don't mind," and finished pumping. I just thought to myself, "Why would anyone want to sit there while I do this?"

Tracie, Mother of Two and Business Systems Analyst

While attending a mandatory conference that was held at a local hotel, I asked the staff if they had a spare room where I could pump. They were kind enough to let me use a penthouse suite that was vacant. Unfortunately, unbeknownst to the desk clerk, the suite was scheduled for some maintenance. While pumping, the maintenance men began banging on the door to be let in. Next the phone started ringing because they couldn't figure out who was in there when they had it all locked up. Luckily I finished my "business" before they managed to get in and I wasn't caught with my shirt off and my boobs hanging out.

Gail, Mother of Two and Psychologist

I made the mistake of forgetting my pump at home. At around two in the afternoon, I realized that I was in serious trouble and stood up to go to the bathroom for some tissues. Just then, one of my partners walked in and, POW, both of my boobs exploded through my sweater, which was just the perfect color that there was no possible way to cover it up. My entire front was soaked to the point that it was dripping down into the crease at the base of my bra and I could even feel it seeping into my belly button. I sure made an impression that day, just not the intended one!

Michele, Mother of Three and Lawyer

Pumping at work was a nightmare! I could not believe that there were no accommodations for working mothers at my job. I worked in an office of cubicles, so pumping at my desk, I decided, was out of the question. So I used the bathroom. Only problem was the only outlet was by the sink where I would have to stand and watch all the women wash their hands and primp in the mirror. So I stood there with my hooters out, pumping action in high gear, and made sure to say hello to everyone who came in. HOW EMBARRASSING! And I'm sure that it was more uncomfortable for them than it was for me! Finally, after several weeks of this, the maintenance man rigged up an extension cord that allowed me to reach to the shower area where I could sit down on the shower bench and be somewhat secluded from the women who came in to use the bathroom. The only telltale sign that I was around the corner with my pump was the very familiar sound of the pump echoing in the silence of the bathroom. By the way . . . I got to become very familiar with everyone's bathroom habits (So-and-so doesn't wash her hands), and of course, I knew when someone had an upset stomach. GROSSSSSSS!

Kathy, Mother of Three and IT Consultant

There was only a single bathroom at work so I would go in there. All of my female colleagues knew the routine. I would make sure no one needed the bathroom before I got started. I would sit on a chair, strap both cups on (held in place by the nursing bra), and read magazines for about twenty minutes while the Medela did its work. I kept this routine up for a few weeks even AFTER I stopped pumping—just for the break and the quiet time in the workday. No one knew, and I wasn't about to tell them.

MaryBeth, Mother of One and National Sales Manager

Pumping at work was always an adventure. Besides spilling milk all over my desk, I had a coworker almost pour my breast milk into his coffee! I was mortified.

Aisha, Mother of One and Human Resources Director

Pumping at work has been interesting. My office has no locks on the doors, and people are constantly coming in and out to drop things on our desks. That was easily resolved with a note I would tape to the door indicating privacy was needed. The hard days were the ones when my officemates were in the office; I couldn't very well kick them out of their own office to pump, so I would have to find an empty office. One time I got locked into someone else's office and the building super had to let me out. On a different occasion, I was trolling for a free office, and in the process my boss made fun of me and my breast pump bag and said, in front of my colleagues, "Oh, trying to get out of another meeting, are you?" and then he started laughing. Apparently when I went to pump, someone else in a meeting implied I was not pulling my weight because I was always pumping. I mean, was she kidding? I pumped three times a day, with one of those times being on my lunch. Pumping takes fifteen minutes. Give me a break. I guess in a fast-paced legal environment there is little understanding for motherhood and everything that goes with it, from pumping to taking a day off work because your kid is sick.

Danielle, Mother of Two and Attorney

● ●

Signs That Have Proven Not to Work

While they may seem obvious, the following signs proved ineffective:

Privacy Please

Please Knock

On Special Projects

In Use

Knock If Urgent

Women Only

THEN YOU GET IT DOWN, AND YOU CAN DO ANYTHING WHILE PUMPING!

As with anything, practice can make perfect. Remember those first few fumbling attempts with the breast pump? Tubes everywhere, milk dripping in places it shouldn't go, having the suction up to high, which made you squeal, and you holding both bottles to your boobs looking down while your nipples did things that NATURE DID NOT INTEND.

Well, all it takes is a few weeks and you're a pro. And why would working moms waste any time? What can you do while pumping?

- E-mail
- Call friends
- Make conference calls (just try to mask the *sh-sh* noise)
- Press "Control-Alt-Delete" one-handed
- Drive (with your handy-dandy cigarette lighter adapter for the pump, of course)
- Catch up on reading—whether that's a contract or *Us Weekly*

Taking Multitasking to New Heights

• •

I hate to admit it, but the best time for me to pump was while I was driving to and from the field when I was a sales manager. In the morning, I'd get in my car, hook myself up, put my seatbelt on, and drive (and pump) away. It usually wasn't a big deal, although I constantly had thoughts of what people would think if I got in an accident and was unconscious and the paramedics saw me all hooked up! The only times it was a problem were when I'd get stuck in traffic and a semitruck would pull up next to me and I would try to make sure they couldn't see in the car. The other times it was challenging were when I'd hook up on my way out of a parking garage only to have to pay at the cashier to exit. The attendants couldn't see anything because the pumps were UNDER my shirt, but I got a lot of strange looks because they could see that my shirt was poofy and they could HEAR the pump . . . God only knows what they were thinking.

Chris, Mother of Two, and Pharmaceutical and
Marketing Sales Professional

I can do anything while pumping and often did. It was best when I could do the New York Times *crossword puzzle.*

Elisabeth, Mother of Two and Television Marketing Professional

My favorite thing to do while pumping in the middle of the night was sudoku. I would turn the light on very dim, just enough to see in the dark so I could sudoku it up.

Jennifer, Mother of Two and Advertising Sales Representative

There is nothing I didn't do while pumping. I even got on my bike trainer and pumped and made work calls. Now that's multitasking: pumping, working, and exercising all at the same time!

Petra, Mother of Two and Medical Sales Account Executive

I e-mailed a lot. As a matter of fact I got so used to e-mailing while hooked up that I would forget that I was pumping, and the bottles would overflow onto my work clothes—what a disaster!

Yvette, Mother of One and Human Resources Professional

I can do almost anything rigged with my MacGyver hands-free pumping setup made of four elastic hair bands. I found the idea on the Web and it is the best hands-free solution ever. I did e-mail, phone calls, charting in patients' medical charts, light stretching, and yes, even commuting. I pumped hands-free while driving to work. How satisfying to arrive at work after a twenty-five-minute drive with eight ounces ready to chill.

Renanah, Mother of Two and Clinical Psychologist

HAVE MILK, WILL TRAVEL

Just when you think you've got it nailed, that dreaded phrase "business trip" will come up. Or even worse, "trade show" or "sales conference." It's as if they know how to push you to the brink of insanity, and next thing you know, you are going to find yourself on a four-night trip to some exotic locale like Phoenix, Las Vegas, or Orlando. Not only do you need to sort through trying to pump while on a business trip, but getting through TSA with a cooler full of breast milk is a lesson in humility. Yes, technically you can do it, but that's not a fun conversation to have.

I was pumping while at a conference and had to leave every four hours to go pump. Everyone looked down on me for it. When I was at the airport, leaving, I had a cooler that I had bought for all the milk I had pumped. I was gone a week. And come hell or high water, I

was bringing some of it home. The man at security in the airport pro-
ceeded to throw my cooler over to send it through the X-ray machine,
and it burst open and all the little plastic bags came tumbling out and
burst open all over the conveyor belt and the floor. Milk was every-
where. And I was in line with all of my work colleagues. I picked
up the cooler and what bags hadn't opened, closed it all up, and
walked away.

Heidi, *Mother of Two and Creative Professional*

● ●

Supplies for Pumping on Business Trips

- Your electric double pump and all related parts. Get ready to check a bag!
- A battery-operated single pump. Great when you need to pump on the fly. It fits in your handbag and you don't have to carry the faux briefcase.
- Batteries for any and all pumps.
- An extension cord tucked in the zipper pocket of your suitcase with the cell phone charger. (Really, it will afford privacy and often the luxury of sitting down!)
- Hands-free pumping bra, bustier, halter, or kit (see list referred to earlier in the chapter).
- An insulated lunch bag with ice packs (if storage is not included with the pump).
- Breast milk bags (one or two bags for each pumping session per day).
- Nursing pads (three to four pairs for each day that you will be away).
- Medela Quick Clean sterilization wipes. You can wash everything in the hotel sink and lay it out to dry, but the wipes are a good idea to make sure it's all truly clean. Leigh didn't have a lot of luck with the microwave bags while out on the road.
- Brown paper bags and a Sharpie. One bag for each day you are out on the road.

Tips for Traveling and Pumping

It's all in the preparation. Make sure you have all of the supplies. Explaining to colleagues why YOU MUST find the closest Babies Я Us because you are missing a "part" while trying to conduct business is just not dignified.

- Invest in a battery-operated pump. And have a stockpile of batteries to bring with you EVERYWHERE.
- If you're going to travel a long distance, keep the hand pump or single electric pump at the ready. You never know when you're going to need to take the edge off due to traffic, crying babies—not yours—and yet another de-icing of the wings.
- When you check into the hotel, ask the front desk to send someone up to empty the minibar. You'll need the space to keep the milk cold and why be tempted by all of that junk food and alcohol?
- No minibar? No problem! Inform the hotel that you have a "medical condition" that requires the use of a refrigerator for "medication." They'll be too embarrassed to ask, and before you can say what your condition is, a refrigerator will be delivered!

Pumping Disasters

• •

I was traveling for work after the birth of my first child. There I was on the road with two colleagues—both male. We were racing from a meeting to the airport and in serious danger of missing our flight. And I NEEDED to pump before getting onto that plane. I ended up pulling out the pump in the backseat of the rental car and imploring them not to turn around. With my "business" taken care of, we ran for the plane. I'm not sure they ever recovered, and I'm sure their wives think I'm a nut.

Aimee, Mother of Three and Business Development Executive

My first trip was when my son was seven months old. I literally flew around the world over the course of two weeks. I was still nursing, but didn't want to lug my electric pump around the world so I brought only the hand pump. Halfway through the trip, because of stress and the crappy hand pump, my milk just STOPPED. The same day I got my period. It was a bit overwhelming on every level. I decided to smoke a cigarette and drink some wine since it no longer mattered.

Hilary, Mother of One and Clothing Designer

Have Batteries, Will Travel

On one of many trips I had to make during the first year of my son's life, I took the double pump, which my best friend named "the double nip grip," for obvious reasons. I felt ready to knock the business out of the park. Unfortunately, pumping while on a rigorous schedule of meetings proved to be a nightmare. I would have to carry that awful fake briefcase with me to all my meetings, and then I would excuse myself at a business lunch while everyone was ordering and go into the bathroom, pray for a quick letdown (close eyes and picture darling rooting baby), and get my "business" done in ten minutes. I'd then walk back to the table and rejoin the conversation. This scenario would repeat again at dinner. It got old and pumping was always on my mind. After four days of pumping five to six times per day, it was time to go home. Unfortunately, in the rush to the airport I missed a pumping session and ran for the plane. I boarded the flight at JFK only to sit on the tarmac for an hour before takeoff. All I could do was wait until we reached cruising altitude so I could beeline it to the bathroom and pump away. At this point it had been a good six hours since I'd last pumped, and I was starting to get a little backed up, if you know what I mean. Upon arrival in that glamorous airplane lavatory, I set up shop (pump in the sink, me sitting on the can) only to find that the batteries in my pump had gone dead. Somehow I'd left a switch on and I was out of luck. I nearly burst into tears. In fact, I did. I skulked out of the bathroom and begged the flight attendant to ask around for batteries. She obliged to no avail. Well, six hours later I landed at SFO in my black Michael Stars shirt (which by now was getting more soaked by the minute), ran for the news shop, bought some batteries, and headed into the "family" bathroom. At this point I had become engorged and I had rocks all over my now watermelon-sized breasts. I went into the bathroom, all modesty gone, and just pumped and pumped for a record-breaking nineteen-ounce yield (yeah, that's over two cups). Needless to say, I never made that mistake again.

—Leigh

TO TOP IT ALL OFF

So you've got the multitasking and the traveling nailed. But let's face it: being a working mom can be a bitch. Being a working mom lugging around an extra briefcase can be a bigger bitch. Being a working mom with yet another task, namely, milking yourself like a COW, is a bitch and a half. But you can do it. It's for your baby, and if you decide that it's what your kiddo needs to thrive, then lose your inhibitions, throw your tits to the wind, and go for it. And when that office asshole mentions that you're taking too much time "off," you have our permission to slip him some breast milk in his coffee.

6

Call the Help Desk—
You Need Your Password!

THIS ISN'T GOING TO BE PRETTY

Going back to work after leave sucks. There's no getting around this. At the very least, you now must leave the house wearing actual clothes rather than sweats and flip-flops. To top it off, you're about to leave your precious baby at home with a total stranger while you slog it out at work. The cruel reality is that you often have no choice in the matter, especially if you need the paycheck. For those whose circumstances beyond their control are driving them back to work, it can feel like someone is ripping their still-beating hearts out of their bodies and then taunting them. But many look forward to the adult interaction, the unencumbered trips to Starbucks, and the fact that they're no longer watching their kiddo roll around on the floor for hours and hours on end. Must leave the house!

It doesn't matter whether you wanted to go back to work or you HAD to go. After two months, we're all in about the same place: acceptance. The playing field is leveled. Either you got used to the fact that you left your gorgeous child at home with someone you don't know or you realized your fantasy about going to work and enjoying some adult conversation was just that—a fantasy. Office politics are still boring.

For those of you dreading your return to work, it is possible to approach it with a somewhat positive and constructive attitude. There are things to look forward to, despite the fact that your baby just smiled at you for the first time while you were on your way out the door.

Good Things About Going Back to Work

- You have conversations with people who respond with actual words.
- No more poopy diapers. Or at a minimum you're changing only half of them! That's something to smile at! Yippee, no more ass-wiping from eight a.m. to five p.m.!
- You can eat without the interruption of the dropped binky, the vomit, the crying, the diaper change, etc. . . . Just you and your plate of food . . . ahhhhh.
- Your brain can now focus on things bigger than which size diaper to buy or is that a rash or how can I get my pinky far enough up the kiddo's nostril to dislodge that ginormous booger.
- You can outsource housecleaning and skip the gourmet meals—all guilt-free.

- Your greatest accomplishment of the day has a fairly good chance of being more than the requisite two loads of laundry.
- It's familiar. Whereas the first maternity leave was uncharted waters.

You Either Think It Sucks a Lot, or You Think It Sucks Only a Little

* *

Just enjoy being dressed and showered without the looming threat of being spit up on.

Hilary, Mother of One and Clothing Designer

I remember bawling every time I had to drop my first son off at day care and seeing the cribs lined up like it was an orphanage.

Jen, Mother of Two and Sales Account Manager

Honestly, I was thrilled to be back at work. And I think that was the biggest surprise for me. Every other mom I worked with kept coming by to make sure I was OK (bless them) . . . But seriously, it didn't bother me at all that my son was at day care while I was at work. I needed that piece of myself back.

Kelly, Mother of Two and Marketing Manager

* *

So If It Sucks, How Do You Deal?

If you're in the camp that feels like going back to work is the worst thing that's ever happened to you or to your child, there are ways to deal (besides just "Suck it up, lady!") A few words of advice that seemed prevalent from all of the moms we interviewed:

1. **Compartmentalize**. Some of us are better at this than others, but here's the general idea: You can't really be stressing about your kid's bowel movements while you're trying to sell a new project. And the same goes for home life. When you walk in that door to that smiling face, immediately pulling out the PDA is not recommended. Unless it's to let the kids play Bubble Wrap or Scribble, but even then, it's barely forgivable. There's a time and place for work and home, and you do your best to turn on and off when appropriate.

2. **Take a deep breath and come to terms with the fact that your kids now have a life outside of Mom.** For some moms this happens when their kids first go to preschool or kindergarten. For working moms, this happens with the first day-care drop-off or nanny exchange. It's tough to realize that you're not there every minute and your child is experiencing firsts without you. But unless you can bring your kid to work, you need to deal. Acknowledge it makes you sad. Now get over it. Did anyone else really believe that their kids took their first steps when Mommy was actually home AND watching? Like suckers, we did. Tell your child-care provider to let you experience the firsts, as in "Don't tell me if she rolled over today; I'd just as soon see it tonight at home myself and pretend that it was the first time."

3. **Trust in your child care**. You spent a lot of time trying to find the perfect child-care situation, we're sure. But this is the true test. Chronic worrying about your kid's safety, happiness, and care will surely create a bad situation for you upon your return to work. Hard to be productive when you're obsessing that the nanny is mindlessly watching TV and chatting on her cell phone while your five-month-old is trying to figure out which of your house keys fits in the electrical socket.

4. **Get the nanny to send a picture a day those first few weeks.** We know that you miss the kid. The beauty of camera phones and instant messaging means that you can check in at any time. If

you've got a nanny, see if she can send you a picture of the baby. YOUR baby, not just any baby. It can make your day and suddenly the fact that your boss just yelled at you for missing an imaginary deadline can seem like no big deal. And if the kid is in day care, it's OK to check in once a day (only once!) for the first week or so to make you feel a bit better. They won't start to hate you until week two, when you quickly go from "cute and concerned" to "psycho mommy."

5. **Don't forget the big payoff.** Presumably they are paying you to work. And keeping the bill collectors from breaking down your door can be reason enough to head back. There's also the realization that you enjoy work, and if you're happier returning to work than remaining at home, your family will be happier as well. (See chapter 10 on guilt if you feel like this is rationalizing the fact that you're not at home every waking minute of your child's day!)

WHERE DID I PUT MY ID?

So you've scrounged up your ID and badge in that old purse (goodbye, diaper bag!) and you're back at work. You've either just cried in the bathroom because you're so sad to be back or you just hung out in the Starbucks line for the last hour talking to everyone whose name you could remember. And some you didn't remember. When it's time to actually head back to your desk, plunk yourself down in front of the computer and get to work. You will, we guarantee, have that "holy sh*t" moment. It's a bit surreal. They are paying you to work. You actually have to get back into the game and contribute to the bottom line, and you can't even remember your password to get into e-mail, not to mention that the whole marketing strategy has been completely erased from your mind.

How do you cope with the fact that you are suddenly expected to contribute at work, you can't remember the names of your direct reports, and you spend most of the day daydreaming about your kid's adorable little shoulders while on the verge of tears? Don't sweat it. For at least the first few weeks you can ease your way back in. And then you're going to need a plan. We love plans!

Recognize the Three Stages of Reentry

At least part of your reentry plan should be to acknowledge the emotional turmoil you're feeling as well as the fact that what you are experiencing is not unique. You can learn from the weary-eyed women who have gone before you, and there have been lots. Have faith that they made it through and so can you.

Stage 1: "Holy sh*t, I'm back at work." Yes, you are actually back on the job. That's your computer and your desk chair and your pens and notebooks and those people over there are your colleagues and they are SICK of towing your ever-increasing weight. And you need to be productive or they might take all of those nice pens away. Hi, and welcome back!

Stage 2: "What the hell is going on here?" You've probably been gone a good long while. It's impossible to know what's going on because so much has changed. People have taken over your tasks, your accounts have been managed by others, decisions have been made, and shockingly life went on without you. You're playing catch-up and feeling like a dumb-ass. Admit it, if you interviewed for a job right now, you'd be in some serious trouble.

Stage 3: "Holy sh*t, I really AM back at work." For us, at least, there was that moment a few weeks after we started, around the time we moved back to a full-time schedule, when we realized that this was the rest of our lives, or at least the rest of our lives until our next maternity leaves. It's a painful realization, one that can most definitely bring you to your knees and potentially cause you to hit the sauce for a few nights.

Tricks of the Trade
from the Been-There-Done-That Crew

How do you minimize the chaos of returning to work with all of the angst, the guilt, and the total cluelessness that go along with it? A few tried and true tips:

- **Delete all.** We know that you're going to be overwhelmed by e-mails when you get back. You'll probably have at least three thousand of them. The first leave Amy painstakingly went through ALL of them and looked for the important ones. The second time around she realized that if it were important, the person who sent it either had solved the issue already or would send her the e-mail again. She decided to go for the full SHIFT/ HIGHLIGHT ALL/DELETE and never looked back. And no one ever said a word. So much easier.

- **Take ten.** You are truly exhausted, we know. The sight of you is making US tired. And you're stressing about pumping, the kid is still up at night, and you now have to do your paying job. It's nuts and there's no way that you should expect yourself to go from burping the kid on the couch (really, no need for critical thinking . . . thump, thump, thump) to studying a profit-and-loss statement (ouch). Bake some time in for breaks, for walks, for any excuse to get out of the office, and give your brain time to breathe. Catch up on training materials or the new employee handbook. Guaranteed to quiet your aching brain. Use your pumping breaks to do a few deep-breathing exercises. If you're not pumping, LIE and say you are pumping. Now you've just earned yourself two fifteen-minute breaks. You should feel better already. But what happens if you've got a classroom full of kids or a job that makes breaks hard to come by? Hmm, that is tough. We recommend you use those recesses wisely, take care of the biological needs, spend just a minute by yourself to take a breath, and just pray the whistle blows fast. Believe us, it's going to be hectic and you are going to need these breaks. Any break is a good break. Even if you end up curled in the fetal position under your desk or hiding in a closet to take a few breaths. No shame.

. . . .

I knew I would be tired. But you don't know tired until you have only had four hours of sleep, still have to pump, AND manage to do a database restore.

Sheila, Mother of Two and Database Administrator

. . . .

Mommy Brain aka Baby Brain aka YOU'RE DUMB!

There is such a thing as mommy brain. People joke about it, but come on. You think any normal person can go through nine months of growing a human inside her gut, give birth, suddenly have to feed a screaming banshee every two hours, have life completely turn upside down, and then return to work four months later like normal? Beyond the fact you just went through a scene straight out of Mutual of Omaha's *Wild Kingdom*, you are now trying to work while bringing up another human. You've got worries you never thought existed— feeding schedules, bowel movements. "Is the nanny going to get here on time?" "Is that stomach flu going to end up infecting the entire family?" And on and on and on.

. . . .

Everyone talks about placenta brain—the expectation that you get fuzzy once you get pregnant. Nobody prepared me for the 70/30 split post-birth. I have been back to work for seven months, and no matter *how much I have to do at work or how crazy my day is, I still feel that my brain is always in 70/30 mode: 70 percent of my brain capacity can compute work activities and 30 percent always seems to be in the mommy/household never-ending loop. (I wonder if he's sleeping OK? Is he having trouble pooping today? Oh, I need to write the nanny's check. Sh*t, we're almost out of milk. I need to call the electrician. And on and on.) I know for sure that my husband does not have this struggle. I know this because reminding him of his to-do's is part of my 30 percent list.*

Melissa, Mother of One and Marketing Manager

• •

Mommy Brain Remedies

Those first few months, you need some mommy brain remedies, surefire tricks to help you get through the struggle of having to remember your boss's name and what they asked you to do twenty minutes ago.

- **Write it all down.** We don't know about you, but post-kids we lost our short-term memory and were unable to follow complex directions. And by complex we mean two steps or more. (Measure warm water, put in two scoops of formula . . . Wait, how many scoops did I put in?) You need to be obsessive about writing stuff down. Otherwise you won't remember and you'll look like an idiot. It's OK that you aren't at the top of your game. But no need to broadcast it.
- **Find friends.** Find somebody to tell you what's going on. Reconnect with your old work friends, particularly those who have already experienced this reentry madness. When life starts to get too hectic (say on week two), these same friends are available to cover for you when you miss meetings, come in late, or

generally just totally forget what you were supposed to do. Find a friend who isn't much of a talker but can at least offer you an office to camp out in every once in a while, just to find a relaxing place to rest. You're going to need to rest a little those first few days back. Your brain has just gone from zero to ninety mph and it's sucking some serious wind!

- **Walk fast, carry lots of folders, and look busy.** When in doubt, just look busy. Makes you feel better and gets them off your trail for at least a few hours. See chapter 7, "Fake It Till You Make It," for more helpful hints.

We promise you it will get better—eventually. In a few months you'll be so used to juggling so many things, you'll become a no-nonsense model of efficiency and getting things done. But it's still a good idea to keep writing things down.

THE TRAIN HAS LEFT THE STATION

We spent those first few weeks nodding as if we knew what was going on, all the while wondering what everyone was talking about, and desperately trying to remember what the hell we did before we left on leave. We were filled with confusion and doubt. Confusion because we weren't sure if our brains had died or atrophied, but something had clearly happened to them. Doubt because we were trying to find our way back to our old roles and just felt like we were all thumbs. Our teams had just survived without us—in fact, surprisingly well—and we had no earthly idea what was going on and how we were supposed to contribute. Bumps on a log. Or more accurately, names on the list of downsizing opportunities. There are a few scenarios to which you can return (see the table that follows), but regardless, you still need to wipe that clueless look off your face and OWN your role.

Reentry Strategies—Don't Get Run Over!

	Where have you been?!	We (kind of) missed you!	Have you met Susie? She's fantastic!	You want your old accounts back?
Scenario	You left and the team is pissed! It was miserable without you and they are looking for revenge.	You delegated responsibilities and the team ran with it. You are now officially irrelevant in any decision-making processes.	You hired a temp to replace you and it turns out that she's a rock star. And she's out for your job AND this PYT (pretty young thing) is a whole lot cheaper!	You turned over the accounts you spent THREE YEARS cultivating and now it seems no one wants to give them back.
Solution	Immediately start to take on incoming fire and do some damage control. Take the team to lunch, listen to them complain, and pretend like you care. You don't need the entire team to quit just because you're back.	Go in gradually, or risk becoming the awful boss who micromanages. Have confidence in your abilities, but take some time before you ruthlessly squash their big ideas.	Get a grip on yourself and come out swinging. You've got at least a few more months' experience than she does in the job. The only thing this ladder climber has on you is more sleep!	You've got a sales plan to meet! **Get your accounts back!** Demand a plan for taking them back on. Hell, just bust in on a few calls uninvited if that's what it takes.

Regardless of the situation to which you return, you can't help but feel that the train has left the station. Any conversations or decisions that you hear about during those first few weeks are probably not meant for you to derail. You need to figure out how to jump on the moving train—without getting run over and ending up a bloody mess. We're not saying totally check out and just keep nodding when the team plans to scrap the entire marketing plan in favor of sponsoring a roller derby. Or smile sweetly when your boss lets you know that your former accounts will now officially become the property of someone else. We're just saying that you might have the opportunity to lie back a little and not immediately need to drive the train or risk hijacking it.

There's a transition plan to get you back in the game. We separated ours into a 30-day plan and a 45-day plan. If it didn't help us actually get integrated again, it certainly made us feel as if we were giving it our best shot.

The First 30 Days: Jumping on the Train

- **Listen to everyone and ask questions.** When someone says something you don't understand, or you feel like you need context, ask the question. Don't feel stupid. You have the perfect excuse—you were totally checked out with a baby latched on to your breast and no sleep. As long as the questions are asked intelligently—i.e., at the proper time and in the proper context—you're going to be allowed to keep on asking. Warning: There are such things as dumb questions, as if you didn't already know that. Asking the dates of the upcoming sales meeting when the last twenty minutes were spent discussing its every detail qualifies as dumb.
- **Balance keeping the team empowered, but YOU relevant.** Ooooohhh, this one is tricky. Your team just survived without you and made decisions without you and totally filled in for you. And now you want to come waltzing back in and take all of that authority away? You self-important, insecure egomaniac! So you've got to balance inserting yourself into the decision-making

process without undermining their authority. Ask them to catch you up on what went down while you were out. Ask them to bring you up to speed on what's coming down the pike. And by all means, try to figure out a way to keep some of the authority with them. Remember that you're going to need to screech out at 5:00 p.m. in order to make the day-care pick-up and you'd rather have some decisions delegated to someone who still has the ability and motivation to stay past 5:01.

- **Find friends who can give you the straight story.** You checked in with your boss. You checked in with the team. Now it's time to find out what really is going on. Who's getting along with whom? Who is about to quit? Who was secretly angling for your job while you were out? Which office affair is heating up and whose wife just found out about it? This political non-sense is critical information. You do not want to be caught step-ping into a minefield. During your first few months back, you do not have the emotional bandwidth for one more ounce of turmoil.

- **Check in frequently with your boss.** Don't be annoying about it, but if you were checking in every week before you left, try to spend these first 30 days checking in twice a week. It will make you feel more on top of it, and it will make your boss feel like you're fully dedicated. Did we mention that you shouldn't be annoying about it? No one likes a brownnosing kiss-ass, even though you are going to need all the help you can get. In a fight-to-the-death head-to-head battle, the you who just returned from baby bliss would never survive if pitted against the pre-kids working you.

The 45-Day Plan (That's right—you get only two more weeks to pull yourself completely together.)

It's officially time. You need to start pulling your own weight or you're going to get run over by the train—not just hit, but pulverized.

You can only count on the kindness of others for so long. The goal of the next two weeks is to get back into the game and remind everyone that you are one FANTASTIC worker bee.

- **Contribute and make decisions.** You've got four weeks of knowledge behind you and are ready to start barking out commands. Have the confidence to act like you know what you're doing. And if anyone questions your authority, say something like, "Well, you didn't tell me that." It's now OFFICIALLY everyone else's fault that you don't know what's up.
- **Start taking over some projects.** There's a risk that you might be late to day-care pick-up, but it's time to be taking on some meaty assignments and show that you actually deserve your paycheck. Pick wisely on your first big new thing since coming back. It's got to be manageable. You need to be successful and you also need to be able to pump two to three times a day, make it home for pick-up, and maintain your sanity. We cannot recommend anything that will require extra travel. That's just masochistic and your husband may kill you.
- **Stop checking in with your boss.** Fly free, baby. Both you and your boss want some freaking autonomy. Go back to your regular touch-base schedule and skip all the ass-kissing. Now they actually want to see the work. They hired you to get the job done and now it's time to do it.

There's No Shame

It's inevitable that you're going to have at least an embarrassing moment or two upon your return. Leak breast milk all over, forget to make an important meeting, come into work with spit-up on your shoulder, fall asleep in a meeting. It's going to happen. We want you to know that there's no shame. You can stop being embarrassed for that time you forgot your colleague's name, excused yourself to go "potty," or called your boss "honey."

You are from this point forward absolved from guilt for the following:

- **You forget your password.** Do you think any working mom can remember her password? All it takes is a four-day weekend and we've forgotten our password and the number to the help desk (yes, it is H-E-L-P, but sometimes even that slips our mind).

- **You cannot remember anyone's name.** Even though it's Leigh's profession to remember the name of everyone she meets—as well as his or her favorite candy, date of birth, life partner's nickname, and Social Security number—even she couldn't remember names when she came back. She still can't. That should make you all feel better. Really.

- **You feel dumb and totally lost.** Ummmm. Who doesn't those first few weeks of returning to work? We've all been there. Get over yourself!

- **You spend your time pumping, daydreaming about the kid, or calling day care to check in.** We ended up spending an inordinate amount of time daydreaming those first few weeks. Good thing day care didn't have a webcam. Who wouldn't rather spend their time thinking about nibbling on baby shoulders than doing the three-year plan? (Is Amy the only one with the baby-shoulder fetish?)

- **You don't spend every waking minute thinking about your baby.** That was a shocker to us as well. We had just spent four months changing every diaper and feeding every meal. Suddenly we were liberated and we actually could go five minutes without thinking about the kid. Shocking. Once you get over the initial surprise, it's possible to move on. We promise that you will not forget to leave work and pick up the kid. We absolutely promise.

PART-TIME ~~LOVER~~ WORKER

The part-time schedule . . . God, it sounds so fantastic, doesn't it? That gradual transition from stay-at-home mom (SAHM) to working mom. The ability to get your laundry done and still make money. The chance to get to the grocery store on a Thursday instead of loading the weekend with chores. More precious time with your darling baby. Yes, it sounds great. And it can be great, but there's something you should realize about part-time schedules. They are rarely well defined and can be a colossal pain in the ass unless you do some serious boundary setting.

The pitfalls of a part-time schedule are many. We're sure the following sounds familiar:

1. **You're being paid for four days a week, but you're really working five.** Who needs that? But when your boss calls to say that he needs something NOW, it's hard to tell him that it's actually your day off and you'll get back to him the following Monday. This is what we call part-time pay, full-time headache. The reality is that in today's work culture, we are all available 24/7 through technology and work outside of traditional office hours.

2. **You can't get anything done anywhere.** It's tough to get involved in a project, let alone finish it if you're waltzing in the door every other day. It only caused us to feel schizophrenic—a huge problem if you're already feeling mentally unbalanced. Now you feel like you're bad at both, screwing up with the kid and working late at night every night to maintain the part-time schedule.

3. **You are considered expendable.** Oh, we know that this sounds harsh, but trust us: In tough economic times, the woman working three days a week has a target on her back and is going to be considered a nice-to-have rather than a need-to-have. Yes, that sucks, but it is true. This is America and we're not exactly

known for our socialist tendencies. Part-time momployee =
downsizing opportunity. Don't say we didn't warn you.

So how do you manage the morass of the part-time schedule? Four
days a week might be your answer. Less chance of being caught by
the partner on one of your "off" days, thereby making you work for
80 percent of the time for 60 percent of your pay. Less chance of dropping EVERYTHING midstream. And less chance of being considered a nice-to-have rather than a need-to-have. Put it this way: You're
just taking a lot of three-day weekends in a row. Who doesn't deserve a
three-day weekend? The key is to get the job done. Face time is important at certain times, but at the end of the day, results are what matter—
or should matter—to your boss and the people you work with.

If you can't say no to your boss, then screw it. And if you can't help
checking and responding to your e-mails 24/7, double-screw it. You
will not actually be working part-time. If you are being paid for a part-
time schedule, you may have to try to "not work" as many working
hours as you possibly can in order to make up for the off hours that you
do work. Be flexible, so to speak. We're quite sure that it will add up to
thirty-two hours of work when all is said and done. If you can deliver
results by working from home one or two days a week—while still getting paid your full salary—you may be better off than trying to work
part-time. Even one day a week at home creates more flexibility for you.

THE UNFORESEEN BENEFITS
OF RETURNING TO WORK

*I was amazed how nothing seemed to bother me at work anymore. It
seemed as if nothing was really as important as it was before my son was
born. If I didn't return an e-mail or phone call that day, there was always
tomorrow. What was really important was waiting for me at home.*

Jennifer, Mother of Two and Teacher

There's a dirty little secret about returning to work: You have perspective; i.e., you don't really care about the minutiae as much as you did before. It takes a working mom to know that that's actually a good thing. Why, you might ask, would my employer want to know that I don't care as much as I used to? Frankly, we're firm believers that it makes you a better employee. Okay, we're revealing a bit much here, but we are somewhat neurotic. We would spend hours awake at night freaking out that we messed up an analysis or gave someone poor directions. Obsessed. And then we'd try to go to work the next day completely exhausted and freaked out that we'd messed something up. We needed to relax. And we needed to only sweat the BIG stuff.

Having kids forces you to care less about the unimportant time-sucks that can dominate a workday. You physically have no more space left in your brain to obsess about the market share data you collected last week. Is it the right data? Is the source reputable? Is the study recent? WHO CARES? Really. You now have the ability to sit back and determine if the decision is going to change if you update the market survey by a few hours. Don't sweat it. If being a working mom doesn't force you to prioritize and focus on only the big issues, nothing else will. NOTHING!

YOU'RE BACK AND NOT REALLY BETTER THAN EVER

We're not going to lie to you. You probably aren't better than ever. Especially at first, but you'll get there. You're a smart cookie and even though you're currently wearing your kid's breakfast on your shoulder, the people at work will soon realize that you're back, you're good at your job, and you're pulling your weight. That's all you can ask for. Working moms emerge as the most efficient employees in any organization. There is simply too much motivation to focus on the big things, do them right the first time, avoid wasting time, and finally get home to see our kids.

Fake It Till You Make It

(Looks Are Everything)

Delusions

- I'll fit into my work clothes in time for my triumphant return to the office.
- Those aren't boogers on my shoulder. Just a little lint.
- No one noticed that I just fell asleep in that budget review.
- My colleagues don't realize that I'm sneaking out at 5:01.

So now that you're a frazzled working mom like the rest of us, how are you going to keep it all together? Or at least the appearance of having it all together? We've found one indispensable trick—when all else fails, fake it!

We're not condoning insincerity. We're advocating survival. Sometimes survival is convincing your colleagues and yourself that you've got it all together, despite the fact that you've had no sleep, your nerves are raw, deadlines are fast approaching, and all you can think about is the fact that you're going to be late in picking up the kids since the meeting is running really, really long and the moron across the table from you just started talking about some new rule he thinks you should run by Legal.

Why do we think faking it is important?

1. **No one cares.** Suck it up because regardless of how tired you are, how stressed, no one cares that you weren't able to get on e-mail last night because your kid had trouble going to sleep. You need to stop thinking that your boss or your work colleagues give a hoot that you're tired, cranky, and on the edge of tears. They pay you to work.

2. **If you need the job, we want you to keep it.** If that means buying you some time at work by giving you a few the-dog-ate-my-homework excuses, then so be it. You need to look like you're on top of it so they don't fire you or put you on "performance review," i.e., "We're watching your every move and although we say there's a path to the right track, you're really a step away from being canned."

3. **Breathe deep and say a few *oms*.** Not to sound like a couple of fanatics about *The Secret*, but we actually believe that you can visualize your way to looking like you've got it all under control. Smoke and mirrors, ladies. If you keep telling yourself that you've got it together, you just might trick yourself into believing it. We have.

4. **You have to feel good about yourself if you want to be happy.** If that means covering up your dark circles with an inch of spackle, go for it. If that means wearing the same outfit three days a week because it makes you feel fantastic, great. If that means demanding that you get exercise on your lunch hour, go ahead and sweat it out!

5. **Buy yourself some time.** Sometimes you'll find that you might have been faking it in the beginning, but before you know it, you'll actually be on top of it or looking great or having fun. We swear. Faking it gives you the few weeks/months/years you need to actually get it together.

PERFECTION IS A CRUEL MYTH

The golden rule of faking it is letting go of perfection. If you are actually trying to do everything perfectly, you are not, by definition, faking it. It's too much self-imposed stress and will land you one stop short of the loony bin. If there was ever a time to cut yourself some slack, this is it. If you stop caring about dust balls and fancy meals and stop believing that your child will be forever disadvantaged if he or she doesn't go to ballet, soccer, swim lessons, AND Spanish each Tuesday and Thursday, you might just be able to make it until the kid learns to be a bit more self-sufficient. Or drive—whichever comes first.

You need to find yourself some shortcuts and you need to be okay with those shortcuts. Take a deep breath. Relax. Focus on the important things and try to figure out what you can fake your way through.

FAKING IT AT WORK

When we returned to work from maternity leave, we truly had no clue what was going on and would sit in meetings completely unclear on why we were there. We thought that was as bad as it would get, until the post-maternity-leave glow wore off, and we were faced with the daunting reality of the daily grind at home. It was hard to convince people we were awake in meetings and we struggled. Never mind that we were the ones who called the meetings.

So how do you survive, or better yet, continue a successful career trajectory? Even assuming that you're holding it together the vast majority of the time, every once in a while you're going to need to pull some sort of trick out of your hat to make sure that everyone believes you're fully engaged.

Tips for Faking It at Work

Keep the PDA handy. We don't care which brand you use—BlackBerry, iPhone, Palm Pre, whatever! This handy little sucker is going to keep you in touch with what's going on at work wherever and whenever. The beauty of having it fully hooked up with your work e-mail? You can be sitting in the doctor's waiting room with your pinkeyed child and still be available to answer that e-mail bomb. It's going to be a brief response, but it's a response. Note: This same tactic can also be used for less noble pursuits—like sneaking out early to get the grocery shopping done before you have to get the kids. Or sneaking out for a pedicure.

Figure out a way to work a little later just a few nights a week. If you can manage it, try to stay past the 5:30 p.m. whistle just one or two nights a week. This has two advantages—one, you can actually get some extra work done. Two, if you can make that one night a week visible to everyone around you, they might just forget that you screech out at 4:59 every other night.

If you have to work late, milk it! Occasionally, despite your best efforts to power your way through lunch to get all of the work done, you need to stay late. It sucks, but use it to your advantage. Once the dust settles, make sure you casually mention to everyone you know how late you worked. This strategy is best used infrequently and with the utmost subtlety. You don't want them to see through you. Note: This is NEVER recommended where the vast majority of workers do work late every night and your one late night will make you look like a poser.

If you know that you're cutting out early or coming in late, make up for it (kind of). So you know that you're going to be late. Let's say, for instance, that it just took you thirty minutes to drop your kid at day care because of a severe bout of separation anxiety, which required you to pry the kid off your legs. You're going to need to take the edge off with a foamy latte before heading into the office. Use the aforementioned PDA and do a few e-mails in the parking lot. Then head to the coffee shop. You've left a trail of evidence that you were on e-mail when required. You've got your alibi, even when you pull up with the steaming latte. And you're caffeinated and calm.

If you have to be sneaky in order to sneak out, get good at it. So you have to leave a little early to get the kids, get dinner, or buy some sunscreen because school is telling you you're the only parent who hasn't managed to bring it in yet. Leave the lights on. Leave your laptop on at your desk. Remember, you have your PDA. Leave a coat or a big purse/ bag in an easily seen location. Don't walk out with your coat on and dry-cleaning under your arm. Mark a meeting in your calendar. "Business review" is both vague and important-sounding. Perfect, now high-step it out of there.

Five Elements of a Great Excuse

1. It's realistic.
2. You aren't throwing someone else under the bus (bad karma).
3. There's no way to prove it, even if they suspect guilt.
4. You don't sound defensive.
5. It buys you some time.

Have these responses ready. They might be somewhat transparent, but we doubt anyone is really going to call you on it. And to get truly good excuses, try to find a willing accomplice at work. The most likely candidates are other working moms. Everyone needs a good alibi.

Answers to "Where is that _____?"

Excuse	Notes
You didn't get that e-mail/voice mail? I must not have pressed "Send"! Let me get through with my next few meetings and I'll send it to you later today.	Sounds like you did the work. Also buys you some time. Downside: Makes you sound a little ditsy.
The analysis is a bit trickier than I originally thought. Let me review it one last time and send it to you shortly.	Sounds like you're conscientious and responsible. Downside: Can't be used on simple projects.
I'm so sorry. I was set to finish it this morning but I just walked in from the doctor's office. I had to bring _____ in for an unexpected visit.	You get the sympathy vote and you're technically not throwing anyone under the bus. Downside: If your kid knows your boss, and can talk, you might be in trouble. "Annual exam" can be substituted in this case.
I know it's a bit later than I wanted, but we had a few fires come up that needed to be put out. I'm on it and you'll get it soon. (Note: The answer to "What fires?" is "Oh, you don't want to know! Don't worry, we took care of it.")	Great excuse because it makes it sound like you handled another annoying problem, thus saving your boss's ass. They love that.
Oh, I've been BURIED by a special project . . . Operation Ring of Fire. Don't tell anyone you heard that from me.	Not entirely realistic. But tons of fun. Best used on underlings or those not within your direct reporting structure.

Answers to "Where were you? Where have you been?"

Excuse	Notes
Did you not get my e-mail? I had to speak with _____ this morning about that other project.	Never suggest you sent an e-mail. Too easy to prove that you didn't. This is a BAD excuse.
One of the kids woke up sick today, so I had to call in backup child care.	You get a bit of sympathy and look superdedicated because you left your poor sick child with some stranger. Make sure that no one can blow your cover, including your kid.

Excuse	Notes
My last meeting ran late. I got back as soon as I could.	Suggested only when you have a willing accomplice to back you up. Or when your boss doesn't know ANYONE in the last meeting.
My e-mail/voice mail has been on the fritz. I'm not sure I got that. When did you send it?	Recommended only at companies where IT is truly unreliable. You must have precedent to pull this off.
I'm not feeling well. The kids have had an awful stomach flu and I was afraid that I was getting it. I think I'm fine, though. Do I look okay?	Fabulous excuse. Watch them all immediately back off. Again, be careful that no one can rat you out.
Nowhere. Why? Who's looking?	Ballsy, for sure. Sounds a bit defensive, and not recommended if you're in line for the next round of layoffs.

Stay on Message

Let's face it. I'm a PR professional, and it's not uncommon for reporters to put me on the spot. Being good at my job requires that I often rely on canned statements in order to buy some time. I guess it wasn't so hard for me to adopt this practice in all aspects of my life. It became obvious that surviving this period of time would require me to fake it a little.

When I returned to work, it was surreal. The pace seemed so fast and I seemed so slow. My biggest misconception was that I thought people would go easy on me for the first few weeks as I reentered the vortex that is my job. No such luck. When I realized that there would be NO break-in period I suffered a mild panic attack and just naturally starting faking it. It made every day more of an adventure. I gave people what they wanted, e.g., "Nothing is going to slip through the cracks." I just stayed on message. I came up with quick snap-backs that I would use over and over again until I got my professional mojo back. Here are some examples. Go ahead and tweak them a little and call them your own!

Q: *Did you get my e-mail last night about that issue?*

A: *I did and thank you. I'd love to discuss it further, but I'm ten minutes late for my next meeting. I'll shoot you an e-mail by the end of the day summarizing my thoughts. I'm sure that will be more helpful than me yammering on in the hallway.*

Q: *I still haven't received that report. Is there a problem?*

A: *That's odd, I finished it yesterday. I wonder if I inadvertently forget to hit "Send"? Huh—let me check and resend it. (Buys you time to actually do the thing you clearly forgot to do.)*

Q: *How's everything going now that you're back?*

A: *Great, I'm so excited to be back. One of my business ideas is finally getting to the starting line. It's so gratifying! (The question is a TRAP. They want you to say the baby isn't sleeping, that you are guilt-ridden and an overall wreck.)*

Q: *I haven't seen you on the eight a.m. sales call. Where have you been?*

A: *That's true, I'm on another piece of business right now. I'm calling in when my schedule allows.*

Q: *I just talked to So-and-so, and he and I agree on the way forward. What do you think?*

A: *Well, I don't want to talk out of turn. That project is very important to my boss, so let me check in with her first and get back to you.*

You get the picture!

—Leigh

For the Masters

Once you get really good at faking your way through the basics, we're not opposed to advanced fakery. When vacations are all dedicated to family visits, and life is starting to overwhelm you, we are not opposed to sick days. You'd best be extremely confident about how you're doing at work. If so, calling in a sick (of it) day to rest at home, get on some errands, and pick up the kid early can be highly rewarding. After one of those, you just might be able to make it to your next vacation.

● ●

Don't tell your boss everything you are going through. Fly under the radar. Do your job even if it's at a minimum. No one else knows but you . . . for now. Don't beat yourself up for being distracted. You've had a baby!

Marcia, Mother of One and Sales Manager

Always appear to be on e-mail late at night. Answer people late and early in the morning. Then people tend to ignore when you roll in at nine-fifteen.

Heidi, Mother of Two and Creative Professional

I try not to yawn in front of people.

Tracie, Mother of Two and Business Systems Analyst

Always put on a happy face and never let them see you sweat, literally!

Laurie, Mother of Two and Advertising Sales Director

● ●

Feeling Good About Yourself

● ●

I really don't look good at work anymore. I used to look fab—not a hair out of place, clean fashionable clothes, makeup just so, and always manicured nails and waxed brows. I shudder at my post-kid brows,

chewed nails, and dandruff-covered shoulders. Just today, a colleague
pointed out the hole under my arm in my sweater as I sat back and
clasped my hands behind my back in a group meeting. Thank God I
happened to have shaved.

Amy, Mother of Three and Research Analyst

We swear we're not crazy superficial. OK, maybe a little. Regardless, you're not going to find either one of us obsessing about nail color or hunting down a zebra print purse to match our zebra pumps. There is simply no time to care. But we do both try to keep people from running away screaming when they see us. More important, we both try to keep ourselves feeling good about our outward appearance and our health. And most important, we believe in the power of Spanx. They render you "ass crackless" and squeeze your stomach in until it's (almost) taut. If you're lucky, no one would ever believe you had a baby.

If you feel good about yourself, then others are going to sense that confidence and just assume that you've got it all together. Even, as we've already established, if you don't. You're faking it, remember?

There are a few key areas where you can work on feeling good about yourself: your beauty routine, your clothes, and your health. Now, you'll notice that these aren't listed in order of importance. Health is the hardest to fake. Let's start with the others because we're not in the mood for difficult subjects.

YOUR BEAUTY ROUTINE

The cosmetics industry makes fortunes off us poor working moms. Who needs concealer more than the mom who just spent all night up with her kid and then has to suffer through some long presentation the next morning? But it doesn't just begin and end with concealer. If you want to trick everyone into believing you're on top of it, you're going to have to keep it all together, from your hair to your eyebrows to your toes.

Cover It Up—Literally

Under-eye concealer: Covers dark eye bags and all other unsightly blemishes. Saves us from looking like the living dead. Pick a brand you love and stick with it.

Two-in-one lotions and potions: Who needs two lotions, when you can get away with one! And if you buy sheer tinted lotion, you don't need to spend time trying to figure out if your neck matches your nose. If they made three-in-one potions, or four-in-one lotions, we'd be all for it. Or a "press-on face" kind of deal, where we could just press a cloth to our face and look like we spent thirty minutes actually doing our makeup. That would be worth a few extra bucks.

Lipstick: Useful for distracting your audience from those bags. You know it works when you get loads of compliments every time you make this feeble attempt. Beware. Don't put it on tired. Amy's been known to kind of miss her mouth and look like a clown for the rest of the day.

Mascara: Although we're not convinced that Maybelline hasn't completely pulled the wool over our eyes, we're so desperate that we'll believe others can actually see our long, luxurious lashes and miss the rest of the haggard face. If you do nothing else, please put on mascara. It's a D effort, but at least it's an effort.

* *

Concealer and mascara are essential to my working-mom face. The concealer hides the bags under my eyes and the mascara draws attention away from the bags. And Visine gets rid of the red in my eyes!

Aisha, Mother of One and Human Resources Director

* *

I Still Refuse to Wear Foundation . . .

I am horrible at being girly. I am a spaz at makeup and typi-
cally end the day with smeared mascara and smudged lip-
stick. I'm also impatient and can't tolerate more than three
minutes in the bathroom each morning. I get ready so quickly
in the morning that I routinely set land-speed records, mostly
because I skip huge chunks of the normal beauty routine.
Leigh recently informed me that I should be moisturizing my
neck. Who knew? And what is exfoliator anyway?

Now, I'm not saying that I can get away with it. I can't. Far
from it. And after kid number two, it became painfully obvi-
ous that I needed to pull myself together to avoid losing the
confidence of my colleagues. The added benefit—when I finally
got with the program—was that when I looked in the mirror, I
wasn't bummed out by the huge black circles under my eyes.

I also now blow-dry my hair. Didn't used to but I got this
new cute and sassy haircut and tried to get away with walk-
out-of-the-house-wet hair. Leigh told me I was "limiting my
fabulosity," which translates to "Lady, you look like crap.
Clean it up." Now I sacrifice my speed records to hot air.

On weekends, I do none of the above. My family forgives
my dark bags. My husband has a matching set.

—Amy

Mom Hair

We used to define "mom hair" as some sort of short, boring cut
that looked like you could burn a hole in the ozone given how much

hairspray was required to keep it in position. It never dawned on us until now that it was possibly the EASIEST haircut known to women everywhere. Short, simple, and once you shellac it down, you don't have to worry about it for the rest of the day.

Well, none of us want to look boring. And popular opinion now frowns on burning holes in the ozone layer with Aqua Net. So what to do with the hair? We don't care what length it is, just make sure that it's cute, it makes you feel good, and it's EASY. Curlers, flat irons, pomades, and blowouts are all the enemies of the working mom. And if you're coloring your hair, stay on it. Calico cat isn't a look to strive for. Invest in a good haircut and color. And if you can't afford either the $200 cut and color or another 4.5 hours of babysitting for the four hours required to sit in the chair, try touching up your roots at home. Ask your hairdresser (and if she's a mom she'll understand) for the most flattering, low-maintenance style for you and tell her it's hard for you to come in every six weeks for touch-ups. She may be able to recommend some tricks or good home kits for you to use in between visits.

Other Beauty Musts

An eyebrow wax: Nothing says "I'm at my wit's end" more than shaggy brows with those pathetic little straggly hairs that hang out somewhere between your eyelid and the rest of your eyebrow. Plus, the super-arch makes you look awake, even when your lids are drooping dangerously low.

Your toenails: We ask only that if there is even the slightest chance you'll be wearing open-toed shoes, or taking your shoes off, you get rid of the chipped polish. You instantly appear to have it together when you've got a pedicure. Nasty toenails equal woman on the verge of a nervous breakdown. You can be on the verge, but try not to telegraph that with your toes.

Perfume: Although not for everyone, it can mask that stench of sour milk that unfortunately can accompany you after a small boob leak. Or after the kid spits up formula on you right as you leave the house. Who cares what your cubemate thinks? Spritz it up.

WARDROBE MALFUNCTION

Clothes matter. Really. To see us while we were working on this book might cause you to doubt that. But when it was time to roll out in public, we'd desperately try to pull it together, thank you very much! We don't care in which profession you earn your paycheck. If you look and feel like a schlub, it's going to be really tough to convince everyone else at work that you can still handle your job. You don't need to sacrifice comfort, but if you are trying to pass off those sweatpants as "cotton trousers," think again. They're all on to you.

It all goes back to fooling yourself into believing you've got it all under control. Sometimes all it takes is an outfit that makes you smile and suddenly you are walking that catwalk again like you own it. Or a necklace that blinds everybody to the fact that you didn't wash your hair this morning.

Wear clothes that fit: First things first; if you're wearing clothes that are too tight, or too big, you're not going to feel so great. It's hard to feel cute when the button on your pants is digging into your gut and giving you gas. Lose the weight or get new clothes. After our first kids, we both got new clothes. We were already bummed about leaving our kids. No use in also being bummed that we couldn't lose those last five pounds. That took another year or so, emphasis on the so.

Layer: Spit-up. Boogers. Drool. Muddy shoes. Sticky hands. Poo. These are the everyday hazards of your morning routine. And we can't begin to count how many times someone has asked us, "What is that on your shoulder?" Rather than going through seven costume changes each morning, just put on your last layer only after you've kissed the kid good-bye for the day.

Make yourself feel snazzy: Cute clothes and shoes serve only one function. They make you feel good and help you play the part. You love them while you're wearing them, and when everyone else gives you compliments on your outfit or your snazzy pumps, you actually forget that you're faking it. We're not saying buy Prada. We're saying get some clothes and shoes you love. Faking it does not include faking that you have some fancy bank account. We said "Fake it" not "Be a fraud."

Bedazzle them: Who can pay attention to your sad, tired eyes when you're blinding them with that sparkly necklace? Or that fabulous scarf? Necklaces, scarves, earrings, bracelets, headbands, eyeglasses (even if you don't need them), whatever—accessories are essential elements in the fake-it game. Even if you don't have time to think, grab one from a pile and throw it on. ALWAYS accessorize.

• •

Invest in some great outfits that make you feel like a professional hot mama! Even when you're tired and dragging, a fancy outfit will make you hold your head up high.

Miki, Mother of One and Recruiter

Buy lint rollers in multiple packs from the warehouse store. Keep one in your bedroom, one in the downstairs bathroom, one in the car, one in your briefcase, and one in your desk drawer. Especially helpful to dog owners! It's hard to look professional and be taken seriously if you've got dog fur and crumbs all over you.

Alex, Mother of Two, and Event and Marketing Director

• •

My Uniform

I'm addicted to Theory clothing. Okay, I haven't bought any recently due to the economic meltdown. But when I feel flush with cash, I've got to be one of their best customers. After kid number one, I was feeling large and in charge and I dragged my husband with me to buy some new clothes that actually fit and made me feel good. I got a few key pieces that immediately went into heavy rotation. One pair of pants that I bought were "magic pants." Every time I wore them, people told me I looked thin. Magic pants.

I never thought anyone would notice that I only wore this small collection of clothes. But Leigh noticed and called it my uniform. Although predictable, it was the perfect uniform. Looked cute, made me feel good, and came across as professional. Plus, I didn't have to think when I got dressed each morning.

—Amy

THE HARDEST TO FAKE . . . YOUR HEALTH

We're the first to admit that we are absolutely NOT the experts in health and fitness. Sad to admit, but we actually get winded walking up the one flight of stairs at work. We don't want that to happen to you. But moms, especially working moms, do not have time to get sick. You already took all your sick days when your KIDS were sick! Working moms need the physical and mental stamina of a marathon runner. Remember, this isn't a sprint. The more you take care of your day-to-day health, the better you will feel, the more energy you will have to get through each day, and the less cranky you will be.

- Try to eat healthy (freebasing cheese quesadillas never got anyone back into her size six pants . . .) and for energy. You don't need a sugar crash in the middle of the day when you're already reeling from lack of sleep. Then again, when you are tired and have no time to make your own breakfast you're more likely to pick up that donut. We know, we know—it's a catch-22. But in all honesty, the better you eat, the better you will feel. Or take a multivitamin and call it a day. Again, not experts.

- Try to get some exercise. Not a ton. Just enough to make you feel like you accomplished something that day or, in our case, week. We sadly try to convince ourselves that the one-block walk from the parking garage to the office is exercise, but we're not dumbasses. We know that we're lacking in the exercise department. The fact is, getting some exercise is going to give you more energy and make you feel better mentally. Of course, "Who the hell has time?" you might ask, as a working mom. We ask the same question. Tell your husband you will all be happier if Mommy gets some exercise time a few days a week. If he has any sense, he will want you to feel good and be healthy.

- Try to drink enough water. This, anyone can do. A lot of the time when you think you are hungry, you are just thirsty, and when you think you are tired, you are just dehydrated. Ditch the soda and keep a big glass with you at all times. It helps, we swear.

- When you can, get some sleep. You won't get enough. Just get as much as you can. Don't stay up late watching Letterman. That's what TiVo is for.

- Don't regularly drink yourself into a stupor. That one should go without saying, but we wanted to just gently remind you . . . and ourselves.

Find an eating and exercise plan that works for you. There are plenty of experts out there and enough channels on cable TV that someone has GOT to be airing a workout show at any given moment of the day. Recently Leigh got her groove on with Core Rhythms, the equivalent of trumping and Jazzercise all rolled into one. We're not health gurus, but we're smart enough to know that you need one. And when you get one let us know, because we need one, too.

• •

To me, happy and beautiful go hand in hand. I have made a commit-
ment to myself (and everyone in my life because I am less of a bitch
when I do this) to run at least two to three days during the workweek.
I get a little less sleep and I might be thirty minutes later to work, but I
am happier, therefore nicer, feel prettier, and am more productive than
if I am a martyr all week and never work out. There is NOTHING
pretty about me come Friday if I don't work out!

Gabrey, Mother of Two and Creative Director

• •

WHEN ALL ELSE FAILS

Faking beauty, wardrobe, and health can still sometimes not be
enough. So what do you do when you're still looking and feeling like
the dog's dinner? Drugs! Okay, that's grossly simplifying it, but we
feel the need to save you from yourself and give you some sources for
when all natural methods fail.

Your Drug of Choice

Caffeine. Lots of it. In all forms. We're all for it.

Visine. An essential tool when sleep-deprived.

Gum. It can keep you awake and masks your coffee breath.

Cucumbers, raw meat, gel packs. Anything that will keep your
eyes from being puffy. We're not picky. As long as it works.

Happy pills. All joking aside, if faking it is failing you, it might
be time to look deeper and see if professional help is in order. It just
might be the kick-start you need. We aren't saying to medicate your
problems away, but read chapter 9 about Crazy Eyes and if it sounds
real close to home, get thee to the doctor and tell him you are feeling
a little "off."

• •

I discovered Starbucks mochas! I could use an IV with caffeine running through it at the rate I'm escalating and embracing my coffee addiction.

Debbie, Mother of Two and Marketing Executive

• •

FAKING IT AT HOME

No, we don't mean faking that, you dirty bird! We mean faking yourself into actually having fun. Have you ever noticed that when the to-do list gets too long, you start to focus on the to-do's rather than having fun and enjoying the shockingly little amount of time you have with your family? Or you start to dread the routine that has become your life? The word "drudgery" comes to mind. Well, it's time to fake yourself out. You might just catch yourself starting to have fun.

Things You Can Fake at Home

Pretend the errands are done. Tough to do, but if you stop stressing about the fact that the milk is down to a few drips you might actually find some time to hang out with the family or even get some time to yourself. You'll find a way to get the errands done eventually. Whether it's you who actually does them or you outsource to friends, family, or paid professionals, they will get done.

Pretend you're not tired. Go hang out with your friends. Not every night. Just once in a blue moon. You'll have fun and that can make up for the one night of a little less sleep. The next day, when you're suffering through the consequences, just remember the fun you had.

Pretend you want to spend time with your husband and kid. Who hasn't dreaded coming home at one time or another? But fake enthusiasm for the 1,012th reading of *Surprise, Thomas* or *Princess*

Belle and we know that you'll end up having a good time. And if date night sounds too daunting, try to suck it up. Ten minutes in, you just might remember why you married him.

THE OTHER RULE OF FAKING IT

So we now know that the golden rule is to let go of perfection. There's another rule, which is closely related: Take it slow. Sometimes it feels lousy to fake it. In your old life, you were on it and there was no need to resort to tricks to make yourself and others see that. Those days are gone now. Get over it. They'll come back. But not for a while.

Before you start to get all bummed out, remember that it goes in waves and stages. One day you're going to wake up and realize that you're no longer faking it. You are on top of it. And better than ever. For real.

Part III

The Crash

8

The Realities of the Working Mom: Business Trips, Diarrhea, a Leaking Roof, Pinkeye, Hand-Foot-and-Mouth Disease, Whining Employees, Pouting Husbands, and Other Issues That Drive You to the Brink of Insanity

---

Delusions

- Business trips are a vacation; I'll finally get some downtime.
- My kids really don't get sick that often.
- The cable company has plenty of convenient weekend appointments available. And I don't need Internet access until Sunday.
- No one can tell that I've been up ALL night with the baby.
- Even though the kiddo is puking, I can still pull off this conference call from home—thank God for the mute button.

In case it hasn't yet hit you in the face with a brick, you're still the go-to person for everything in your work AND home life. We'll discuss all that unfairness for which you inadvertently signed up here. Yes, sadly, somehow you must not only hold down a job, just like your spouse, but except for those few lucky bitches who married enlightened metrosexuals, we'll bet you're pulling a teensy, weensy bit more than 50 percent of the weight around the house. From our survey, you're lucky if you are pulling only 60 percent (and based on every conversation we've ever had, most women claim between 70 to 80 percent), and that being the case, you need to be prepared for the events that will turn your well-oiled family machine into total chaos. Hell, even if you were splitting it right down the middle with your hubby, total household insanity is just a boogie-nose away.

We *thought* we were pretty prepared for working life after the children came, but the truth is we didn't have a clue. We didn't realize how little it would take to bring us to our knees, while simultaneously screaming an unsavory four-letter word. It's a fine line between chaos and control. A sick kid is enough to send you from feeling like you've got it all licked to batsh*t crazy. But add a business trip and a house crisis, and the tears start flowing. One would think that these occurrences would be rare, like a category 5 hurricane, but unfortunately they happen with unwelcome regularity. Why didn't any of our girlfriends warn us? What happened to the secret sisterhood? If only we had known, perhaps we wouldn't have spent that first eighteen months feeling like we were the only ones in perpetual crisis mode. So, ladies, don't get caught with your pants around your ankles, because we're telling you—the sh*t WILL hit the fan. Now it's up to you to decide what to do about it.

CHAOS MAKER #1:
BUSINESS TRIPS: READY, SET, DISASTER!

For many women, the job involves travel. Pre-children, it was a godsend. Off to New York City, all expenses paid, entertaining clients, checking out the hotspots, everything in the name of business. It was fun. So fun, we coined it a "workation" and signed on for more. Post-children, those trips can be torture, especially if you happen to be breastfeeding and the trip is a six-hour cross-country jaunt. Just the thought of the preparation that will be required to get out the door makes business travel akin to an armpit wax. At a minimum you are going to have to write a to-do list and map out who does what on what days. At a maximum it is going to involve an Excel spread sheet, a few carefully arranged rides, help from other families, several hundred dollars, and the alignment of the planets to pull it off without dropping some balls. The mere thought of it gives us agita. Here's the good news: now that we've fine-tuned the art of preparation, a well-timed business trip can be a working mom's salvation—cue room service.

⬤ ⬤

I don't travel for work, BUT sometimes I wish I did! It sounds pretty nice to have a hotel room with a big bed all to myself. Don't have to make dinner, don't have to pick up the house, don't have to feed a child, don't have to put him to bed—all I'd have to do is lie in that big bed, order room service, watch reality TV, and fall asleep and sleep through the night with no interruptions—sign me up!

Miki, Mother of One and Recruiter

⬤ ⬤

Preparation Is Everything

A word of caution, ladies. Think about your out-of-town preparation strategy, because whatever you do the first time will set precedent for each subsequent trip. We have heard some crazy stories—OK, we're guilty, too—about what women do prior to going on a trip (pre-cooked meals in the freezer, laying out a week's worth of children's clothing wrapped in tissue paper, and coordinating six rides for soccer practice). We thought *we* were neurotic, but some of you, to judge from your actions, must truly believe your husbands are idiots or totally incapable of taking care of the children. We agree that it doesn't appear to come as easily to them, but with a road map most men can pull it off. Just not the way you would do it. In this case, his way, unless it's unsafe, is going to have to do.

* *

I've learned to lighten up a bit, and I finally realized I gain more out of doing so. It's not the end of the world if the kids are not in bed exactly at nine p.m. or if my husband allows them to eat cake for dinner and breakfast. If that is the worst thing that happens, then I'm really lucky.

Michele, Mother of Two and Property Manager

* *

So how do you prepare? What should you do or not do? In order for you to be effective on your trip, you are going to need the confidence that everything is OK at home (i.e., no one is playing with matches or smearing chocolate cupcakes all over your kitchen walls). So what do you need to do to make sure that no one's head flies off? Some of you are lucky enough to leave a blank check on the counter and high-step it out of there, and others take it to extremes with meticulous Excel spreadsheets. Whatever you decide, just put it in writing so your phone doesn't constantly ring with annoying questions and problems.

* *

Recently, while out on a business trip, I got off to a bad start. Monday a call from the grade school to tell me my six-year-old was being bullied and Tuesday a call from my au pair to tell me my daughter fell and almost broke her neck. Two days of emotional pain for me. VERY hard to hear, and as a result I came home.

Wendy, Mother of Two and Sales Director

* *

Here are our suggestions to help out your better half, or the nanny, in your absence. We'll assume that it's your husband who's holding down the fort, given he's a much cheaper date than the nanny.

Setting Hubby Up for Success

- Leave him a printout of your itinerary on the kitchen counter (for all we know he's deliberately sending your e-mail to the spam folder).

- Leave him a printout of the schedule on the days you will be gone. Include all pertinent information for each child. Give him the broad strokes and a few mommy secrets if you are feeling generous.

- Include information on what goes on at the house in the schedule (UPS deliveries, housekeeper, maintenance issues, etc.). Don't stop everything because you are out. The last thing you need is a whole pile of chores to do when you get back. Provide him with the name, e-mail, and cell phone number of a friend who can help him if he gets in a real pinch. He is responsible for all communication and coordination with the assigned backup person. No need to play operator from the other side of the country.

- Leave a stocked house if you can pull it off: milk, cereal, diapers, and all the fixings to make the lunches. While you are at it, get the man a six-pack of beer or some wine. Lord knows he's going to need it! You do, too, after a week alone with YOUR kids.

- Agree to speak once a day (let him call you) so you can talk to the kids and catch up.

- Let child-care provider/school know that you will be out of town and to call your spouse if there are any emergencies or issues with the children. Not much you can do while on a cross-country flight. And that's a hell of a voice mail to get first thing off a plane.

- Make sure he has health insurance cards for the kids in case they need a doctor's visit.

- Make sure that your cell phone is going to work. Nothing is more frustrating than landing in Canada and finding out that your service doesn't cover international calls.

- Set up a Skype account or iChat or something similar. On a five-week tour of your Asian factories, it's going to save you both money and your sanity.

	School Things to Bring	School Activities	Home
Monday	Napping supplies (sheet, blanket in pillowcase). Lunch box, coat.	Monday is share day. Jack to bring a "share" that starts with the letter of the week. *See newsletter pinned to kitchen corkboard for letter of the week. Put share in share box and retrieve at the end of the day or all hell will break loose.	Leave a note for the UPS man that he can leave our package. I tape it to the front door and sign it. If you don't do this, you'll need to pick up the package at UPS 9 to 5, M thru F. IMPOSSIBLE for either of us.
Tuesday	Brown bag lunch* (field trip), coat, permission slip.	Jack will be going on a field trip to the zoo. No lunch box, paper bag ONLY. You must meet Michele (Spencer's mom) at school and install Jack's car seat in her car. I've arranged for her to drive him. She will take him back to school when the field trip is over and you'll pick him up at school. Her cell phone number is: xxx-xxxx. Unless you want to take him to the zoo, you better have him at school at 8 a.m. SHARP. They will leave as a group at 8:15 a.m.	
Wednesday	Lunch box, coat.		Housekeeping day. Leave $80 in cash in envelope by front door. Strip the beds and get the sheets into the wash. The housekeeper will do the rest.

Other Activities	Notes	Medicine
Try to do the flashcards to help Jack with his D sounds. You flip the cards and if he says it right, he gets to keep that card. If he doesn't, you get to keep that card. The goal is for him to "win" all of the cards.	School drop-off is at 8:00 a.m., no earlier. Pick-up 5:45 p.m., no later. The moms frown on bringing the kids before 8:00 a.m. . . . looks bad. Don't do that! Don't forget to sign in and out each day and retrieve lunch box and coat for next day. NEVER let Jack take his "lovey" to school to sleep with at naptime. He can be quite convincing but don't give in. Loveys include his pug dog aka puggie, doggie, Blackie, the lion, the lamb, or his Dalmatian, Spot. Loveys NEVER leave the house PERIOD. Check both folders (art and communication) at school and bring contents home. Make sure nothing is time-sensitive.	Give the prescribed dose at breakfast and at dinner. Put the medicine in his lunch box so school will give it to him at lunch. You need to fill out a permission slip so they can give it to him. It's in the office.
	Check both folders (art and communication) at school and bring contents home. Make sure nothing is time-sensitive.	
	Check both folders (art and communication) at school and bring contents home. Make sure nothing is time-sensitive.	

	School Things to Bring	School Activities	Home
Thursday	Hot lunch day. YAHOO. No lunch to bring today. *Make sure you put karate uniform in your car so you are ready to roll when you pick him up.		
Friday	Lunch box, coat.	**HIBERNATION DAY!** After learning about bears all week, the kids will hibernate today in a tent at school. The teachers have requested they wear their pajamas. Find cute ones that fit, preferably without stains.	
Saturday	N/A		Comcast coming between noon and 4 p.m. to figure out what is wrong with the TV in the office.
Sunday	N/A		
STUFF YOU SHOULD KNOW	Wake Jack daily at 7 a.m. Rushing him will only backfire on YOU.		Dinner nightly at 6:30. Bedtime no later than 8:30. PLEASE! Baths are every other night after dinner unless really dirty. (Swimming, in Leigh's book, counts as a bath.)

Other Activities	Notes	Medicine
Karate at 5:45 p.m. See schedule and location on kitchen corkboard.	If Jack starts complaining that he is scared, bribe him with an ice cream cone and he'll snap to. I take him to the grocery store right by the karate class after it's over. *I know you're working late tonight. I've arranged to have _____ pick Jack up and bring him home. She gets $15 an hour. And round up!	
Silly Wiggle Singing & Drama Class at school.	Not that you were planning on it, but DON'T pick him up before 5 p.m., as he has the class from 4 to 5 and he loves it and will not leave before it's over. Check both folders (art and communication) at school and bring contents home. Make sure nothing is time-sensitive.	Take napping supplies home to be laundered. This includes sheet, pillowcase, and blanket.
Charlie and Ryan's birthday party from 10 a.m. to noon. Invite and present are on Jack's dresser. He is so excited! Parents are Stephanie and Brad. You've met them at the grocery store. Try to pretend to remember.	My flight gets in at 5 p.m. United Airlines flight 15. Should be home no later than 6:30.	
	Pick four books to read before bedtime, and if the story is too long, skip some pages.	

I hope you notice that we didn't suggest cooking all the meals and freezing them in advance and making all the lunches. Your spouse can handle those matters. Or he can call the pizza man each night. Trying to do all of that stuff and get ready for a big trip is too much. TRUST your husband and try and relax a little.

Let's hope leaving him this many clues will result in success. You've done your part.

·   ·

I'm lucky enough to have a husband who handles all the details and I never look back.

Teri, Mother of Two and Visual Merchant

I wear two watches and keep one on "home time." Before I implemented this solution, I unknowingly called in the middle of the night and woke EVERYONE up, the unfortunate result of a miscalculation of time zones between the United States and India. What a disaster!

Julie, Mother of Two and Finance Manager

·   ·

Get the Hell Out!

Now it's time to leave. Stop obsessing, stop worrying, and get the hell out of Dodge. Whatever you've forgotten is now someone else's problem. That being said, the feeling we get when we are finally in the car en route to the airport is equal parts terror and giddy little girl. The hard work is behind us and now we are going to sit on a plane, read some magazines, watch a movie, have a well-deserved drink. Oh, and did we mention sleep alone in a big hotel bed with no interruptions. Oooooooooh!

When you are out on the road you have to surrender control to your circumstances, which often include canceled flights, crappy hotels with cockroaches, and unsuccessful business meetings. Isn't that enough? Don't add the additional stress of trying to control every-thing at home while you are traveling. You need some boundaries so you are not the go-to person for everything when you are out of town. That's just not realistic.

A big part of the letting-go process is emotional. We'd suggest you save yourself thousands of dollars in therapy and take our word on it. Trust us; it will be OK. Letting go includes informing teachers and child-care providers that you will be out of town and instruct-ing them to call your husband should something come up. Yes, this does include emergencies. While this might seem unnatural and a bit heartless, having them call you during a true emergency isn't going to help anyone. What are you going to do? Make the flight from NYC to San Francisco in two hours instead of six?

Things You Clearly DON'T Need While Out on the Road

- Calls from hubby asking *you* to call the school to let them know he will be late. Uh . . . NO. In the time it took him to call you he could have called the school himself!
- Bug-infested hotels, lame room service, cockroaches, spotty Wi-Fi, and $15 potato chips from the minibar.
- Your spouse or the babysitter putting the kids on the phone and all you hear through the torrent of tears is "Mommy, when are you coming home?"
- Calls from school regarding issues with the children. (Kiddo bit the teacher, peed his pants, refused to eat his lunch, and on and on and on.)
- Calls from the nanny indicating she is sick.
- Any house problems—leaking roof, busted water mains—DON'T want to know. Call spouse.

- Sickness of any type. Colds, flus, the runs . . . they all suck.
- Calls from hubby to inquire what to feed the children. The answer is FOOD!
- Texts that simply read: "We need you home."
- Questions that begin with "Have you seen the . . . ?"
- Technical issues with the very gadgets that are supposed to make your trip easy, including poor-performing cell phones and trouble connecting remotely to work servers.
- Employee drama of any kind. Why must things always flare up while you are out?
- A call from your boss asking you to come in to the office after you land. Little did he know you had a whole spa day planned. ARGHHHH!

If you are mildly passive-aggressive, like us, we'd suggest that you rip these pages out of the book and leave them on the counter for your husband to see, along with the schedule. Now you are on your way to smooth sailing.

Now It's Time to Enjoy Yourself

We know business trips can be hard, but they can also be an opportunity. When else do you have the luxury of being alone, without kids, in a nice hotel? Never, so if you blow this opportunity by getting a good night's sleep or catching up on e-mail you are truly a fun sponge. Fulfill your work obligations, knock the business out of the park, do what you got to do, and then disappear.

You heard us right. For God's sake, ladies, it's time to do all of those things you dream about doing on the weekend but can't because you're guilted into spending all day with your kids. We don't want to hear that you're tired. We're tired, too. But you can sleep when you're dead. Now it's time to pull some fast ones!

Some Ideas to Make *Business* a *Pleasure*

- Get a mani/pedi with the extra massage. Why rush, right?
- Sit at the bar at a local hot spot, sip wine, and hold court.
- Go to a movie. A real one—not *Shrek*, not *Cars*. A movie all for you!
- Visit a museum and get inspired.
- Sit in the coffee shop, drink your coffee while it's hot, and read *The New York Times* cover to cover.
- Get some exercise. Use the hotel gym or try a new Pilates class. OK, we'll admit we've never done Pilates, but it sure sounds good. You're bound to feel better.
- Find a local Borders or Barnes & Noble and devour the magazine section for free.
- Enjoy a nice dinner out with a friend—no interruptions.
- Take a hot bath in the hotel, but only if the bathroom is up to snuff.
- Shopping, anyone? Have the concierge point you in the right direction and freshen up the wardrobe.
- If we can't convince you to go out, then go ahead and get in your pj's, order room service, and catch up with all your best friends on the phone. Cherish the feeling of long, uninterrupted conversations.
- Most important, be on your own agenda.

It's OK to do something for yourself. In fact, we insist. Don't waste your precious free time holed up in your hotel room filing e-mail or going to another boring work dinner with colleagues you can see any day of the week. And no matter what, throw the pangs of guilt out the window. It's a colossal waste of energy. If you can't learn to seize a little mommy time, you are not going to make it. It's that simple.

You're Crazy If You . . .

- Make all the meals in advance, label them, and organize in the freezer so dear hubby doesn't have to "deal."
- Choose all the kids' outfits, wrap them in tissue paper, and lay them out for the days you'll be out.
- Buy gifts for the kids each time you are away to assuage your guilt. Just to be clear, this is for you, not them.
- Call home obsessively to make sure everyone is adhering to your plan.
- Ask a family member or friend to pop in on your husband to make sure the kids are clean and the house hasn't burned down.
- Give up a business class seat to sit in a middle seat in coach to get home a whopping two hours earlier. What are you thinking?
- Even THINK about bringing your family on a business trip. It just doesn't work.

I had to go out of town for a six-week trial. The weekend before I left was spent cooking meals, packing all of the lunches, labeling them, and stacking them neatly in the extra refrigerator in the garage. I washed all the clothes and set out shoes, socks, and undies for each day and jammies wrapped in tissue paper with a little note or packaged with a book. I came home to find only half of the meals eaten, the toys, books, clothes, and tissue paper scattered throughout the house, and the boys unbathed. My initial reaction was to cry, to feel completely unappreciated and like the worst mother ever. Then I realized that they could actually survive without me (even if it wasn't to my standard) and finally I let go. It freed me up to play with them and enjoy our time together versus always just "doing" for them.

Michele, Mother of Three and Attorney

It's a dreaded ordeal for my husband when I need to travel. Once when my daughter was two, I needed to travel to New York for four days. It was eight years ago when the economy was booming and the reason for this particular business trip was a "get to know your colleagues" conference—so a fun trip overall. Knowing this, I think my husband was actually offended that I would leave him to go "have fun." I called him from my hotel room one night and he was quite upset with me. He actually blamed me for his clumsiness the night before, which had resulted in him breaking one of his favorite bobble-head sports guys. The reason: if I had been home, he wouldn't have had to get up in the middle of the night to attend to our crying child; he wouldn't have stumbled in the dark, bumping into the dresser, thus knocking his "toy" over and breaking it. Men! And I thought I was leaving only one child behind.

Michelle, Mother of One and Research Project Director

My husband and I both travel for work but always managed to coordinate trips so that one of us was home with my daughter. One time neither of us could change our plans and we were both going to be away for one night, so I asked a good friend to spend the night. We were both set to come home the following afternoon, but the weather had other plans. I was in Columbus and tried four different flights. I finally boarded a plane that was set to go through La Guardia. We flew for a couple of hours but mostly in circles, until we were running out of fuel and were forced to land in Pittsburgh, where I spent the night. Meanwhile I was panicking about who was going to take care of my daughter. Our daytime babysitter had plans that couldn't be canceled, and I was desperately trying to get ahold of my husband and my friend. My husband's flight from Nashville was very delayed but ended up getting him back to Boston—many hours late. Fortunately I was able to get ahold of my friend, who went back to my house and took care of our daughter until my husband got home around midnight. I felt awful and vowed never to have both of us gone at the same time again!

Jean-Marie, Mother of Two, and Marketing and Operations Professional

I accidentally dropped my cell phone in the toilet so I couldn't take my husband's frantic phone calls about the two-year-old throwing up at day care, in his car, etc.

Jenn, *Mother of Two and Employee Benefits Consultant*

CHAOS MAKER #2:
OH, NO . . . SICK KIDS!

You'd think, based on the number of pages heretofore committed to business trips, that no other event could wreak as much chaos. Oh, how we wish that were so. We are now going to cover another chaos maker—sick kids—and as is not the case with business trips, there's no telling when a particular instance of sick kid may begin or end. As the saying goes, "If it ain't ants, it's roaches." Just when you master the business trip you'll be humbled by sick kids. If you're lucky, you'll survive.

For dual working parents there is no phone call you dread more than the sick kid bomb from school. We liken it to getting bitch-slapped. It comes out of nowhere and it hurts that bad. Really it does. The conversation usually goes something like this:

School: Hi, Mommy, this is Miss Carla from preschool. I'm afraid little Jack is sick today and you are going to need to come get him immediately.

You: Oh, my goodness. What's going on? Is he OK?

School: Well, he had two loose stools in a row and we're certain he has a tummy bug. It's going around.

You: Are you sure it's not the fact that he ate some prunes and corn on the cob for breakfast today?

School: Absolutely not. This is a virus. The clock is ticking; you have thirty minutes to come get him, chop chop. We don't want anyone else getting sick. Oh, and don't forget our policy on sick kids.

You: What do you mean? He doesn't have a fever?

School: Well, we treat diarrhea the same as a fever. Jack must be diarrhea-free for twenty-four hours, and since it's already noon he can't come back until the day after tomorrow. Have a great day.

You: Uh . . . OK, I'll be right over.

Just seeing the school's phone number on caller ID is enough to get our hearts racing. It's one of two things: your kid is hurt or sick. Be forewarned, the minute you answer the phone the clock starts ticking. Our daycare gives you one hour to pick up your Typhoid Mary once you've received the call. So word to the wise, let it go to voice mail, immediately check voice mail, then call back in thirty minutes. Now you've got one and a half hours, assuming it's just a minor illness. If you are really in a bind (e.g., the big budget meeting is in one hour), let it go to voice mail and then call your husband and beg him to call the school, scrap his day, and deal. Now he knows what it feels like to get the call, followed by all-out panic.

Now obviously, if your kid is genuinely sick, we do not recommend sandbagging. Got fever, pinkeye, lice? Run like hell. Save sandbagging for the times when your kid has a boogie nose but it's not fluorescent green or your kid has a soft stool, not to be confused with loose stool. Got the difference? It's a fine line between spit-up and projectile vomiting.

If you get the call and your kid is genuinely sick, we're sorry. Your life is about to suck on many levels. What now?

Putting My Negotiation Skills to Good Use

Each time a kid is too sick to go to school, or we get the dreaded call from day care to come pick a kid up, we instantly go into negotiation mode. Usually I get the call. I then instantly do some quick calculations. What did hubby say he was doing today? Did it sound important, or not? Is he working on a big project? Is there an actual client in the room with him? If he's got a client either hovering around or coming in to meet with him, I don't bother even trying. If not, then I call him and try to coerce him to get the child(ren).

- *I point out that he can work from home while the sick kid watches movies.*
- *I swear that if the child is sick tomorrow, I'll be the one who stays home.*
- *I beg.*

If there is a chance that he can spend any time at home, we try to do the fifty-fifty split. I'll go to work until lunch, then race home and relieve him, and then he heads in for the back half of the day. It's messy and stressful, but it works.

—Amy

You've Got Thirty Minutes Before You Have to Leave Work—Here's What to Do

- Check your calendar and cancel the rest of your day. You heard us right. This means all meetings and calls. You cannot conduct conference calls from home with sick kids if they are awake. If your kiddo passes out or can be occupied with *Finding Nemo*, you can try to jump back in. But don't count on it. Check your schedule for the following day; chances are it is toast, too.
- Change your outgoing voice mail and e-mail to reflect you are out of the office.

- Pack up your computer (if you have a laptop) and take any files you will need with you. On most occasions, you will be out at least another day. But you can work at night and when your kid is sleeping.
- Speak with your boss. Let her know your plan. If she is not available, send an e-mail. Answer calls and respond to e-mail when reasonable. It's not your boss's problem YOUR kid is sick. Don't give her reasons to question your work ethic.
- Call your child's doctor and schedule an appointment for that day if possible. It's worth the stress and the hustle because if your child isn't really sick and/or contagious, the doctor can write you a note and get you back in school.
- Call your spouse and put him on notice. Someone is going to have to take off work; don't just assume it's going to be you (unless that is your agreement). Plant the seed and see if he might be able to stay home tomorrow.

So now what? Who stays home? Based on the response to our survey, it's going to be you, so suck it up and move on. We know, it's NOT fair, but why waste time trying to get your husband onboard for sick-kid relief when it's probably not likely? Perhaps you can take turns and evaluate on a case-by-case basis. Perhaps one of you has a job that is truly inflexible? We'd really recommend you discuss this before you check your kids into school. Come up with a few backup scenarios, because if you are anything like us, sick kids will put you on the fast track to a working mom meltdown coupled with a little marital strife.

Backup Plans
- Mom or Dad takes sick day and stays home.
- Mom and Dad split the day: Mom home in the a.m., Dad in the p.m.

- Employer offers emergency/backup child care and you check in.
- Partner up with another mom at day care whose child has pink-eye and take turns staying home. Now you are only on the hook for half of the sick time.
- Call in a babysitter/parents in a pinch and forget to mention the epic bout of diarrhea the little kiddo just had.
- Ask your retired parents or other family members to help you out.
- Have an all-out, knock-down, drag-out marital fight only to realize Mom is staying home . . . AGAIN.

Key Phrases You NEVER Want to Hear When Determining How to Handle Sick Kids

- My job is more important, so . . .
- I make more money, so . . .
- Your day would be easier to reschedule.
- Why can't you just call in sick? He wants his mother.
- I have a really busy day. It's just not possible.
- I'm supposed to play golf today with my clients.
- Not my problem.

It's pretty likely you are going to be on sick detail, so get your head around it and formulate a plan. If you are lucky, you won't get sick until the kids get better. God have mercy if you all get the tummy bug at the same time.

• •

Sadly, my first reaction is to pump the kids with children's Tylenol and send them off to school with lots of hope and hugs. When the school's number shows up on my work phone, I stare at the number for way too long and sometimes it goes away. Usually it returns repeatedly. Then

guilt sucks me in, I get in my car, and I scoop up my feverish wonder
only to be told, "Don't come back for forty-eight hours." Sh*t.

Amy, Mother of Three and Research Analyst

When I first started my job (reentered the work force after a six-year
hiatus), my daughter got sick at school and the school tracked me
down. I did not want to leave since I was new on the job, so I called my
husband, who was working close to home that day. I thought it went
off without a hitch until he called me ten minutes later just to "confirm"
where her school was.

Joellyn, Mother of Two and Teacher

It's always Mom. I dumped a conference call this week because I was
working from home with a sick kid and my son started screaming in the
background and I wasn't confident "mute" was really on so I panicked
and aborted the call.

Marcia, Mother of One and National Sales Manager

· ·

The Perils of "Working at Home" with Kids (Because They Are Sick or the Child Care Fell Through or It's Just What You Have to Do . . .)

"Working at home" with sick kids is a bit of an oxymoron. There
are occasions, however, where you truly have NO other options, and it
sucks. If you find yourself in this predicament, you are going to need
to get creative.

· ·

I have to run a seven a.m. conference call every Monday. This requires
me to hire a babysitter for one hour, because I can't get the kids to
school before the call. The kids still want to be with me, so I am often
leading this call with three little kids in my office, on my desk, or in

my lap while I speak to every office head and practice area for thirty minutes about the state of our business. Last week, I traced my three-year-old daughter's hand at least a hundred times to keep her quiet while I was talking. Thank God it worked.

Kelly, Mother of Three and Management Consultant

On one occasion I had to work with my eighteen-month-old daughter close by. I had to take a long conference call, and when it was over, I realized she had eaten an entire sleeve of Oreos.

Jenn, Mother of Two and Employee Benefits Consultant

• •

How the Hell Am I Supposed to Keep This Kid Occupied?

- TV—lots of it
- Movies—get out the entire Disney library
- Unlimited time on the Wii, Xbox, or Sony PlayStation
- Endless supplies of Popsicles and Jell-O
- Errands (if they aren't vomiting)—why not kill two birds with one stone?

This is not a good time to rate one's parenting skills, because trying to get anything done with sick kids is going to require some less-than-admirable parenting. So set the judgment aside and do what needs to be done. But remember, your child is sick. Do only the work that is absolutely critical and then surrender to your role as nursemaid.

If you must take a conference call, we have two words for you . . . MUTE BUTTON. Use it at all times and only take it off when you need to speak. We heard the funniest story—probably not too funny to the woman implicated—about a mom at home with sick kids: while on a conference call, her kid announced, "Mommy farted." We can only imagine the shade of red her face must have been. So don't expose yourself to any unnecessary humiliation. Use the mute button, go hands-free if at all possible, and be ready to dump the call if the going gets tough.

CHAOS MAKER #3: YOUR OTHER KIDS (EMPLOYEES AND HUSBANDS)

We hate to overstate the obvious, but we changed after we became working mothers. We are sure many of you have experienced the very same thing, which we'd sum up as less patience at the office for petty crap. So to all you employees out there, here is the deal. We have babies and kids at home; we don't need them at work. And we are quite certain our bosses feel the same way. So grow up, buck up, do your jobs, and save the constant complaining and tattling for someone who has the time to listen. We are now one hundred percent laser-focused on getting our jobs done in the limited time we have to do them. We simply can't indulge our employees like we used to. There isn't a spare minute, but if there were we'd use it being productive and so should you.

As managers we don't mind constructive feedback, don't mind troubleshooting, and don't mind brainstorming sessions. What we do mind are employees who whine and complain like children when they don't get their way. But how are we supposed to respond when you march into our offices and tell us that you're bored? Really? That's why you are in here? Sounds to me like it's time to do some goal-setting and pile on some extra work. Now that you are back at work, you need to use every minute possible being productive. Be clear that you'd like the exchanges with your team to be solutions-oriented and focused on an area of business importance. Schedule weekly touch-bases at an agreeable time, stay focused on the agenda, and don't exceed the allotted time.

And last, be kind, professional, and courteous ALWAYS. It's not your employees' fault that you made a choice to have kids and work. So don't take it out on them. How are they supposed to know about the crazy morning you've had (highlights: washing Junior's banana-prune breakfast out of your Mary Janes, then discovering you'd forgotten to put a diaper on him five seconds after he "made" on your Berber carpet, which immediately required stain treatment!)? When people are standing in your doorway yammering on about something you can't fix and you feel your blood begin to boil, just politely interrupt them by informing them you are on a very tight deadline (i.e., get out of my space; time is a-wasting).

And what do we do about pouting husbands? It's tough to be them. They just aren't getting all of the attention they used too, are they? Unfortunately, unless you know a way to clone yourself, we don't have the solution. When you figure it out, let us know. When he starts dumping on you about his day, the bills, office politics, and the oil change he needs, just metaphorically change the channel and tune him out. Sounds a little mean, but trust us: he's doing the same thing to you.

THE FINAL CHAOS MAKER: HOME OWNERSHIP—THE AMERICAN DREAM (OR IS IT?)

That pile of bricks you own is one of the biggest time stressors of all. Life would be so much easier without all of the house crap blowing up when you least expect it. The world isn't designed for working people when it comes to house maintenance. If you rent your apartment or home, chances are your landlord will handle most of this stuff. Lucky you. You have just avoided a minefield of problems. But if you own a piece of the American Dream, it's likely you are going to be responsible for its maintenance. It's unavoidable. For the same reason your husband can't take the kids to get their shots or drive for the field trip, he won't be able to be home to receive the plumber to fix the toilet the kids shoved a stuffed animal down. I'm guessing somehow, some way, you'll be motivated to get that toilet up and running.

Home maintenance is inevitable; it's the busted water mains and frozen pipes that are killing us. Things break, and kids—well, they accelerate the rate at which things break, and now you have to figure out how to cram a toilet repair into the middle of an already impossible day at the office.

Here are some options:

- Ask the vendor to give you a one-hour courtesy call on your cell phone, and instead of taking a lunch hour, run home and let him in.
- Ask for a small window of time. Noon to 2:00 p.m. is OK; 9:00 a.m to 5:00 p.m. is NOT.
- Ask if they do service calls on Saturdays, early mornings, or evenings. You'd be surprised, many do.
- Ask a good friend, neighbor, or SAHM (that's "stay-at-home mom," for those of you not in the know), if she can let someone in and wait. Trade her for wine, a play date, or babysitting on the weekend.
- Take a day off work and handle a bunch of things all in that day. So not fun, but a lot less stressful.

DON'T SCREW YOURSELF

You are supposed to be a smart, educated, working professional. So what in the hell were you thinking when you decided to fire the nanny with no backup? This is what we would call a "dumb-ass maneuver," and we've heard about lots of them since we embarked on the journey of writing this manifesto. Ladies, it's hard enough out there. Do we really need to remind you not to screw yourself? Apparently so, and with that in mind, here are a few things you shouldn't do:

- Start any significant change or transition on a Monday. No "Ferberizing," no moving to a big-boy bed, potty training, taking away the binky, etc. Save that for Friday, so you can have the weekend to build momentum and have cocktails when the going gets rough.

- Don't fire the nanny without backup unless it's a matter of safety. Reprimand her and start an all-out search!
- Don't cram your calendar with too many personal commitments in one week. Two things are enough; the third doctor's appointment will trigger a stress-induced fit if you are anything like us.
- Don't be difficult with the teachers at school; not only will you pay the price, but your kids will, too.
- Control your schedule. If you have a choice of when to travel, try not to be gone at the same time your husband happens to be traveling. Sometimes you have no choice, but when you do, don't do this to yourself and your family.
- Don't try to do it all so you can save money. If you're trying to save a few measly bucks by having the nanny show up an hour later, get over yourself. The stress of trying to pull off a conference call with the kids running around is surely worth the $14, give or take a few.
- Don't think you can work while trying to make dinner, give the kids a bath, put them to bed, etc. Compartmentalize. Wait until they are asleep and then hop to. The BlackBerry is convenient, but DON'T BE ITS BITCH.

The hardest thing for type A women is to know their limits. Once you figure out what triggers your tantrums, you'll be on your way to smoother sailing.

Crazy Eyes and Other Signs That You've Officially Lost It

Delusions

- It's normal to think that driving into oncoming traffic is easier than going home and facing the bedtime routine.
- Getting laid off sounds like the solution to my problems.
- My boss did not notice that I just bit the head off the waitress while we were out for a business lunch together.
- No one else can remember what happened last week, either.
- It's going to get easier; I just have to get more organized, like the other moms.
- Crying once a week is normal; it's just my hormones.

Every working mom has suffered a crash. A total meltdown. A trip to the loony bin or at least the serious consideration of one (it sounds a lot like a spa vacation!). Welcome to the club. What took you so long?

If you haven't already suffered one yet, there is an incredibly high likelihood that you will. There is too much going on, too much to juggle, too much responsibility, and too little time. We're not talking simply about being brought to tears—that happens far too frequently to qualify as a full-scale meltdown. Basic tears are reserved for things like these: the new school schedule is going to wreck your life, you just forgot to buy milk for the third night in a row, your child just accused you of being a bad mommy because you forgot pajama day, and on and on and on. Those are practically everyday tears. There's nothing spectacular about them.

A full-scale meltdown is the slow leak that happens from that day you start back to work again until the daily grind and the pressure of so much sh*t to do just piles on and fundamentally jiggers your DNA/chromosome-thingies and changes you from an otherwise perfectly friendly, normal woman to a raging lunatic who cannot tell her head from her ass, her husband from a punching bag, or her kids from a to-do list. How do we know? We have experienced it all. We've lived Crazy Eyes and are back to tell the tale.

CRAZY EYES

You know Crazy Eyes. You've seen them. Potentially on yourself even. They are the eyes of a woman who's barely hanging on to her sanity while desperately trying to shore up work, home life, and basic personal hygiene. How do you get them? Without almost daily vigilance, they will simply just come naturally. And for all you eternal optimists out there who don't see this happening to you. . . . go ahead and read this JUST IN CASE. We love your confidence, but we feel obligated to prepare you. Imagine this, and it probably sounds familiar: you're racing to get out the door to get the kids to school, you just noticed that someone plugged the toilet with a superbouncy ball, the conference call starts in thirty minutes, and then your youngest pees his pants. He told you it was coming, but you were too frazzled to pay attention. Now, press "rewind" and repeat in a continuous loop with subtle variations every day for about six months. Crazy Eyes.

Is It Normal to Be Thinking This?

How did I know that I had the Crazy Eyes? What got me to that point? It was as simple as trying to take on EVERY-THING. When my younger child was six months and my older child two and a half, I was doing ALL of the drop-offs, ALL of the pick-ups, ALL of the lunches, ALL of the din-ners, ALL of the baths, ALL of the bedtime routines, etc. And working a full-time five-day-a-week schedule. I was spending my weekends obsessing about how I was going to find time to get to the grocery store, get up to Costco, and steam carrots for the boys' lunches. I did it without even thinking at first, but by the time my youngest was hitting a year, I was in full-scale meltdown mode. I was thinking a head-on on the Golden Gate Bridge was somehow easier than facing yet another slog-fest at home. Really. I'm not joking.

I didn't realize how bad it was until I met some girlfriends for a weekend getaway. This statement alone should scare you. I just admitted that I thought driving into traffic was a good idea and I didn't know how bad it was. To me, the weekend getaway was the answer to all of my prayers . . . wine, friends, a fancy hotel room, ready access to pools and spas, and trying on Jimmy Choos at every store in the Bel-lagio shopping arcade. After two days, I was going to come back completely refreshed and ready to face another year of the grind. That doesn't sound realistic, does it? Now I know. Then I didn't.

On my way home from the airport, the palpable dread began creeping in and then I fell asleep while driving on I-580, which is a really bad thing. The next day I ran into our garage and tore the front end off my car. A week later I was driving my husband's car and rear-ended someone. And then I walked into Leigh's office with the full-on realization that I had totally and completely lost it. All she said was, "You've got Crazy Eyes." And then she said, "It's time to call in the big guns and get some professional HELP."

It was the best thing I ever did. I spent months on the couch and walked away with tricks that would help me avoid (ahem, postpone) a second meltdown—if only for a few years. When I feel myself slipping into Crazy Eyes (my trigger signal is that I start to obsess about errands on the weekends), I pull myself out by stopping something—one less chore, a few declined birthday party invites, sending the boys the hell out with their dad for a bike ride, etc. Somehow, I take a breath. It works.

Oh, and I got a babysitter two nights a week because I couldn't do it on my own anymore. She saved my life.

—Amy

How Do You Know When You've Completely Lost It?

You might think it's easy to recognize when you've got the Crazy Eyes. Wrong. By definition, having Crazy Eyes suggests that you are not thinking rationally. You've been rewired to think that stress, lack of patience, moodiness, and constant tearfulness are the new norm. Therefore, you think it's perfectly normal to find yourself in any of the following situations:

- You're not organized like you were pre-kids and you keep losing things—important things like checks to deposit, your cell phone, car keys, and the microwavable mac and cheese you just pulled out of the grocery bag and now can't seem to find anywhere, but will later find stuffed in the freezer.

- You obsess about all the things you need to do. Lists are everywhere, and you actually put stuff on the list that you've already done just for the satisfaction of checking it off and gaining some control over your life—do laundry, defrost chicken, call your boss, breathe, wash hair, pee. Check, check, check.

- You get the kids fed, bathed, story-timed, tucked into bed, and fast asleep before it dawns on you that you haven't taken off your coat.

- You run over your laptop in the driveway. Funny, as it just happened to one of us, but it has in fact happened to at least three people we know. FYI, laptops do function after you run them over.

- You've been rehashing old fights with your husband (things like he's breathing too loud, his mother calls too often, he doesn't share the remote, etc.). These are things that got settled the first two years you were married, and now you're just kicking the proverbial dog to make yourself feel better.

- Your toddler throws spaghetti at dinner and you throw it back. And then come to your senses and wonder if child protective services comes after women who throw food at their kids while you clean up the gargantuan mess you made.

- Your team at work is now totally afraid of you. You can hear them asking each other, "What kind of a mood is she in today?"

- Your husband won't let you order at restaurants anymore because you're such a bitch to the waitress.

- Your two-year-old just asked for cereal and you started screaming that he needs to be more independent.

- You are always, always in a bad mood.

- Calling your friends sounds like too much work. In fact it IS too much work. Talking takes time and you have none.

- You would consider jury duty, a minor car accident, or mandatory surgery a welcome respite from your daily existence. Root canal, anyone?

- You cannot relax until everything you think you could be doing is done. When your kid asks you to play soccer in the backyard, you say you can't because you've got to vacuum up all the hair from the bathroom. Never mind that you've spent only twenty minutes with him all day.

Should any of the above sound familiar, it's very likely you've suffered, or are currently living with, Crazy Eyes. Now it's time to figure out what got you here.

• •

I once yelled at my boss and told him I did not care about jeans today. He asked if he was annoying me and I just blurted it out.

Allison, Mother of Two and Merchandiser (of jeans!)

When am I not overwhelmed and reduced to tears? When I leave my daughter in the morning and she is crying, "Mommy!" When I ask my husband to get a towel out of the closet and he tells me he does not know where the linen closet is.

Suzanne, Mother of One and Salesperson

• •

Why Didn't I See This Coming?

Crazy Eyes are not a sudden occurrence. They don't happen like a freak flash flood or an earthquake. They are a much slower and more deliberate natural disaster. The kind that you could see coming, if you just paid enough attention or had any time for self-awareness. Like hot lava slowly creeping down a hill. You've got enough time to avoid it. Just pull your head out of your ass and look around. THERE'S HOT LAVA CREEPING TOWARD YOU! DANGER!

Shockingly, most of us don't see it coming. Why is that?

First, no one told you that you'd get Crazy Eyes, so you're not on the lookout. While you're pregnant, no one wants to tell you how bad everything can be because they don't want to freak you out. It's too late, anyhow. They want you to think everything is going to be sunshine and happiness and that you will be totally blissed out by this motherhood thing. Kind of like those dirty little secrets about breastfeeding. Only your dearest friends are going to tell you that the early days hurt like hell and can be a complete pain in the ass, and for the first month you're going to be a fumbling idiot. Everyone else is going to tell you that it's a hundred percent fantastic. Liars!

Second, your pursuit of perfection makes it almost impossible to admit that you might be losing control. We know that you're in pursuit of perfection because what working mom hasn't at least tried for a day or two to be perfect? The perfect worker bee—never lets a deadline pass or a budget get blown. The perfect mom—clean, well-behaved, well-fed, fabulous kids who have every opportunity in life. The perfect wife—dinner on the table, house spotless, in shape, and sex every Wednesday and Saturday nights. We've all watched enough *Oprah* (OK, maybe it was just during maternity leave) to know people-pleasing and perfection are the curse of the modern woman. But it takes a deliberate effort to let go of perfection, and if you're not proactively slacking, you won't notice until it's too late that you're in over your head.

Finally, Crazy Eyes come on when you're overwhelmed, and it can take a while to get you to that point. The daily grind creeps up on you so slowly that you don't know you're in deep until it's too late. You're used to taking on everything, so it just keeps piling on and piling on and piling on until you blow.

All of these factors together can create the Crazy Eyes behavior described above (the running over your own computer, the biting off heads of employees, husbands, waitresses, etc.). But you're not going to know you've got the Crazy Eyes until you've blown up spectacularly. Typically the full-scale, crazy-lady meltdown is brought on by events that continue to stack up and stack up until you just can't take it anymore, and then with one tiny little event, you will completely and totally come UNHINGED. Let's hope it's in private, but it probably won't be. It's like having your water break—chances are it's going to be messy.

So What's Going to Slowly Drive You over the Edge? The Long-term Stresses That Lead to the Blowup

- **Chronically sick kids.** Ask any mom with kids in day care or preschool about illness, and she'll tell you it's a slow grind that's going to get you. Colds, the flu, strep, lice, you name it. All it's going to take is one more ear infection or one more bout of projectile vomiting, and you will be driven completely over the edge. You'll be on the phone with the after-hours nurse, or in line at the pharmacy, and you'll either completely bite this poor innocent bystander's head off or you'll be reduced to a puddle of uncontrollable tears over the fact that your insurance company doesn't pay for this type of medicine. Either way, the madness/sadness will be mixed with horror and embarrassment. How the hell can I be screaming at the pharmacist?

- **Child-care disasters.** We don't need to tell you that when the child care falls apart, on top of everything else, it's going to create a colossal disaster. When you can't get it right, it's a stress that eventually will completely and totally do you in. You have to leave work early in order to pick up the kid because the in-home day care decided to close again or the day care is unexpectedly closed for Columbus's Father's Day or the nanny calls in sick with a family emergency or you just can't find someone you trust with your precious little child. You'll slip off the ledge on which you were perched. Let's just hope you don't scream too loudly at the woman you'll be sheepishly handing your kid over to tomorrow morning at seven on the dot.

- **Promotions or new projects at work.** Please don't think we're suggesting that your career shouldn't keep on flying. If your career is flying high, we're rooting you on. We're making the obvious observation that more stress at work can trigger the Crazy Eyes. When the boss calls with a demanding task, the only question is if you'll finally be having your mental break at work or at home. We hope for your sake and the sake of your fancy career that you lose it at home. Spouses and children can be a lot more forgiving than an angry CEO, believe it or not.

- **Lack of sleep.** Whom are we kidding? The best way to guarantee Crazy Eyes is to continue to live life in a perpetual state of sleep deprivation. Haven't you heard that sleep deprivation is a torture tactic? The human brain was not designed to function after sleeping only four hours (interrupted at two-hour intervals by screams of "I WANT MY BINKY"). One of your poor, unsuspecting kids is going to innocently try to crawl into bed with you at three a.m. and you're going to go ballistic. The volume of your psychotic break will determine if the neighbors will be waking up as well.

- **A nasty commute.** It's no fun to slog it out a few hours a day when you could be doing much more productive things like hanging out with the kids, sleeping, etc. You can try to convince yourself that it's your Zen time, but we're going to have to call you on that. There is no possible way that slogging it out in traffic, being crushed next to a bunch of strangers in a train, or driving endless hours while you think about all of the other things you'd rather be doing is good for your long-term mental health. Oh, and please don't bite the head off the person next to you on the train when it stops in a tunnel for a twenty-minute break.

- **Busy, lazy, sick, or clueless husbands.** They might not deliberately be trying to drive you to the loony bin, but their lack of assistance can do you in. Being the good spouse, you'll probably suck it up for as long as you can. But you'll lose it and this same guy who forgot to go to the grocery store on his way home is going to have his head handed to him by the dragon lady who replaced you.

The Final Straw: Embarrassing and Totally Real Events That Were Considered the Last Thing a Working Mom Needed Before She Fell into a Pit of Despair

- Your flight home is delayed.
- Nanny calls in sick; it's a day-care "vacation"/school closure.
- Husband forgets to pick up socks/clean dishes/fold laundry.
- TiVo failed to record *Gossip Girl* and it's your one night of guilt-free TV time.
- There's no milk in the house.
- Your employee just quit.
- Child wakes up at three a.m. and will settle for no one but Mommy.
- They preempted your favorite TV show with a presidential press conference.
- You're out of wine.
- The school asked you to drive on the field trip but just changed the time, so you can't get on that important conference call.
- You realize that back-to-school night is scheduled during a client dinner.
- It's ten p.m. and your kid is just now asking you for homework help.
- Karate class requires that you find someone to hem the kid's gi.
- You're all dressed for work and your kid just puked up her breakfast . . . on you.
- You forgot to pick up the dry cleaning and now there's nothing to wear . . . nothing.
- The car will not start.
- The sewer is backed up.

The list can go on forever . . .

Dinner Party Drama

*It only took nine months and the slow drip of working moth-
erhood had rendered me chronically irritable. My husband
wasn't a tremendous help. He hadn't seemed to notice this
major shift in my personality, or chose to ignore it, and kept
piling on the responsibility: "Honey, did you do this?" "Honey,
can you do that?" And then the final insult: "Honey, we're
going to have a gathering on Saturday for one of my absolute
heroes in medicine. Would you mind pulling together a menu
for sixteen—nothing fancy?" I couldn't believe my ears. In
fact, I had homicidal thoughts about hitting him in the head
with one of my fancy Le Creuset cast-iron skillets but thought
better of it, only because our child deserves a father. It was
Sunday and he was talking about sixteen people sitting down
at my dinner table in six days for a dinner that consisted of
"nothing fancy." Well, unless the man wanted Happy Meals
on paper plates, there was going to be some effort needed, and
he knew it. The only problem was the next day was Monday
and I had a little problem called A FULL-TIME FRICK-
ING JOB and it would take me all week to pull this "simple"
gathering together AND chase after a toddler. As I started
thinking of my to-do list, the shopping, the prepping, the
table-setting, and the need for a babysitter, I could feel my
blood BOILING. And there he stood: "Leigho [as he calls
me], what's wrong? I'll be home the day of the party around
four p.m. to help, I will totally help." Little did he realize that
the party he was envisioning would require all-week preparation, party rentals, and multiple grocery store stops, not
to mention kitchen help. Him arriving two hours before the
party would be of NO help whatsoever. I don't know exactly
what I looked like in that moment, but apparently I had*

CRAZY EYES. Not just your garden-variety Crazy Eyes: these apparently were Crazy Eyes of the Hurricane Katrina caliber. I was desperate, overwhelmed, and uncertain of how I was going to cope for one more second. My husband tried to comfort me and I came unhinged like a child in the toy department of Target when you tell him you came for laundry soap and aren't leaving with the 500-piece Star Wars trilogy Lego set. I was inconsolable and screaming to the point that I was spitting. It was then that my husband articulated something he had probably been thinking for months. "I just want my old Leigho back. I just want my wife back," to which I barked, "I don't know what happened to her, she's dead." Clearly I had a penchant for drama, but it was obvious to both of us in that moment that I was combustible TNT or, as my therapist discerned, hyper-responsive. My reaction wasn't proportional to the situation and I needed to take the stress down about nine notches. Sometimes it takes coming unhinged, hitting the bottom, to realize you need to chart a different course for yourself. One that is a little less hectic, a little more fun, with the occasional sit-down dinner for sixteen.

—Leigh

HEY THERE, CRAZY LADY— THERE'S NO SHAME!

It's almost inevitable that you got the Crazy Eyes, and we hope that you can see that. We hope that you don't feel like you've failed because you haven't. The pathetic, tear- and snot-filled, hysterical downfall of the working mom is inevitable. But Crazy Eyes are not a terminal disease; there's a cure. It is possible to recover and emerge better off than you were before. Yes, you heard us. Better. And depending on your feelings about the joys of motherhood, you can easily argue that you are better than you've ever been. For us, personally, our answer depends highly on how much sugar the kids have ingested in the last two hours.

We also hope that if you haven't gotten the Crazy Eyes yet, you're not passing judgment on those of us who have. Karma is a bitch.

Mr. or Ms. Fix-It/Happy Pills

So you've got the Crazy Eyes, or you're about to get them and you know it. Now is the time to fix the issue. Before we go on, it's time to figure out how critical this situation is.

It's time to ask yourself if you're seriously OK. How bad is it? Are you a babysitter and massage away from getting your mojo back or is this situation going to require the need for a psychiatrist? Be honest. You can be in deep enough to need a serious break, or you can be in much deeper. There's no shame in either situation, but the remedy can be a bit different. There's a big difference between a girls' weekend and the big guns (therapy, happy pills, a reservation at the Cirque Lodge—hello, Lindsay Lohan and Mary-Kate, or some combination thereof).

Fixes for the Not-So-Bad Total Meltdown	Fixes for the Complete and Total Meltdown
Regular exercise	An immediate visit to a qualified professional for therapy, happy pills, or some combination thereof
Predictable and guilt-free time to yourself	
Occasional weekends away from husband and kids	The unequivocal support of your spouse to stick around until you get it together
Massages, yoga, acupuncture, and all other hippie-dippie cure-alls	More help
	Even more help
	And everything on the left side of the chart

How serious is it? Only you can tell. You're the one having the breakdown, but there are a few people to trust who can give you honest advice and help you sort out if you've got to book a few weeks at the Cirque Lodge or can simply and deliberately get some of this load off your back to get back to normal.

Your husband. This poor guy is currently suffering through the horror of living with you. Sit him down and have an honest conversation: Have you totally lost it? Are you acting like yourself, but just an angrier version? Or have you totally been replaced by either a zombie or an angry wench from hell? One step further: if he does think you've lost it, does he have any creative ideas to help get you out of this mess?

Your best friends. These are the ladies who have known you forever and can tell you when you've gone over the edge. They'll probably also be the ones who can help you figure out how to get yourself out of this hell. If nothing else, they can at least take you out for drinks and a night off from the routine.

Your mom. You know from personal experience that nobody loves you more. She's a good one to help you figure this out. Chances are that she went through her own version of Crazy Eyes when she was raising you. Just be warned: Telling your own mother can create responses that range from immediately jumping on a plane to help all the way to long diatribes on "I don't know why you're doing this. Why can't you just stay at home!" and other not-so-helpful tidbits.

Now Get Yourself out of This Mess—Forever

So you've fixed the situation for now. How do you ensure that you're not going to "go there" again? No guarantees. Anytime life changes a little, you are at risk—at risk of taking on more, at risk of juggling too many things, and at risk of losing your mind at soccer practice because one of the moms just asked you to bring oranges and it seems totally unreasonable.

We have come up with some questions to ask ourselves—and some behaviors that we recognize as the coming onslaught of Crazy Eyes. We'll fully admit that until we went through Crazy Eyes, neither we nor our husbands really took this stuff seriously. All it takes is half a year of trying to recover from the Crazy Eyes to take it more seriously. Maybe our husbands saw how bad it could get and now realize that they have to take an active role in helping pull us out. Or maybe all of those months of therapy made a serious dent in the checking account and they don't want to waste the cash again. Whatever the answer, it's a lot easier to get help now.

The Key Question to Keep the Crazy Eyes Away

When you're feeling at the edge, ask yourself: Do you really need to do that, whatever it is—from cleaning to having houseguests? If you don't need to do it, then don't. Find a way out of it. You don't need to make excuses. Just say no. We've said no to the following all in the name of saving our own asses:

- Visits from family, either yours or your spouse's, when the timing isn't convenient.
- Birthday parties, for either the kids or the adults.
- Helping friends of friends with business plans, marketing advice, informational interviews, etc.
- Play dates. The only exception are drop-off play dates when you're the one doing the dropping off.
- Entertaining your husband's clients, either at your house or at a restaurant.
- Clean houses, fancy meals, and all other June Cleaver activities.
- Home or self-improvement projects that would be nice to do, but would most likely suck out all your free time.
- Socializing with people who are not your real friends. When times are tough, casual acquaintances, aka the "B list," are things of the past.

- Self-imposed pressures to be perfect. You are not perfect, so get over yourself and save the cash that you'd spend on the couch for some new shoes.

Sometimes, despite your best efforts to trim the fat in your life, the Crazy Eyes start to creep in. How can you tell they're coming? It's time to keep a vigilant eye out for the onslaught.

Tips That the Crazy Eyes Are Coming

Amy	Leigh
Starts to obsess about errands rather than hanging out with her kids. When her husband comes home and gives her a hug and kiss, gets irritated that he just interrupted her dish-washing activities. Starts to dread the nighttime routine with the kids—especially bedtime.	Aha moment is when she starts manically cleaning the house (it's so obvious EVERYTHING in her life is out of control and this is her feeble attempt at control). Too many weekends are scheduled with back-to-back commitments and no downtime and she gets panicked just looking at the family calendar. Everything her sweet husband does irritates HER (uh—NEWS FLASH—it's not him).

And What Amy and Leigh Do to Hold Off the Crazy Eyes

Amy	Leigh
Tells her husband that she's about to lose it and goes on strike for a few nights. And feels no guilt when she hears the kids screaming, "But I want Mommy" from downstairs. They need to figure out that their dad is perfectly capable of bringing them water and showering them with kisses. Forces herself to get some exercise. Not a lot of exercise. Just enough to feel like she did something for herself (that's about three laps around the block for anyone who's counting).	Combs the medicine cabinets for any happy pills left over from the postpartum jag years ago. Goes into LOCKDOWN mode. Lockdown mode requires that all plans be canceled in a last-ditch effort to shore up mental state. Two weeks are the minimum but has been known to go on lockdown for a month. The results are guaranteed. Less stress = happier mother, happier wife = happier person.

Amy	Leigh
Takes a guilt-free hour to get out of the house. This doesn't mean grocery shopping by herself. This means something fun like a trip to the coffee shop, a pedicure, or even window-shopping at the fancy mall.	Warns husband where it's headed and implores him to get some skin in the game or ELSE. Just the thought of her losing it (again) is enough to get him motivated for just long enough for her to recover. And then it happens again!

THERE'S HOPE

Yes, Crazy Eyes are likely coming and they truly do suck. But we hope this chapter has helped you with a few things: One, you aren't alone. Two, there's no shame. Three, there's a way out of it and a way to prevent it from happening again. It took a good long time to get you into this mess, and it's going to take a while to get out.

From those of us who have seen the Crazy Eyes and come out on the other side, here are a few final thoughts:

1. Be careful when you ask a working mom on the edge if everything is OK. Timed incorrectly, that's just going to end up with you getting your head chewed off. Or she might just burst into tears uncontrollably. Be ready.

2. When a working mom looks like she's going to lose it, gently offer some help. God knows when you find yourself screaming at the PTA meeting, you just might want to see a sympathetic face and, if you're lucky, someone to offer you a drink or a smoke or something to at least take the edge off.

3. Don't judge. For all you eternal optimists out there, your time will come, and when it does, we're here for you.

The Guilt Is Killing Me!

The topic of guilt is so overpublicized it's tempting to not give it any more air time. But every time we try to tamp it down, it rears its ugly head again. Based on any given conversation with fellow moms—working or not—guilt is still en vogue in many circles. There are inherently two camps: Kids . . . what kids? Or our camp— self-anointed guilt addicts twelve-stepping their way to recovery. And working mom guilt, in our humble opinion, is the MOTHER OF ALL GUILT. How can we not all be going nuts when we're spending all of our waking time feeling guilty?

"I'M A WORKING MOM" GUILT

Here's what you need to understand. Modern motherhood has become inextricably linked with guilt and working motherhood just ups the ante. As working moms, we are forced to leave our babies in the care of someone else at an early age, and that is guilt bomb number one. They just add up from there.

There are two main reasons all of us are working moms—either we need to work or we want to work. Either situation can create guilt.

"Need to work" guilt. "Oh, how could I possibly have put myself in this horrible situation where I have to leave my kids?" Umm, get real. Do you realize that you are in the same boat with the vast majority of the U.S. population? Get over it.

"Want to work" guilt. There are many subtleties to this kind of guilt, but it is not as easy to get over because working is entirely your choice. Yes, you are choosing to put your children in the care of someone else. Yes, you are voluntarily going on that business trip. Yes, you are begging a SAHM to schlep your kid from school to soccer and back again and taking advantage of the fact that she chose not to work. But get comfortable with your choice and move on. A woman happy and satisfied in her career is a good mom, too, and is setting an example for her kids that work is a valuable part of life and something that can be enjoyed—not just endured. And since when is being financially independent something to feel guilty about? In today's world you never know what will happen, and knowing you can feed your kids and keep a roof over their heads if necessary is nothing to sneeze at.

How can we be so certain about either? We fall firmly in both camps! OK, if we gave up our rock-and-roll lifestyle (i.e., basic cable) and moved to Greater Podunk, we might have a chance of surviving on one salary, but last time we asked, our husbands had no desire to move. And neither did we. So let's be honest and say we both fall into the camp of want-to-work.

When Do We Feel Guilty About Being Working Moms?

A lot of times, but it really goes in waves. Whether you're working because you want to or because you have to, it's when the routine gets a little out of whack that we're most likely to feel we're failing, either at home or at work. And the guilt goes both ways: I'm not working enough and I'm not parenting enough.

- When your child asks, "Mommy, can you stay home with me today?"
- When your kid is sick, but you've got to leave him with the nanny anyway. Important meeting.
- When you have to ditch work early to pick up the kids and you leave the team to pick up the pieces.
- When school is begging for drivers for the field trip and you can't drive. And some SAHM has to drive twice the kids and her day is going to suck . . . all because of you.
- When you just can't stay for the six p.m. meeting.
- When you cut the business trip short because you've got to make it home for a birthday party.
- When the kids beg to have you pick them up instead of the nanny, or your husband for that matter.
- When another mom asks you, "What are you doing for the summer?" and the answer is, "The same thing." The kiddo goes to day care; we don't get a "summer."
- When you do the math and realize that your kid has a longer day than you.
- When your kid has to miss the birthday party that starts at three p.m. on Friday.
- When your kiddo's first steps are recorded on video by the nanny.
- When day care puts your kid on the phone because he needs to ask, "When are you going to pick me up tonight?"

- When you explain to your mother-in-law that you've picked a nice day care for your kid, and she looks at you like you're checking her grandkid into a dog kennel.

REGULAR MOMMY GUILT

It doesn't matter if you're a working mom or a SAHM, guilt doesn't discriminate. We think mommy guilt is born out of unrealistic expectations and lies—there, we said it! Lies! You have a preconceived idea in your mind as to how you want to raise your children. Good manners, church, family dinners, little TV, and so on. Then you actually have a kid and all bets are off. You realize that the days are long, that twenty-four hours means 1,440 minutes of being on call for these little bundles of joy. Suddenly you realize that having kids is hard and, uh . . . time-consuming. Those little bundles of joy can get on your nerves, and do, and TV can all of the sudden become your best friend—and that's when it starts going sideways. Things don't turn out how you thought they would, and somehow you are to blame. Immediately you think, "What's wrong with me?" The answer is NOTHING. Mothering is hard work. It's a full-time job and then some. It doesn't come with a manual, and there is a lot to learn on the fly. Of course, you are not doing it perfectly, so GET OVER YOURSELF. When is the last time you started a new job and were firing on all cylinders on day one? We suspect the answer is never. Mothering is a work in progress and the minute you get your kids to stop eating their boogers, they'll start with the potty talk, or the ultimate insult—the teenage years. This is not a job you are ever going to master, so you may as well align your expectations with the job and cut yourself some slack.

Healthy Guilt—When You Really Should Feel Bad

You see, there is healthy guilt and unhealthy guilt. Healthy guilt comes from a place of real sadness, a true regret for choosing a behavior that hurt or caused problems for someone you care for. Had too

many drinks and slept with your best friend's husband? You're enti-
tled to some guilt; in fact, wallow in it, you shameless hussy.

On the flip side, unhealthy guilt is a persistent and daily feeling of
shame or inadequacy. That you "should" be making different choices,
that you "should" be a perfect mother but aren't. That you "should"
be coping better. That you "should" put everyone else's needs ahead
of your own. Before you know it, you are "shoulding" yourself right into
guilt's grip. Or worse yet, "shoulding" all over yourself! The majority of mommy guilt falls into this category. Now that we truly understand and appreciate the difference between healthy and unhealthy
guilt, we are one step away from a full recovery from this powerful
addiction. We're certain there is hope for you. Trust us, guilty mom
syndrome (GMS) is not going to get you anywhere. We'll admit that
it's HARD to give up the guilt. It's almost as if we enjoy it. It's as if we
moms think it makes us look like we are superdedicated and always
striving to be better. The reality is it really only makes you look like
an insecure martyr. Get over it. Get a backbone, and gain some confidence in your choices. If you can't assert yourself here when the stakes
are so high, we worry about your ability to advocate for yourself in
the workplace. Really we do. As we would say, get your balls off the
shelf, tuck them back into your pants, and speak up for yourself.

Leigh's Lessons in Avoiding Guilt

One day I woke up and discovered I had become a resentful,
overworked, guilt-ridden (chubby) mom in need of some help. I was
feeling guilty about everything. (Was I a good mom, was I doing a
good job at work, was I spending too much on babysitters, and was
day care the right thing? Blah blah blah.) Then and only then did I
learn how to navigate the never-ending river of guilt so that it didn't
envelop me or, worse yet, rule my life. It was a bit of an epiphany, but
after lots of agonizing, I realized that if I wasn't doing any long-term

harm to myself, my kid, my family, or my friendships AND I could afford my choices, then I was OK. No guilt necessary . . . move on.

Ever since I realized that guilt is a self-absorbing and destructive behavior, I've become pretty darn good at avoiding it. You should, too. It's so liberating. Don't worry about what everyone else thinks, including your husband. He'll get used to the idea of you taking care of yourself, and I'm pretty certain he'll love the more calm and rested you—and chances are he'll get more sex!

Let It Go!

It's easy to say, "Just get over it." But it's actually just about that simple. Guilt isn't real. It's in our heads. You just need to turn off the "Guilt" and turn on the "Who gives a rat's ass" switch in your brain. OK, we're simplifying just a bit, but it's time to come to terms with it and move on. How?

Six Steps to Put You on the Path to Guilt-Free Mothering

- **Form close relationships with other moms whom you can share your experiences with.** Make a promise that you will be honest with one another; keep one another's confidences, and listen without judgment (OK, try). This includes keeping your big mouth shut when your friend tells you she hasn't slept with her husband in months and is OK with his porn habit because it gets her off the hook for sex. Unless you want the entire school community knowing that you take your morning coffee with a double dose of Zoloft, you better keep her secrets so that she will keep yours. Forming these types of friendships is probably the most important thing you can do as a woman and mother to normalize and validate this tangled mess of emotions that is now your day-to-day life. We can assure you that these conversations will mark the beginning of a real friendship, because now that you've come clean about your mental state, you are about to get an earful in return that will make you look and feel like Carol Brady.

Any moms who perpetuate the "mask of perfection" (MOP) are not welcome. They are fake bitches who make sport out of making you feel inadequate because it takes the focus off themselves. Do not waste a minute of your precious time with them. You can often recognize these women by the fake smiles plastered on their faces. They scrapbook and chronicle every burp and fart from their children and make you feel terrible because you don't. They are constantly baking something for the classroom and kissing the teachers' asses. They would NEVER admit their honest feelings and therefore are not deserving of knowing yours. What it boils down to is that they are insecure, and the only way they feel better about themselves is by making you feel like a less than enthusiastic mom.

- **Be realistic with your expectations and you'll have a better chance of meeting them.** It's when we come up short that guilt creeps in. Don't aspire to accomplish stuff that is out of your league. You know what we're talking about. If you can't bake, don't all of a sudden try to become the Ace of Cakes for the kid's first birthday party. You'll end up feeling like a huge freaking loser, and you'll still need to go out and buy a cake. Wasting money and time is dumb. We can't imagine you have either in excess. Remember it's all about managing expectations. Aim low and then you can be delighted when you exceed your expectations, instead of the other way around.

- **Ask for help instead of assuming that all the other moms seem to do it all themselves.** Trust us, those other moms have more help than they are 'fessing up to. Their lies are contributing to you feeling less than. These are the kind of women whom you don't need as friends.

- **Accept your shortcomings and do not dwell on them.** Mothering is a marathon, not a sprint. It's going to be a long eighteen years if you hold yourself to a perfect standard. Banish the word *perfect* from your vocabulary. We hate perfect people—they can't possibly be happy because they are too busy being perfect! Prior to having kids, we used to glare at those moms with dirty-faced kids who were always grabbing their crotches. Where was their motherly pride? Recently Leigh looked down at her kid and just laughed out loud. He was about four months overdue for a haircut, hadn't had a bath in days, but was smiling ear to ear. Relax and let kids be kids. They need not look adorable all of the time.

- **Listen to your own voice and trust your instincts.** Stop worrying about what every other mom is doing and all of the newfangled parenting trends. If you want to circumcise your kid, then shut up and do it. Who cares what everyone else is doing? Stop driving us all nuts with your consensus building, neurosis, and self-absorbed guilt trips. YOU are the parent. Make a decision and live with it.

- **Change the word *guilt* to *regret*.** Don't you feel better already? It's as simple as semantics. Regret does not carry the same emotional toll as guilt. Regret is simply another way of saying, "It was the best I could do . . . at the time." Do not allow any other person's reaction to your parenting control your actions or feelings. Here's an example:
  - "I regret that I didn't scrapbook my child's first year of life."
  - "I regret that I wasn't able to attend the sixth field trip of the year."
  - "I regret that I let my kid wear the same pair of pants to school so much that the seat ripped out while he was on the monkey bars."

You see how easy that was? For all of you Catholics out there, it's like going to confession: voilà, you are instantly absolved of any further guilt!

Dumb-Ass Things Moms Do to Alleviate Guilt

We've all done this. Recognize it for what it is and try not to do it regularly. You really don't want your kids thinking that your role in their lives is to be at their constant beck and call and to fulfill their every need. And if you are always trying to assuage your working-mom guilt by buying them crap, throwing insane parties, and trying to keep them happy, this is exactly where you are headed. Kids know more than they let on, and if you are trying to overcompensate, they will sense it and then take advantage of it. That's not a lesson you want to teach them.

We've all done some dumb-ass things to make ourselves feel better. Don't worry, you're not alone.

• •

I hired "Princess Belle" for my daughter's third birthday and invited the whole class (we started the trend). Last year, she wanted a Babar birthday party, and I actually thought for about five minutes about whether I could figure out how to get an elephant to a city park in Cambridge. Then I spent grotesque amounts of money to pay a lady to host a "safari" in the park, and even more to put not only Babar but also Celeste on the birthday cake (in 3-D) because of the look on my daughter's face when I suggested that Celeste could be drawn on with icing.

Debbie, *Mother of Two and Marketing Executive*

I feel guilty not being one of the many stay-at-home moms who help out at school, so I try to at least do my share of participation and help drive for a field trip or bring in snacks for an event. I volunteer when I can, but I notice no matter how hard I try, I'm still never part of the non-working-mom clique. There is one and I'm sure other working moms notice it!

Michelle, *Mother of Two and Property Manager*

I have broken the seal and now I routinely bring my kids a treat from every business trip. It is awful! The first thing they do when my husband or I walk in from the airport is push us aside and dig through our bags.

Gabrey, *Mother of Two and Creative Director*

• •

You Caught Me, Now Get over It

All I know is, when I'm sitting at the nail salon getting a pedicure and my husband calls me on my cell phone, I immediately panic and blurt out that I have an important meeting and, uh, can he pick up our son from school? It's like it's too selfish to admit that I'm sitting somewhere getting my feet rubbed and neglecting my kid. I know this kind of thinking is nuts, but it was my reality for the first two years of motherhood. I lost my way, lost my sense of self, and was constantly wracked with guilt about my choices. If that sounds familiar, I know where you are headed and would like to help you chart a new course, unless a nervous breakdown sounds especially appealing.

—Leigh

THE GUILT IS GETTING YOU NOWHERE

Do you feel guilty if you do the following?
- Get a pedicure
- Spend quality time with a friend over a glass of wine and some dinner
- Get some exercise (alone)
- Work late so you can meet that big deadline
- Spend money on yourself
- Take time for yourself
- Spend money on child care so you can have a moment's peace

If you answered yes more than no, you are a guilty mess and need help. It's time to pull yourself together and get over it. We want you to be a happy, well-adjusted working mom. That way your kids will be happy and well adjusted, and they will STOP showing off all of those fancy toys you keep buying them. Really. You're making it tough on the rest of us.

Your Career—The Sacrificial Lamb

O K. We've got one thing established: You're working and you are NOT going to feel guilty about it. Or you are going to feel guilty about it, but you're going to deal. But here's the kicker: even when you've come to terms with the fact that you work and you either like work or need the money, there's still a great deal of angst involved. Goal-oriented career gals that we are, no one told us that we'd have to sacrifice a few things when we became working moms. Well, maybe they did tell us, but we TOTALLY ignored them and it came as a shock. Sacrifice? Sacrifice!

We were told that we could have it all. But "they" didn't tell us we'd have a few ego blows in the process. Or a few moments of

"Holy crap, am I doing the right thing for my kids?" When something particularly nasty goes down, like a last-minute you-gotta-go business trip to Asia when someone comes down with a little case of pneumonia, there's no getting around the simple fact that you cannot devote both a hundred percent of your efforts to your career AND a hundred percent of your efforts to your kids. That's two hundred percent. No math majors here, but even we know that's not possible.

So what gives (besides your sanity)? We're not here to judge, but ask yourself this question: How many women do you know who are on the Grand Poobah track and are working forty hours or less a week? About zero last time we looked around. We're not saying this is acceptable. God knows we'd love the part-time CEO job of Google, Apple, or Louis Vuitton. But it's the reality in which we find ourselves. Sacrificing something—whether that is time with the kids or the promotion—is the world as we know it.

There's a spectrum on which you can find yourself when discussing career. And there's a whole different kind of sacrifice that comes with each end. We call it Grand Poobah Versus Coasting.

Career Track	Grand Poobah Track	Middle Ground (We're not sure it exists!)	Coasting
Angst	I can't believe I just gave my four-year-old a cell phone. The nanny sees the kids twice as much as I do. I've missed four out of five of the last family birthdays.	What angst? Everything is fabulous!	My boss graduated from business school five years after I did! I've been doing the same thing for five years and I'm BORED. My brain is atrophying.

Career Track	Grand Poobah Track	Middle Ground (We're not sure it exists!)	Coasting
And what you need to pull it off	Stay-at-home husband, husband who's coasting, or some serious outsourced HELP.	Job-share, part-time partner track, or one of those other mythical situations.	Patience to believe that you'll be able to get back on track someday.

WE KNOW THAT WE'RE CONFLICTED— PLEASE STOP POINTING THAT OUT

So which end of the spectrum are we on or would we like to be on? Well, it depends on the day you ask us. Before you go off and start to psychoanalyze us, trust us, we've done it for you. Debated with ourselves. Listed the pros and cons. Looked at the logistics, run the budgets, understood our options, done the soul-searching, and come to some albeit temporary conclusions about our careers:

It's tough to admit, but we lost a bit of that fire in our belly when we had kids. We'll admit, we wanted to be Grand Poobahs. The hours we used to work back in the day before kids were a source of great pride. We would obsess at night about work stuff, itching to get in the next morning and solve the problem. We'd think about the next logical step in our careers and jockey for position. Then these precious human beings came along and turned our worlds upside down. Instead of obsessing about work from one to three a.m., now we worry that the kiddo's cough sounds awful or we just sleep because we're so crazy tired. Working seventy hours a week would mean less time with the kids and less sleep, and we've already established that we're tired. Getting to Grand Poobah sounds like a dream temporarily put on hold.

But it really sucks that we're not on the Grand Poobah track; in fact, it irritates us. We want to be on top of our game. Hell, that's where all of that education and those years of work pre-kids were supposed to lead. It doesn't help when male or childless classmates are regularly flouncing around with "Chief Bullsh*t Officer" on their business cards. We'll be the first to admit that it annoys the crap out of us when we have to say something like "I'm sorry but I have to go—day care closes at six p.m. sharp" when something major is being discussed and/or decided. It's our career and we actually care about it. But we'll fully admit, when it's something unimportant and it's time to go pick up the kids, we have no qualms at all about ditching and not looking back!

But who's going to pick up the kids? So, even if we wanted to be on the Grand Poobah track, the simple fact is that our husbands have already chosen careers that bring them home late at night and give them extremely limited flexibility. Yes, we could split up the trips and the late nights fifty-fifty, but the truth of the matter is that we've elected to be the person who is "there." There are those couples with equally high-powered careers, and kudos to them. And there are those couples where the mom is the primary breadwinner. We've elected not to go down those paths, at least not until our husbands get laid off. Therefore we will not be taking the position that keeps us away from home four nights out of seven. And did we mention that it sucks that we're not on the Grand Poobah track?

We're coming to terms with this whole sacrifice thing, as you can see. And we're probably not there yet. We want to be able to have it all. The fancy title, fancy paycheck, and all of the free time in the world to kiss our kids good night, see every piano recital, and drive them around to soccer practice. It has slowly and begrudgingly dawned on us that it's not humanly possible . . . at this very moment in time.

YOU'VE GOT FRIENDS

We're willing to call anyone who won't admit to having even fleeting questions and doubts about her career a liar. Have the women who have thrown themselves into their careers whole hog never wanted to just walk out the door at three p.m. and pick up their kids from school? Have the women who are coasting at work never wondered what it would be like to revisit the days when they had a chance in hell of a promotion? There are no such absolutes. We have had those moments of doubt and we're human. It's the "grass is always greener over the septic tank" theory. When the going gets tough, the other option always seems more appealing, if only for a second. Just ask the stay-at-home mom who's on her three-thousandth trip to the Palace of Jumpies in a desperate attempt to keep her kids entertained. We'd bet she'd give anything to trade places with you for just an hour or two, no matter what your job, and there are those days where we'd kill to be her.

Handy Phrases to Tell Yourself When You're Feeling Conflicted

So what do we do to come to terms with our altered career paths? We think there are a few kumbaya/self-motivational/namaste things to tell yourself to make you feel better.

If I Am Happy and Satisfied in My Career, I Can Be a Better Mom. I'll Sure Make a Better Role Model

That's right. We think we're better moms because we work and actually like our jobs. Call it a personality disorder, but work is an important part of who we are, and if work isn't going well, the family feels it. If your job isn't making you happy, then it's time to put some effort into finding one that will. Doesn't matter if you're coasting or you're shooting up the promotion track. When Mommy kicks ass at work, that's a good message to send to the kids—boys or girls, doesn't matter. What's cooler than an ass-kicking mommy?

• •

It's something that tugs at me, but each time it's offered, I have taken the advancement because I know it's really my expectation of myself (not the company's) to give more than a hundred percent to whatever I'm doing, whether it's the job, the kids, or the family.

Carolin, Mother of Two and General Manager

• •

Some Years I Coast, and Some Years I Kick Ass. Everything Goes in Waves, and It's OK to Take On ONLY What I Can Handle (i.e., Take On What I Can Without Totally Losing My Marbles)

Nothing is permanent. You heard it here for the thousandth time, but it might be a good moment to stop, drop, and think about it. Yes, today you might be working some dead-end job because you need to race home to pick up the kids in time for dinner. But your kids are going to get older and need less child care. Or your mom might move to town or Mary Poppins might drop in and volunteer to take care of your kids for a few years. Whatever happens, there will be an opportunity to put your career back in high gear. And the converse is also true. If you're on the partner track and it suddenly looks like it's going to get a bit longer because you no longer want to work ninety hours a week, it's OK. You're prioritizing, and no one can make that decision but you. And those people who give you a hard time can come see us, and we'll hand them their heads on a platter.

Embracing the New Order

• •

I always thought that I'd want to continue to climb the ladder at work. Now my priority is spending as much time at home as possible.

Moira, Mother of One and Physician

Having kids gave me the permission to care less about my career (for now), and once I got my priorities changed, I embraced the new order.

Renanah, Mother of Two and Clinical Psychologist

I don't do special projects anymore. My priority is to get home ASAP. This doesn't look so good to my boss . . . but who cares?

Jennifer, Mother of Three and Teacher

• •

I Am Not Alone—Others Feel Conflicted, Just Like Me

That's right. If you haven't figured it out by now, everyone else is also going through this crazy existential crisis. We all do it. All it takes is missing a gymnastics recital because you couldn't get out of work in time, or you just plain forgot, or missing a marketing meeting because the kid threw up on you again after breakfast, and you're going to have a little moment debating whether you're doing the right thing. Then your boss tells you that you're not getting promoted until you go back to the ninety-hour workweek you used to put in. All we can tell ourselves is that those moments pass, and the good and the bad all get mixed in together. Before you know it, your kids are going to be graduating from high school and the company will be handing you a gold watch to celebrate your retirement. Yes, the gold watch comment should clue you in that we're also a bit delusional about work loving us back, and you should take everything we say with a grain of salt.

Angst Is in Vogue

• •

It is hard to switch roles. I took a major promotion the week before I found out I was pregnant. I have regretted the decision to take the promotion more than once."

Beth, Mother of One and Publisher

Secretly I harbor a wish that my husband made plenty of cash and I could work part-time without ever having to worry about how much money my salary brought in.

Name withheld, Mother of One

I work part-time and have to say no to appealing and career-advancing opportunities. I am OK with the decision, but not without tension and anxiety. Do I want to step up? Do I need to step it up? When? How?

Lindsey, Mother of Two and Recruiter

• •

And Believe It or Not, It Can End Up Perfect (for Now)

It should be obvious to you that nothing is perfect permanently. The nanny quits, the job suddenly demands more hours, or the kids decide that their entire existence is defined by swim team, never mind that practice is five days a week and you have no way in hell of getting them there. Something happens. And that's the same with whatever job you're doing right now. It might be perfect because it's four days a week or because it's the CEO track position and that's all you ever wanted. But things change and you change and the kids change and you adjust accordingly. You find what works for now. And then you don't cry any tears when it's time to move on.

It's Perfect—for Now

• •

After I got my MBA, I went to a firm that had flexible hours and great four-, three-, and two-day-per-week options for mothers. I hated the job and left after a year to get back into the industry I loved pre-MBA and pre-kids, even though it meant more hours, more travel, more responsibility, and therefore more mommy guilt. I justify it to myself by looking back at when I was unhappy at work or unhappy at home at the end of maternity leaves and saying I'm a better mom when I am around and I'm happy, though with the good job I'm home less. And I can afford to pay to outsource everything, which has to be worth something. And my husband respects me. The list goes on—can you tell I'm rationalizing?

Elizabeth, Mother of Three and Private Equity Investor

I quit my job after having my five-year-old son asked me, "Why are you always on the phone or computer?" and not being recognized by my boss. If there was ever an eye-opener, that was it. My competitive nature still leads me to be jealous of more "successful" working women, but I simply remind myself that the most important compliment I ever receive is that my boys are well mannered and well adjusted. There is always room to get a new job, but I am certainly not doing this mommy thing again!

Liz, Mother of Two and Environmental Consultant

I am not in a tenure-track position. I teach during the school year and then am home in the summer. Very rarely, I wistfully think about being a tenured professor. Almost every day, however, I am grateful for my wonderful job and the balance that I have with work/family life. This is who I am, though. I am a mom first, then a professional second. I wouldn't be happy if it was the other way around.

Sohie, Mother of Three and Professor

● ●

SOME TIPS TO HELP YOU
IN THE WORKING WORLD

So you're working. It doesn't matter how hard or how many days, or where you fit on the spectrum of the mommy track versus the Grand Poobah track, we know that there is a simple rule to keeping it all under control and helping you feel like you're making all of the right decisions: Don't miss the big things. It doesn't matter if those are big things at work or big things at home. Don't miss them. Some have called them rubber balls and crystal balls. Whatever you call them, it's the same idea. We've been lucky enough to get this advice from our own Grand Poobah and have taken it to heart. Some things are more important than others, and if you lose perspective on that, you're in for a world of hurt—tears, career suicide, hurt feelings, pissed-off husbands . . . all of course leading eventually to crack-addicted kids who will be living in your basement for the rest of your life. Just kidding. We're sure it'll only be an addiction to Cheerios.

So what are "big things"? There are a few hard and fast rules, but some internal soul-searching is also required. If your kid lives and dies by movie night, we'd strongly suggest that you consider that a big thing. Same thing goes for your work life. Every company has its own "big thing," and even though you think the meeting is a big waste of payroll doesn't mean you have the option to skip it.

Things You CAN'T Miss at Work	Things You CAN'T Miss at Home
Budget/resource meetings. Any time funding and resource allocation decisions are made, you need to be there. You really want to trust next year's budget decisions to someone else? **Any meeting where a strategic decision is being made.** And here's a hint: A real strategic decision is one that will affect your business for more than one month. Deciding the theme of the Top Sellers Vegas boondoggle is not a strategic decision.	**Graduations (from one school to another).** Ignore those from one classroom to another. Those are faux graduations and considered optional if a true work emergency arises. Any hospitalizations or trips to the emergency room. The doctors need you there to hold the kid down while they give him stitches.

Things You CAN'T Miss at Work	Things You CAN'T Miss at Home
Meetings where you're able to make a meaningful impression on someone who matters. This means you play a big part at the meeting, you have something important to say, and someone who can help get you promoted is in the room. **Things that could get you fired.** Anytime you skip out, make sure that no one can fire you for missing the meeting/day at work. We assume that you want to keep your job.	**Recitals/school shows (as long as they happen fewer than four times per year).** If your kid is starring in any way, you MUST attend. Depending on the event, discreet PDAs are allowed. **The first game of the season, the play-off game, or the game when your kid starts.** Although it would be great to pass the time in the sun and watch all the games, you don't need to go to all of them. Pick the important ones and hang out and chat with the stay-at-home moms. You never know when you might need their help someday with pick-ups or drop-offs. **Parent-teacher conferences.** You are allowed to reschedule ONCE, but missing it makes it a waste of time for the teacher. And PDAs are frowned upon during the actual conference.

And of course, there is a flip side. These are things that you should never worry about missing!

Things You CAN Miss at Work	Things You CAN Miss at Home
Any meeting that can easily be rescheduled or moved. We're definitely not saying to do this repeatedly, especially with the same meeting. But if you can rearrange the schedule to get to the parent-teacher conference, do it! **Networking functions.** There can be a gazillion of these. And you're right, there just might be that one where you land a deal or a new job. But chances are you can miss the nine hundredth networking cocktail party in order to watch the ballet recital.	**Field trips.** There are plenty of them and your day will come. Other moms can cover these for you if you need to bail. They might not be happy that you're a flake, but they can drive. **Recitals/school shows that happen on a monthly basis (as long as your kid doesn't star).** With the advent of overscheduled kids comes the fallout: parents forced to attend dozens upon dozens of events. Chances are your kid doesn't care about them, either. Bail.

Things You CAN Miss at Work	Things You CAN Miss at Home
Meetings with important people where you're just going to be sitting there. This one can be tough to swallow, but if you don't have a major role to play in the meeting with the [insert C-level executive here], it's okay to bail in favor of a more important home function. (See list above. It is not okay to skip out on these meetings in order to meet the dishwasher repairman.) **Any meeting where a decision will not be made and you feel that your point of view will be well represented, regardless.** This describes most meetings. Delegate and get out of the meeting if you must. It's not that important because chances are there will be nine others just like it next week.	**The mid-season baseball/soccer/ whatever games.** We might be revealing our age here, but back in our day, parents did not chase their kids from game to event to game. They dropped us off and picked us up and asked us what the score was. You don't need to be there every game. It will do no permanent damage. **Dinner, the bath-time routine, or reading books a few times a week.** It's part of your routine, too, and it's fun. But here's the deal: You don't need to be there every night. If it saves your sanity or your career, stop being such a control freak and skip it.

Don't Feel Bad When You Want to Call It Quits—These Feelings Can Be Temporary

When trapped in one of those mind-numbingly boring meetings, it's hard not to want to escape to see your kid's two hundredth Little League game. Or when some terribly difficult situation comes up, who doesn't wish they could go home and watch *The Backyardigans* with the kids? But the truth is, we've had those thoughts at home as well. When the kids are going nuts about the fact that you're out of Cinnamon Toast Crunch or you're in a pointless argument about how your son cannot wear his favorite T-shirt because it's currently stuck in the turbo-wash cycle, work can seem like a vacation.

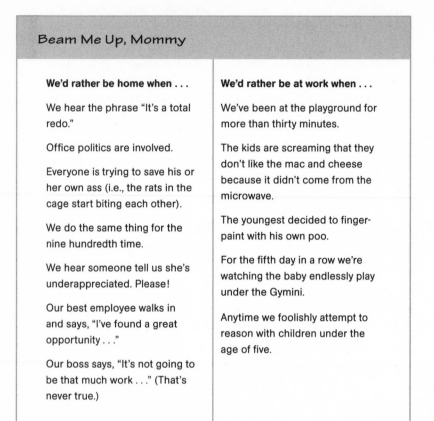

Beam Me Up, Mommy

We'd rather be home when . . .

We hear the phrase "It's a total redo."

Office politics are involved.

Everyone is trying to save his or her own ass (i.e., the rats in the cage start biting each other).

We do the same thing for the nine hundredth time.

We hear someone tell us she's underappreciated. Please!

Our best employee walks in and says, "I've found a great opportunity . . ."

Our boss says, "It's not going to be that much work . . ." (That's never true.)

We'd rather be at work when . . .

We've been at the playground for more than thirty minutes.

The kids are screaming that they don't like the mac and cheese because it didn't come from the microwave.

The youngest decided to finger-paint with his own poo.

For the fifth day in a row we're watching the baby endlessly play under the Gymini.

Anytime we foolishly attempt to reason with children under the age of five.

SO YOU NEED TO TALK IT OUT . . .

OK, we've now determined that we've all gone through these moments of self-doubt and we all agonize over the fact that we're trying to balance family life and raising good kids with a fulfilling career and not-so-fat paycheck. Given all of that self-doubt, chances are every once in a while you want to talk it out with a close confidant. There are some people with whom you should have this chat and others you should probably not see when the tears are about to spill and make tracks in your self-tanner.

Your mom/mother-in-law: A risky strategy. Depending on your age or socioeconomic background, a conversation with your mom could in fact be a minefield of guilt bombs: "Wouldn't it be nice if you could stay at home." "I felt that staying at home with you was one of the most rewarding things I ever did." "I don't really understand what you do all day." "Why can't [insert your husband's name here] make enough money so that you can stay home?" Such remarks can be less than helpful when you're about to lose it anyway. Though there is something to be said for rechanneling anger and frustration to another person and away from the overwhelming challenge you find yourself facing. *(Mom, you've never said any of this to me, and for that I thank you!—Amy)*

Bosses: Never. Never, ever a good idea to admit that you're coasting at work or that you simply don't care like you used to. Especially when everyone else around you is struggling to keep the ship afloat. And if you want to negotiate a part-time position or telecommuting arrangement, make sure that you are on strong emotional and professional footing. If you've just stunk it up at work for the past six months, no one is going to be handing you a benefit like working from home two days a week. And if you're bawling about not being able to handle it all, chances are they'll believe you and seriously question your judgment. Never. Got it? Never come undone with your boss. It's career suicide.

Husbands: Can be extremely helpful and supportive. That's why you married him, right? But remember that if you're worried about money, he is, too. You might want to time the conversation about reducing your paycheck so that it doesn't coincide with the enormous credit card or property tax payment.

Girlfriends: Perfect. Especially girlfriends who have jobs or have worked and have kids older than your own. They've been through it before and have made it to the other side. They can be a shoulder to cry on and probably will give you some really practical advice on how to make it work. A word of caution: stay away from the girlfriends who are kind of judgmental and project their own experiences on you. Thus, when you do something that they did not, e.g., quit work when they didn't or coast when they chose to go for the corner office, you'll get an unwanted earful of extremely unhelpful and unproductive nonsense.

IT APPEARS THAT YOU'RE LOOKING FOR A JOB WITH A BIT OF FLEXIBILITY

The desire for flexibility runs deep with working moms. It must be the reason that so many working moms start their own businesses or search out creative ways to both make money and make dinner for the kids each night. When looking for a job, know your limits and your expectations. This will make both you and your new employer much happier. No point in applying for the Vice President of International Development (i.e., the VP of Business Class) if you've got no desire to spend weeks away from the kids.

- **Does the job involve travel?** How much travel and for how many days at a time? When they say "some international travel," do they really mean "some" or do they mean that you'll be on a first-name basis with the flight attendants on Cathay Pacific?

- **What time does everyone get into the office?** What time do they leave? Are they in the office all of the time, or can you get your work done outside of the office? And when they are in the office, is it face time or are they actually getting work done? Nothing worse than having to hang out until the boss leaves when you've got dinner, *Richard Scarry*, and three loads of laundry waiting for you at home . . .

- **What's your boss like?** Does he understand the challenges of working moms? Is he sympathetic to sick kids and bedtime routines? Or can you tell that his brain is screaming, "Does Not Compute," when you pop your head in to tell him that you need to run because the kiddo just got kicked out of day care with a 101-degree fever.

- **What's your support like at home?** Do you have the help that you need to pull off this new position, whether it's your spouse or your mom, or the money to shell out for help? Without the help to shore you up, it's hard to want to take on anything new.

ARE YOU SO FED UP
THAT YOU'RE GOING TO QUIT?

There is a saying that every working mom is only one bad day away from quitting. And while there are times when there is some truth to that, we are here to save you from yourself. The sacrifice and the constant juggling can be frustrating and demoralizing, and if you've got the option it's tempting to just say, "I QUIT!" If that's truly what you want, we'll support you a hundred percent. Yes, it's hard, and yes, it's going to give you more angst than you ever thought possible. But you can manage this because you know that everything changes. Some unsolicited advice: Think long and hard about taking yourself off the market. It's not easy to get back on track.

What's the perfect job? Hell if we know! Well, actually we do know the answer. Life is going to change, you are going to change, your kids are going to become—shockingly—more or less dependent on you, and the world around you continues to change. If you can find the perfect situation, which means that it's manageable, hang on with both hands. But don't worry when it ends and you move on to the next thing. Haven't you figured out that key lesson of motherhood? ROLL WITH IT!

Part IV

Mommy Gets Her Mojo Back

12

Throwing Money, Mothers-in-Law,

and More Money at the Problem

HELP! I'M A WORKING MOM AND I CAN'T GET OUT FROM UNDER THIS LOAD OF RESPONSIBILITY!

You are a working mom. You have overwhelming responsibilities at work and at home. You are incredible. Bask in the happy glow of being able to do it all. Now, that said, offload and cut yourself some slack. Offloading and flat-out ignoring so-called responsibility is the key to survival. What in the world convinced you that you could do it all— and do it all well? Have you ever seen all of the tasks that encompass your life outside of work? Your other full-time job?

We're not trying to get you fired or divorced or make you lose all of your friends. We're trying to help you get out of a few obligations in order to buy you some sanity. Out of necessity your priorities have changed, but you may not have quite caught up with that reality just yet. We're here to remind you. In a perfect world, under perfect circumstances, you'd love to do it all. But you need to have the courage to cut out the things that aren't your number-one or number-two priorities. It's the only way you're going to be able to achieve what we all strive for: a few minutes of time to play with the kids, talk to your spouse, and enjoy being a family. Or the ultimate goal—all of the above plus thirty minutes of TV and a glass of wine.

We've compiled a handy chart of your responsibilities for your reference. It's overwhelming. But here's the good news. You have a choice for each task.

Mark S for spouse if he is responsible for the task or can somehow be coerced into making it his own.

Mark K for kids if you can force them to take it on.

Mark X for skip it—you don't really need to do this (often).

Mark M for yourself if you think you can and need to do the task.

Mark O for outsource if you're open to forking over cash to get someone else to do this for you.

There are some that probably could be marked with multiple letters, but that's too complex for us.

Here's the trick:

- Too many M's and you'll go nuts. No amount of happy pills or dirty martinis will make up for the fact that you're overwhelmed.
- Too many O's and you'd better have a seven-figure salary to back it up. Or some sort of never-ending trust fund.

- Too many X's and we might end up seeing you on the nightly news: "Fire department called when dust bunnies hold local family hostage."

And if you have enough S's and K's in there, you clearly deserve a gold star. You guys are the Brady Bunch incarnate

OFFLOADING THE DOMESTIC RESPONSIBILITIES

Theoretically, you can offload every single item on the list we've given. Some you'll probably want to do yourself anyway, but we'd bet that a good chunk of the tasks you'd prefer to either delegate or never do again. But whether you are paying for the help, begging for it, or trading sexual favors with your husband for laundry duty, you must figure out a way to delegate responsibility to others. And if you don't figure out a way to delegate, you will go crazy. Crazy. Did we say it enough for you to understand? Crazy. And here's another thing: Just because you're not doing it yourself, or choosing to not do it at all, does not make you a failure. Understood? Have you ever heard someone say, "She's a crappy mom because she never empties the dishwasher?" Didn't think so.

Start with the Obvious

The most obvious, and free, source of help is, of course, your hubby/partner. But asking that person to share the domestic burdens can be such a tangled web that it gets its very own chapter (see chapter 13). In the meantime, we're offering some alternatives to your main squeeze.

Household		School/Kid Activities	
Task	Who's in Charge?	Task	Who's in Charge?
Clean bathrooms (tub, toilet, sink, floor, etc.)		Help with homework	
Mop floors		Purchase supplies	
Vacuum rugs		Attend parent-teacher conferences	
Make beds		Volunteer in the classroom	
Change sheets on beds		Drive for field trips	
Clean kitchen counters		Complete forms, signatures, etc.	
Clean kitchen floors		Do school drop-off/ pick-up	
Empty dishwasher/put away dishes		Find after-school activities and register	
Wash pots and pans/other dishes		Do activity drop-off/ pick-up	
Do laundry—wash and dry		Purchase uniforms, paraphernalia, etc.	
Fold and put away laundry		Attend games/recitals, etc.	
Iron		Arrange play dates	
Pick up/drop off dry cleaning		RSVP to birthday parties, etc.	
Take out trash		Buy presents for parties	
Take out recycling		Shuttle kids to parties	
Wash windows/screens		Plan your own parties	
Shop for household (Costco, Target, etc.)			
Schedule and wait for deliveries			
Schedule and wait for repairs			

Meals		Kid Care and Feeding	
Task	**Who's in Charge?**	**Task**	**Who's in Charge?**
Make breakfast (the kids' and your own)		Get dressed/ undressed	
Pack kids' lunches		Give baths	
Make dinner		Read books	
Clean up after meals		Do bedtime routine	
Bus the table		Change diapers	
Clean the floors		Feed [in the younger years], burp, etc.	
Do the dishes		Schedule doctor/ dentist appointments	
Grocery shop		Take to appointments	
		Pick up prescriptions	
		Dole out meds	
		Manage children's wardrobe, rain boots, winter coats, hats, etc.	
		Take photos and organize them	
		Instill discipline	
		Teach life lessons	
		Ensure happiness	

Outside /Big Stuff		Automobiles	
Task	Who's in Charge?	Task	Who's in Charge?
Weed		Manage ongoing maintenance (routine service, oil changes etc.)	
Mow lawns			
Fertilize		Wash/vacuum	
Sweep		Get car fixed	
Plant new plants		Put in car seats	
Set out/take in patio furniture		Take out car seats	
Clean the gutters		Insure car	
Do minor repair projects		Make sure insurance card and registration are in the car	
Paint			
Fix squeaky doors, missing doorknobs, and so on			

Financial		Optional	
Task	Who's in Charge?	Task	Who's in Charge?
Pay bills		Feed pet	
Balance checkbook		Walk pet	
Pay taxes		Clean pet	
Make a budget		Take pet to vet	
Monitor the budget		Clean pool	
Manage strategic financial planning		Maintain pool	
		Visit family and friends	
		Call family and friends	
		Write thank-you notes, etc.	
		Remember birthdays, anniversaries, new baby presents	
		Socialize	
		Plan family vacations	
		Make reservations (plane tickets, hotel, car, etc.)	
		Coordinate school schedules with vacations	

Call in the Reinforcements

• •

Look. It's impossible to run a household with two full-on careers. It's impossible. You need help . . . Prove me wrong!

Maya, Mother of One and Engineer

• •

Gawd, I Need a Wife

I was traveling once if not twice a month to NYC, and it was turning my whole house upside down. I'm the glue—the one who can be relied upon to pick up my son five nights a week at preschool. When I was traveling, I had to make alternative arrangements each night I was away. It would involve a note to the school giving permission for someone else to pick him up, a spare car seat, an extra set of house keys, and directions regarding "after-school routine" for each night that I was away. Occasionally another mom could help me out, but it wasn't easy. Many moms already had two kids and fitting that third car seat was too much. Plus, I didn't want to take advantage. The pressure was awful and the stakes were high. I was so busy I couldn't even stop and take a step back and figure out what to do. So I cobbled it together one day at a time. Then one night while in NYC my phone rang: it was the babysitter, and something had come up with her kids, so she couldn't go pick up my kid. That's when I realized I needed a more reliable, permanent solution. I reached out to all of my mom friends via e-mail and found the most amazing part-time nanny. Now she picks up my son two nights a week, and I limit the length of my trips to three nights if at all possible.

My husband has to pick him up only one time while I'm away, and isn't so stressed when I'm away. A win-win for all.

Outsourcing pick-ups completely changed my life. Two days a week was all it took. As fate would have it, Amy and I made this change the EXACT same week, and as we spied each other at the office down a long corridor, we just smiled and said, "WE HAVE WIVES!" It was a great feeling to find a solution that was of benefit to me and my family, and the lesson to me was it wasn't black or white, all or nothing; the solution was somewhere in the middle.

—Leigh

Outsourcing: A Dirty Word or a Godsend?

Why does outsourcing household or child-care responsibilities make people feel so guilty? Probably because you were raised to be frugal, take responsibility for yourself, and work hard. Damn that Puritan heritage. Well, get over it. There's a limit to what you can take on.

Here are some extremely viable and guilt-free options for outsourcing, from absolute necessity to luxury.

Housecleaner ($/Close to a necessity): Imagine coming home to a clean bathroom after a hard day at work. Honestly, we challenge you to come up with a better feeling. We know for certain that we'd never do as thorough a job. Not even close. Where are you going to find four hours to clean the house from top to bottom?

Gardener ($/Nice to have): The yard is not built for multitasking. Have you ever tried to weed when the kids are climbing the trees or seeing how far they can jump off the concrete wall without breaking their heads open? Every recent gardening project we've attempted has ended with the phrase "Do not hit your brother with that rake!" We'd much prefer to play with the kids outside rather than scream at them while we wrestle with thistles. Someday we'll train them to differentiate weeds from flowers.

Handy Manny ($$/Nice to have): It's hard to imagine your strong, virile spouse incapable of fixing something. But our fancy college degrees taught us a word to use for this occasion—*specialization*. If your spouse is anything like ours, it will take him six times as long as a trained professional, and everyone is going to be really angry that they wasted the whole precious weekend at Home Depot. If you can afford it, keep the name of a handy man handy and the ongoing list of projects nearby. Once you get to four to-do's, call him up. Stand back and watch in amazement as a trained professional completes the task in a fraction of the time of your well-meaning hubby.

Meals ($$$/Luxury): At the very least you can rely on Trader Joe's and Costco for ready-made meals. But in this day of convenience, there's a shocking number of meal services out there—some with healthy and low-cost options. We're not talking McDonald's, but we're also not talking a personal chef permanently ensconced in your kitchen. Even if it's a few meals a month, it makes you feel so good. It's also the best gift you could ever give to a new mom fresh off of maternity leave.

Personal Assistant ($$$/Fabulous Luxury): Appointments with the refrigerator repairman? UPS delivery getting you down? How about paying someone to deal with it all for you? Sounds lovely and expensive. If it saves you from losing your mind, we're not going to stand in your way.

Let Us Make You Feel Better About Outsourcing

• •

The day I returned to work after baby number two, I was totally stressed out. I had an impossible job and a million things to do at home. After dealing with that for a week, I made a nice sign on pretty paper and listed fifteen items that needed to be done daily or weekly and taped it to the fridge. My husband was furious. Apparently he is "really good at original ideas" but does not "do ongoing mainte-nance well" (i.e., he doesn't do dishes, laundry, or cook). So the next day he outsourced his "jobs," including extending our weekly clean-ing lady to do the laundry and hiring a cook who makes five meals a week. It was a wonderful solution for everyone—I can't imagine life without it.

Laura, Mother of Two and Director of Manufacturing

We finally hired a cleaning lady. I had to beg my husband—and lied to him about what it cost. I just couldn't spend another weekend clean-ing the whole house.

Kelly, Mother of Two and Marketing Manager

We have a meal service that is also a not-for-profit that feeds the homeless (there goes any guilt!). I have no qualms about giving up most cooking until my children can set the table and help with dishes.

Renanah, Mother of Two and Clinical Psychologist

What to Do on the Cheap

It would be fabulous to have all of the help in the world. Sadly, neither of us has figured out how to get all of that help for free. So we make do and greatly appreciate the luxury of getting whatever help we can. But we've employed quite a few low-cost strategies to save our sanity.

Go halfway (or even 25 percent). You don't have to think that everything is black and white. It's not nanny or day care, cleaning lady or DIY. We know that times are tight, and no one has any extra cash to throw away. You have options:

- Use a nanny only a few days a week and fill in with day care.
- Hire a cleaning lady once a month to do the heavy lifting (toilet cleaning, mopping, vacuuming, window cleaning, etc.).
- Hire a gardener twice a year—once in fall, once in spring.

Trade with other moms/neighbors, etc. Didn't someone famous say it takes a village to raise a child? We didn't really get it at the time, but it's become abundantly clear to us now. You do in fact need to rely on other moms, the neighbor, the mailman, etc., to help you get your house in order—whether that's trading play dates or catching your kids racing down the street in an ill-fated attempt to see how far they can get before you notice they are missing.

- Trade play dates once a month to buy yourself just a bit of time.
- Bribe your retired neighbor with a nice bottle of wine in exchange for waiting it out until the cable guy appears.
- Trade services with friends/relatives/neighbors—like preparing taxes in exchange for a few nights of babysitting.

Get over it. The greatest cost-saving tip is to let go of your vision of yourself as über-mom and start to let a few things go. A little dirt never hurt anyone, and you can do miracles with a monthly trip around the room with the Swiffer.

. . . .

I've stopped cleaning in between the cleaning lady. When you are eighty, are you going to regret that you didn't spend more time cleaning?
    Dawn, *Mother of Two and Advertising Executive*

. . . .

Rely on the people who are supposed to love your kids. That means your family. If you have any family nearby, this is the time to swallow your pride and repress those memories of when your brother locked you under the sink. It's time to ask family for help. Typically, parents or the in-laws will step up, but you've got to respect their limits. There is nothing worse than hearing your own mother say, "I need a break from your kids." Ouch.

My Mommy Still Races to My Rescue . . .

I live four freeway exits from my parents. They have saved me on numerous occasions. They will drop anything to pick up the kids on a moment's notice—when I'm stuck in traffic, when I have that "crazy" tone to my voice, or when we have to race to the accountant's office to deal with taxes. Every Wednesday night my mom picks up the kids, my dad whips together a gourmet meal, and I get to waltz in, have a glass of wine, and just relax. It's amazing! They've probably said no two times and they are always thrilled to see our kids, or so it seems to me.

But with that comes the guilt. Am I relying on them too much? Will they start to resent my kids? If I drop the kids off too often, will my parents think I'm a bad mom? It's a constant struggle. I shower them with thanks, fancy kitchen utensils, and gift cards to local restaurants. I tell myself this kind of makes up for it.

—Amy

Child Labor

Your kids might be too young now, but believe us, they can do stuff. Do you remember your own chores? Allowance? Well, the time has come to get your own kids working for you. And until about age eight, they haven't even heard of allowance. Free labor!

Did You Know That Your Kids Could . . . ?

Bus the table. Okay, don't use the good china, but our kids have been bussing the table since age two. We only lost a few dishes. And we didn't realize that they could do this until we saw them do it at day care. Who knew?

Make the bed. Totally doable for three-year-olds and above. And if Amy actually did it herself, she'd probably be proactive about having her kids do it, too.

Make their own lunches. Age five and on. Yes, it's possible. We've seen it done by our friends who are much better taskmasters than we are.

Pick out their own clothes and get themselves dressed. After age four this shouldn't be an issue. But you better give yourself plenty of time to let this happen. Sometimes races are needed to speed the process along. Or if you're willing to go the TV route, no shows until the clothes are on and breakfast is down the hatch.

Take out the trash. Age four and on. At least helping with emptying the trash cans from inside the house. And from five on, getting the trash to the curb is totally within the realm of possibility.

NOW CUT YOURSELF SOME SLACK AND JUST GET OUT OF A FEW RESPONSIBILITIES

So let's be honest and say that there are a few things that you can't necessarily outsource. There are, in fact, responsibilities that fall on your shoulders. Are we saying shirk them? No, but we're huge advocates of cutting yourself some slack and getting tough if it gets you out of a few time-sucking responsibilities. You don't need time-sucks. You've got no extra minutes for that. Time-sucks can sneak up on you from places you least expect it. You've got to be diligent to avoid spending your entire weekend participating in some cockamamie activity that you don't really want to do.

Those Darling Little Time-Sucks, Your Own Children

You may not even realize it's happening, but your own beloved children are very likely slowly sucking your time. Not with fun activities like playing in the backyard or baking cookies—things you would like to do—but with horrific mind-numbing tasks. Our own children are the most amazingly sneaky time-sucks, we know. At an early age, those darlings have figured out how to work you. And sometimes so subtly that you don't even see it coming. If you're like us, you've probably got just a few hours with your kids to eat dinner, bathe, and hang out before they've got to be in bed. You don't have any extra time. Everyone ends up getting stressed and cranky if you let the time-sucks get the best of you. A few examples of the minefield that is your daily routine:

Dinnertime: At our house, an eternity can pass while the kids eat their last green beans. Our trick? Limit the amount of food on the plate. And if no bites have been eaten for five minutes or so, give one warning that dinner is over, and then call time. And the kitchen is closed after the last plate is bussed. Now we are not suggesting you starve your children. Just dole out the food, give an adequate amount of time to eat it, talk about your day, teach manners, and then dinner is over. We are not getting up from the table a million times and turning dinner into a two-hour affair. There is no time for that!

Bath time: It's fun and it's a great time to hang out with the kids. But they love it so much that you can spend thirty minutes rinsing their backs with warm water and winding up bath toys. If their fingers and toes look like raisins, the water has gone cold, and there's more liquid on the floor of the bathroom than in the tub, it's time to wrap it up.

Books: Our kids would be happy to read every book in the house before bedtime. We're big fans of limiting the number of books per night—or limiting the number of pages. There is nothing scarier than rereading a Richard Scarry book for the fourth time when you've got a few e-mails to write after the kids go to sleep.

Bedtime: "Mommy, I need water" or "Mommy, my blankie fell" or "Mommy, watch me jump out of the crib" are annoying when you're trying to wind down yourself and watch a little TV. But they can move you within an inch of completely losing it when you've got some work to do that night. There are entire books written on how to make the bedtime routine work. Read them all. Pick your favorite strategy. Stick to it. Figure out a way to make bedtimes routine and quick.

It Took Me Six Months, but I Did It

One of my most stressful periods as a mom was when our youngest was about two and our eldest about four. Like all new moms, I'd made a ton of missteps with our first kid—including rocking him to sleep in my arms from the day he was born. I knew that it was NOT recommended, but I did it anyway. And I probably asked my husband to take over for me on a total of three nights.

What I didn't realize at the time was that I (and only I) was therefore obligated to be nearby while he fell asleep from that point forward. The falling-asleep routine stretched from about five minutes when he was a baby to two hours when he was four. It was like that cruel story about frogs—if you put them in a pot of water and slowly turn up the temperature, they don't realize when it starts to boil. Well, we all know what happens to those poor frogs. I hadn't realized how bad it had gotten. One day it dawned on me that the reason I was so stressed at night and starting to look at my child like he was the devil was that I had created this marathon bedtime routine.

I figured out a plan with the help of our pediatrician, and stuck to it. The pediatrician told him that big boys stay in their own beds and go to sleep on their own. If he got out of bed, I'd march him back in without saying a word. Sometimes I'd march him back in fifty-plus times. Then my husband and I gave him stars for "good good nights." It took six months before everything was perfect, but it works now. And I got back two extra hours each night. In the world of working moms, that's an eternity.

—Amy

Cutting Yourself and the Kids Some Slack

We don't want you to think we're the ultimate disciplinarians based on our statements above. Far from it. Fairly early on, we discovered, much to our shock and horror, that just like us, our children are not perfect. They aren't always clean, they can occasionally be caught doing something very gross, and they did not manage to do some recommended activities perfectly on schedule, like getting potty-trained ditching the bottle, and losing the binky. Yes, that's our fault. We recognize that as the parents, we are responsible for setting the rules and laying down the law. But we pick and choose our battles.

We are NOT child psychologists, pediatricians, or experts in any way, shape, or form. But to maintain sanity and to take on what we consider the right amount of discipline and rules for our household, we've made our judgment calls. We will eventually get to the binky and the sippy cups and the booger-picking (in fact, very soon). But in our opinion, you have permission to cut yourself some slack. We're one hundred percent certain that your kids won't be drinking beer out of sippy cups and will be potty-trained by the time they hit college.

The Working Mom's Worst Friend

For all of you pet lovers out there, we have a confession. We wish no ill will to animals. We don't care if you have a house full of cats, dogs, parakeets, or ferrets. But we are not pet people at this point in our lives. We're full up with these kids. The thought of taking care of one more living thing scares the bejeezus out of us. So much so that we barely have plants. If after months and months of training, this living creature still can't run the vacuum or clean up after itself, chances are it's not for us. We know what you are thinking—"but pets are so important to children: they teach them responsibility"—and we get that, just not now.

And we're sure that, like our kids, yours are begging, or have begged, to get a pet. If you don't have one yet, stay strong. If you have one now, please tell us that you can at least do the following:

- Get the kids to walk the dog.
- Get the kids to feed the dog/cat/parakeet/ferret.
- Assign poop duty to the kids, or hire someone for poop duty.
- Do everything in your power to offload responsibility for the animal.

And our standard response to "Can I get a dog?" is "Maybe someday." Stay strong.

Just Say No! All Those Other Obligations . . .

I've spent a lot of time and money sitting on "the couch."
Undeniably the best piece of advice I ever got was "Say NO
unless it's an unequivocal yes." Apparently I was saying yes

when it was an unequivocal NO. So take that advice; it really provides clarity, and I've just saved you thousands of dollars in therapy!

—Leigh

Everyone has obligations outside work, family, and friends. But there's something about having kids that seems to ratchet up the obligations about a thousand notches or so. Every time you turn around, there's something to do. So how do you pick your battles? Up to you and totally based on what you consider the priority—or the unequivocal yes. We've got some tips to help you sort through how to remove yourself from a few that are the unequivocal no.

When Asked to Cook Meals or Bake

Although we both secretly aspire to being mini Martha Stewarts and we'd never pass up a well-frosted cupcake, we recognize that bake sales and potlucks are the enemy of the working mom. They're almost impossible to pull off, unless you want to stay up until one a.m. baking brownies. In our households, that's simply not going to happen.

- Pick up prepared food from the grocery store for potlucks. If you are really feeling guilty that you didn't do homemade, put it on your platter and smack it around a little to make it look less perfect.
- Volunteer to bring the drinks, the tortilla chips, or even the napkins and plastic cups. They can sit in your car all day with no adverse affects. Hell, they can stay in the car for weeks if you need them to. And you can even grab whatever is in the pantry instead of making a special trip to the store.

- Dress it up. Mask the fact that you prioritized your to-do list and the bake sale ended up way at the bottom of the list. Buy some cookies and individually wrap them in cellophane for bake sales. Better yet, pay extra to have the bakery do this.

When Asked to Drive for Field Trips

We would love to have the freedom to make it to every field trip. But we are the first to admit that we will never be able to compete with the SAHMs for the Perfect Field Trip Attendance award. Sadly, things like business trips, meetings, and completely burning through our sick time can get in our way. Not volunteering can make you look like a slacker mom. You've got to pick the field trips wisely. Here's how to extract yourself (not quite) gracefully:

- Pick the field trips that matter most to your kid. Your kid loves the zoo? Prioritize that trip and skip the others, guilt-free.
- Volunteer to take only one kid besides your own. You are automatically the most useless driver possible.
- Let slip that it's no issue, but you'll just need to put off getting the brakes fixed. Or casually mention that you just got your license back so you're good to go. (You know we're kidding, right?)

When Asked to Volunteer for the School

Any of us who send our kids to public school know the desperate need for additional resources in the schools. And those of us sending our kids to private school know that tuition would likely double without the sweat equity of the parents. But the reality is that working moms have a hard time meeting the dual needs of the school and their jobs.

- Become the Grand Poobah (coordinator, class mom, graduation committee leader, etc.). Find the job where you can delegate tasks and ensure that others are pulling their weight. This means that you can boss people around via e-mail either early in the morning or late at night. You aren't required to figure out how you're going to get out of that nine a.m. meeting that was just called on the day you were supposed to be helping the librarian restock the shelves.

- Volunteer for the big things. These are the projects that take up a lot of time in one chunk. These larger-scale projects are much easier to plan for, and once you complete one, you can skip out of the smaller projects without guilt.

- Find a task that might be easy for you but perhaps seems thankless to everyone else. Master of PowerPoint or Excel? Lord knows that stuff scares a lot of people, so sign up for that and look like a hero. Your years of consulting will pay off in spades. Perhaps you know desktop publishing. If so, knock out the newsletter in your sleep. It could take a lot less time for you than anyone else could ever dream. And now milk that project for a few months at least.

- Ask for the tasks that you can do at night. Data entry? E-mail solicitations? Update the school website? All of these can be handled once the kids are asleep and the work e-mails are finally done.

- Beg your boss for some time off, or cash in one of those precious vacation days. Given enough notice, we're sure that you can sort through a way to get yourself into the classroom to help. How many times can you hear your kid say, "Mommy, when are YOU going to come to my classroom," before you finally step up?

• •

I had a PTA mom ask if I would like to volunteer some evenings and a Saturday to help prepare for a big school benefit. I didn't respond with words, but opened my checkbook. She said, "No, I'm not asking for money." I said, "Yeah, but will that get me off the hook?"

Stefanie, Mother of Two and Psychologist

• •

When Asked to Volunteer for Any Cause

Oh, there are a lot of causes. And who are we to judge which is and which is not important to you. But ask yourself the simple question: do these people matter more than your own family? We both figured out that even if it's just the occasional meeting, if it takes away from time with family or friends, it's got to wait until the kids are in college.

- If you're rolling in dough, ask if you can write a check instead. We promise it will be less painful than picking up trash for four hours on your Saturday.
- See if they will take someone else as a substitute. Then see if you can coerce one of your single friends to go with the promise of free drinks and plenty of eligible bachelors/bachelorettes.
- If it's a volunteer activity and you actually care deeply, see if there's a way to volunteer the entire family. At least you'll be together while scouring the beach for hypodermic needles.
- Did we mention that they might be willing to take a check instead? Even a small one.

When Invited to Join That Fancy Women's Group

Every city has them—the groups of fancy people. These are the groups that you're supposed to want to be in and the people with whom you're supposed to want to hang out. If you are currently at your limit with kids, spouse, and work and we still have to talk you out of joining these groups, we worry about you. Even so, here's how to navigate the pull toward the popular people.

- Take a deep breath and remember that this isn't sorority rush. It's flattering just to be asked and you really need not get in or join.
- If you really care (come on, really?), ask them if they'll take you in a few years.

- Say no and make your own club with your own friends and kill two birds with one stone—see your friends and check "secret club" off your to-do list.

When the Neighborhood Association or Condo Board Comes Knocking

Everyone has crazy neighbors. We are our neighbors'crazy neighbors. And there can be nothing worse than having to spend time at disorganized meetings debating whether the new guy's window coverings are bringing down property values. You must stay away from these at all costs. Unless you feel like your presence can somehow juice the value of your property by more than 20 percent, do not attend.

- Tell them that you trust them completely and you can't wait to read the fascinating meeting minutes.
- Keep telling them you're thinking about moving.
- Assign a proxy. One whom you trust NOT to vote that everyone is now required to give the doorman the Vulcan greeting.

God Is Going to Punish Me, Eventually

When we had kids, my husband and I decided that we wanted to make sure to incorporate religion into their lives. We picked a church (Episcopalian, the compromise religion) and started bringing our first son to church when he was just a baby. Both of our kids were baptized and we even pulled off a few months of Sunday school. And that's when it all started to fall apart. With a baby and a toddler, two full-time jobs between us, and me within an inch of a full-scale breakdown that would surely require hospitalization, I gave up on church. First, I was used to the Catholic practice of get in and get out rather than chatting it up for a few hours over coffee after the service. And second, at the time I just didn't have the space in my life for anything extra. I'll admit that I occasionally feel guilty, but I justify it by saying prayers with the kids every night before they go to bed. In the Bay Area, that makes us Bible-thumping holy rollers. Hide your children!

—Amy

WHAT HAPPENS IF YOU DON'T HAVE HELP OR DON'T CUT YOURSELF SOME SLACK?

There is no *"no help"* option. If it's a matter of money, ask your family. If you don't have family nearby, ask some friends and make a trade. If you don't have friends nearby, it's time to ask the neighbors and see how you can help one another out. If you aren't friendly with the neighbors and you don't have friends, it's time to stick your head out of the front door and start being social. Or reach out to some local community groups. Look for local mom blogs, mom's groups, or even your community social services groups.

And imagine a world in which you've got help, cut yourself some slack, and gotten out of a few obligations. Now you can actually do the things that you want to do. Isn't that fantastic and an almost completely unfamiliar situation? When push comes to shove, the only things that we really want to do are be with our kids, actually hang out with our spouses, get pedicures, get some exercise, drink wine, watch TV, sleep, and of course hang out with our friends. That might change when we have independent kids and a bit more time on our hands. But until then, we'll use our free minutes for all of the hangout time and sleep we can possibly manage.

13

You Are Not Your Husband's Mother

You've read this far and thus know that we've purposely skipped over the most obvious place to turn for help—your spouse—because getting help from your spouse sometimes requires a bit more effort and emotional baggage. You are both most likely working, you are both most definitely tired, and you are both probably at each other's throats much more than you would like to be. And depending on how you were each raised, you may have some societal issues to get out of the way. It's hard to get help or ask for help when your husband's mother never worked, happily met his every need, and still cooks his favorite meal and insists on doing his laundry when you go to visit.

Beyond just getting help from the man, you also need to stop providing any unrequited favors that come your way. We know that sounds heartless, but you are in this together as equal partners. We'll bet that neither of you vowed to "pick up after you, till death do us part" during your wedding. No point in resenting the man because he failed to pick up his socks . . . again. You just need to stop picking them up for him.

THE OBVIOUS GUY TO TURN TO FOR HELP . . . YOUR SPOUSE

We're not sure if anything can strain a marriage like the combination of one or more kids and two or more jobs. Our fights before kids were about who got to pick the movie that weekend or whether we should open up a bottle of white or red. Now we can have screaming matches about everything from the sour milk in the fridge to whose turn is it to find the binky in the dark (for the third time that night).

We Get in Fights over Only Two Things

My husband and I fight over only two things (seriously): competitive jogging and helping with the kids.

I should explain the jogging thing. He feels the need to always "win" while jogging. This means that if my shoulder creeps in front of him for just an instant, he'll accelerate just enough to make sure that his shoulder is two inches ahead. It drives me nuts. One tragic Sunday morning, I tried to prove a point. Each time he accelerated to get in front of me, I'd do the same. We both ended up sprinting down a quiet San Francisco street with me screaming at him that he was a competitive ass. We don't go running together anymore.

Now let me explain, he is amazing with the kids. Want help teaching the kids how to play baseball? He's your guy.

When the kids want to go to the skate park at eight on a Sunday morning, he's there! Want to teach them to remain calm under pressure or simply be nice people? He's far better at this than me. But he's unable to help with the daily drop-off/pick-up thing. For three years we fought over it repeatedly. I did all day-care drop-offs (since his work was farther away) and all pick-ups (since he'd have to leave at 4:30 in order to get the kids in time). He owns his own business, which would suggest that he has tons of flexibility. But he feels he has no choice but to go the extra mile for clients or work late to make sure that each project is perfect. (Yes, I know that's what makes him good at his job. And yes, I know that his drive to succeed is one of the reasons I married him in the first place.) Each fight would start with me asking him, as nicely as I could, if he could possibly come home earlier just a few nights a week to pick up the kids or make it home for dinner. And each would end with me crying while he stood there and said, "What am I supposed to do? Kick out my clients?"

After three years of banging my head against the wall, I knew I needed to find a solution. I needed help or I was going to go crazy. (Okay, I was crazy.) So I pulled my kids out of preschool two days a week and hired a nanny to watch them. It saved me. (And by "me," I mean my family and me because we all know crazy mom equals crazy family.) Two mornings a week, I didn't have to get them dressed. And two nights a week they were fed, bathed, and in their pj's. The house was clean and the lunches were packed for the next day. And I was able to have at least one night a week to go to the grocery store without kids, finish a project at work without feeling like I was racing the clock, or even see friends over drinks. It was heaven.

So now we only fight about jogging.

—Amy

Now let's be clear: we're not assuming that your spouse's ability to take on domestic chores defines his skills as a father or the strength of your marriage. Your husband might be amazing at dealing with your crazy mother or teaching your kids how to survive in the wilderness with only a roll of duct tape, or he might be the only guy in the world who can make you laugh until your drink comes out of your nose. We will assume that, like ours, your husband is a wonderful spouse and amazing dad. That's all fine and good. We're talking about the daily grind of domestic responsibilities. Unless there's some glimmer of cooperation or teamwork, it's going to bring you to your knees.

You Lucky Bitches!

Now some of you have these amazing husbands who have assumed the lion's share of daily household responsibility. Some husbands regularly cook meals, clean the house, bathe the kids, and take responsibility for daily household chores. We didn't exactly ask about the balance of power (i.e., who makes more money), but assuming that it's pretty close to even, all we can say is YOU LUCKY BITCHES! Don't gloat. It's ugly. And for the rest of us whose responsibilities may not be entirely split down the middle, it's time to ask for help.

Try Not to Hate Us . . . but We've Married
the Perfect Guys

• •

I love that my husband cooks dinner for us every night. It's so relaxing to come home and just be with my daughter and know that he will get dinner on the table for us.

   Theresa, Mother of One and Information Systems Manager

He does more than half! He gets up with the kids in the morning. Makes the breakfast. He reads the stories. Sometimes makes lunch. Picks up a couple of days at school (I drop off).

Debbie, Mother of Two and Marketing Executive

He fills in for me, often. He understands when I'm always late coming home and he cooks dinner. He's the best husband imaginable.

Heather, Mother of One and Pediatrician

"He actually does everything. Laundry, housework, drop-offs and pick-ups from school, and he cooks dinner every night. I'm spoiled."

MaryBeth, Mother of Two and Sales Manager

I've worked my husband to the bone. I've relied on him more than I ever thought possible, and I find it tough to draw the line between my husband and one of my direct reports. He calls me "glory mom." He does all the hard work and I get to swoop in for the hugs!

Teri, Mother of Two and Visual Merchant

But Sometimes He Might Need Just a Bit More Direction . . .

He's pretty good about doing housework . . . if I ask. Could he take it upon himself?

Jennifer, Mother of Two and Teacher

He's actually pretty good. But I'd be over the moon if he could just put his dishes in the dishwasher.

Brianne, Mother of Two and PR Consultant

Just Ask Already!

There you have it. (Un)scientific proof that your spouse is actually capable of contributing around the house, and he probably could do an even better job if you just asked for a little help and gave him a well-thought-out, typed, laminated list of step-by-step instructions to solving life's daily riddles. Laundry, breakfast, lunch, dinner, bath time, birthday parties, birthday presents, grocery shopping, etc. These are all fair game!

So how do you ask for help and start becoming more of a united front against the daily onslaught? Between us, we've tried all the methods below. We're not proud. Just saying that we speak from experience.

How to Ask Your Spouse for Help

1. **The butter-him-up ask:** This must be timed perfectly so as to appear natural and unrehearsed. Otherwise he will see through you and become suspicious, thus saying no when he might otherwise say yes.

2. **The equal-partner ask:** Involves a rational argument that points out why and how you need help. It requires that you depend wholly on your savvy negotiation skills rather than breaking down in desperation. May involve homework like putting all of the tasks on paper and discussing each one. We recommend this one as it suggests that your partnership is on sound footing and that you've recognized you need help before you go crazy.

3. **The dramatic crazy-lady ask.** This often includes lots of sighs, sobs, potentially collapsing in a pile of tears, followed by more loud sighs. We're not fans of this method as it can be less effective and annoying for all those around, including the neighbors. Though embarrassing to admit, we have both inadvertently resorted to this method after a few too many glasses of Sauvignon Blanc.

Uh-oh, I've Seen That Look Before

My husband has informed me that I get a very specific look in my eyes. He knows it before I do, and when he sees it he just snaps to and starts helping because he knows I'm about to blow! I wish I knew what the look looked like so I could replicate it more often!

—Leigh

Both of us married guys who have demanding jobs. Leigh's husband is a doctor with some crazy hours, and Amy's husband is a photographer who owns his own business, also with some crazy hours. All of that sexy professional ambition we saw in our grooms has translated into AWOL husbands when it comes to tackling the lion's share of the domestic agenda. And because we're the type of people who end up voluntarily taking on tasks before stopping to figure out if anyone else could or should help, we ended up taking on too much. We learned a valuable lesson.

Negotiate Hard Up Front

You might have negotiated an amazing compensation package at work. Or figured out a way to ask for (and got) an extra few weeks of maternity leave. Or a work-from-home arrangement. Or part-time work with full-time pay. How in the world could you ever let an entire half of your life just go without haggling over who was going to pick up whom or make dinner or do bath time each night? If you get this pinned down up front, then you are going to AVOID asking, begging, pleading for help later.

It's All Negotiable

• •

Coming from a family with three children, my husband really wanted a third child. I was happy with two—I felt like I could be exactly the mother I wanted to be and still be a part-time editor and writer. After a year of discussion, I realized that—given the right amount of help and a slightly slowed-down lifestyle—another baby would be wonderful. I negotiated hard on the front end so that it was very clear what had to be in place in order for me to be able to take care of him (a surgeon), our two young daughters, and pursue my dream of finishing my Ph.D.

Laura, Mother of Three, and Editor and Ph.D. Candidate

Doug is an incredibly involved, hands-on kind of dad. He's responsible for getting Lucy ready in the morning for day care. He works part-time so that he can stay at home with her a couple days a week, and he takes care of her when I have to travel for business. When I think about it, he really does the bulk of the child care. This was not accidental. When I was pregnant, we had multiple conversations about what each one of us wanted to do—and would have to do—as parents. We decided that since I earn more, I'd take on more of the financial responsibility and all of the household accounting. Doug wanted to be more of an at-home dad. I'm not sure if this arrangement will last forever, but for now it works for both of us.

Kirsten, Mother of One and Software Salesperson

• •

Since negotiating up front fixes many issues and helps avoid unnecessary fights, we suggest using this strategy whenever life changes, even just a bit.

- **New school/drop-off schedule.** Time to figure out who's doing what on each day of the week—before you've done it by yourself for a few months and realize that it's not going to work, and your spouse is fully accustomed to you taking it all on (so that it's going to take a serious effort to dislodge this rock under which you find yourself). It's a lot easier to take on more as time goes on than the other way around.

- **New job (for either of you).** Time to talk through the drop-off/pick-up schedule, the meal planning, the lunch packing, etc. No one needs the additional stress of being overwhelmed with household responsibilities when starting a new job. Trying to impress the new boss becomes a lot more difficult when you're screeching out early each night to pick up the kids. And then, of course, there's the flip side—you don't want to get suckered into suddenly being responsible for all of the household chores when your spouse switches jobs.

- **New child-care situation.** Time to think about how to split up the new responsibilities, or how to take advantage of the situation and offload responsibility. You can also get the new child-care provider in on the act. Switching to a nanny from day care? Negotiate laundry and bath time in the deal. Switching from a nanny to day care? Immediately divide and conquer the tasks formerly performed by the magical nanny. There's a decided difference between a nanny and day care, and you might just get blown away by all of your new to-do's.

YOUR HUSBAND ALREADY HAS A MOMMY. IT'S NOT YOU!

Besides simply getting help from the man, you're going to need to divest yourself of a few extra chores you've likely taken on for your spouse. He's perfectly capable of doing them himself. You can have a husband, boyfriend, baby daddy, same-sex partner, best friend with benefits, or blowup doll. Regardless, the same rules apply: when you hitched your wagon to this guy, he was self-sufficient, most likely over eighteen, finding his own dinner, and somehow managing to wear clean(ish) clothes each day.

But you're a nice lady. You want to help him in every way possible, because you love him, and it's the least you can do. That's all
fine and good, but if you let these favors—putting toothpaste on his
brush, putting all his favorite condiments on his hot dog, hunting for
his missing sock—go too far, before you know it you're treating him
like one of the kids and that hardly gets you in the mood. And then
you start to resent the fact that you're taking care of him, too. It's time
to restore the household balance of power.

Time-Sucking "Favors" That You Don't Really Need to Do for Him

Schedule his appointments with the doctor and dentist.
Amy's husband is notorious in the dentist office for canceling appointments. His schedule continuously changes and he can't plan ahead.
So each time she's in for a cleaning, the receptionist asks for help in
finding a time for him. Hell, no! If she can't even schedule date night,
she's not going to try to attempt a dental appointment. And let's say
she does step in . . . Now both the receptionist and Amy are crazy,
utterly miserable, and frustrated. They are on their own on this one.

Fill his prescriptions. Chances are he can swing by the twenty-
four-hour pharmacy a lot easier than you can, given the kids who need
to be unlatched from the twenty-point harnesses, dragged inside, con-
trolled in the line as you wait for meds, kept away from the Wacky Taffy
and the superbouncy ball in those stupid vending machines, and then
wrangled back into their car seats with bribes and tears . . . yours. See
if he can pick up your pills too while he's at the store; otherwise there
might be yet another kid to drag into the place in nine months' time.

Remind him of birthdays' and send presents/cards. This one
sounds heartless, doesn't it? Chances are you'll feel horribly guilty
if it turns out that you missed his grandfather's ninetieth birthday.
But get over it. This is no reflection on you. If he forgets his sister's
birthday, it's not your fault. And if she thinks less of you because you

missed it, she needs to get over it. He probably forgot her birthday before you got married, and we bet she can confirm it.

Write his thank-you notes. Leigh has done this in the past and it is just ridiculous. Hopefully his mother raised him right and he understands the importance of a written thank-you note. But if not, his poor etiquette is not a reflection on you. Oh . . . and unless you want to be writing your kids' thank-you notes for the rest of your life, you should encourage your husband to set a good example.

Make a separate dinner for him when you just made a different one for you and the kids. Before becoming a parent, we'll admit that we always said that we'd make one dinner a night and everyone would have to eat it. We assumed that it would be the kids bending to our taste, rather than the other way around. Well, that was wrong. Now Annie's Microwavable Mac & Cheese is dinner for all of us some desperate evenings. And given the fact that there are no leftovers when you make microwavable macaroni and cheese, the standard response to "What's for dinner?" is now "Whatever you can find yourself." If you did happen to actually cook, feel no shame in setting aside a plate of English muffin pizzas, deli ham roll-ups, or whatever you cobbled together that night.

Entertain clients at your house. That's what restaurants are for. Who wants to spend her weeknight slaving away to please some fuddy-duddies from Toledo (no offense, Toledo!)? It's flattering that your husband thinks you're so fabulous at cooking and entertaining, but what he doesn't realize is it's going to turn you into a stressed-out bitch. Remind him of this fact and follow that up with some hot new restaurant recommendations and an offer to book a babysitter. Time to introduce him to OpenTable.com.

Clean up his socks and dirty clothes, especially if the favor is never returned. How long can you live in squalor? Think long and hard about this question. If you want this to end, you're going to have to have a high degree of tolerance for squalor. When he runs out of underwear, he's going to get on the wash. Or he won't wear any. Either way, it's not your problem.

Pick up the dry cleaning. Listen, if he's in the car unencumbered by kids or school drop-off deadlines, this is a no-brainer. And isn't most of the stuff in that dry-cleaning bag his? Enough said.

Find stuff for him. Have you heard the phrase "Have you seen my . . ." or "Where is the . . ." in the last twenty-four hours? If you have, we've got a tip for you. Chances are that when you hear either one of those phrases, you jump up and start helping him to look. Well, you need to stop jumping. In fact, don't budge. Pretend you didn't even hear the question. From personal experience, we can tell you that saying, "I don't know" and remaining seated on the couch with the kids while watching *Dora the Explorer* actually dissuades him from asking in the future. There's a great book out there called *What Shamu Taught Me About Life, Love, and Marriage: Lessons for People from Animals and Their Trainers* by Amy Sutherland (Random House, 2008). Read it. We swear it works.

Top Things Working Moms Have Given Up Doing for Their Spouses (Based on Our Highly Unscientific Study)

- Sex or any fun sort of naked activity
- Cooking dinner/cooking fancy dinners
- Doing and/or folding laundry
- Dry-cleaning runs
- Making him lunch and/or coffee
- Listening to him
- Getting input on family decisions
- Ironing (If you don't have time to iron your own clothes, why on earth would you iron his?)

Extracting Yourself from the Equation

The next question is how do you gracefully extract yourself from these tasks that you may or may not be doing. The answer is . . . Just stop doing them. You might need to launch a warning shot across the bow (a few nights of "I'm sorry, but the kids and I already ate" or "I'm going to be a bit busy and not able to schedule your appointment . . ."), but quite honestly, we're big believers in just quitting. The truth (you're just too tired to do it anymore) will set you free! And more important, it will help you see your husband as your husband, and not some giant pain in the ass.

What I Stopped Doing for My Spouse

• •

I quit making his lunch at night and truly listening to his complaining. (I've learned how to tune it out.)

> Aisha, Mother of Two and Human Resources Director

I guess the only thing I've quit doing is fussing over him. I let him figure more things out for himself.

> Suzanne, Mother of One and Salesperson

I've stopped asking for input so that everything can be a "joint decision." Sometimes we just need to seize our power and stop discussing everything to death.

> Renanah, Mother of Two and Clinical Psychologist

• •

"You're So Gross When You're Sick"

Too many comedians, movies, or drunken "moms gone wild" nights have covered the topic of sick husbands. We would bore even ourselves if we tried to delve into the horror of a man with the sniffles. But we feel strongly about providing you with some coping mechanisms.

How to deal with the sick husband?

1. Ignore it. At the first utterance of the phrase "I feel like I'm getting a cold," just ignore it. Don't say anything. Reacting in any way will be perceived as sympathy, thus resulting in more complaining. If this sounds too harsh, you need to make a few visits to the therapist and stop being a crazy codependent enabler.

2. If he repeats himself, show him where in the medicine cabinet he can find Theraflu, cold pills, Vicks, heating pad, nasal spray, and/or an enema. This ought to get him moving in the right direction.

3. Grab the kids and some supplies for the day and GET OUT OF THE HOUSE. This makes everyone happy and with any luck will be reciprocated if and when you are sick.

4. Call his mother and hand the phone over. She will be sympathetic. That's her job.

5. Call your mother. Seriously. A good friend calls her own mom whenever her husband starts complaining. Her mom carts over a ton of minestrone and gives him all the sympathy a man could want. Perfect!

6. Move him or you to the guest room at night; no sense in everyone getting sick, especially you.

"Don't Treat Me Like a Child!" . . . "Then Don't Act Like One!"

I won't lie: I have a nurturing personality, and before my son came along, I channeled all of these tendencies toward my husband. This included packing his lunch, taking care of his laundry, and many other ridiculous tasks. The fact was I had the time and knew I was making life just a little easier for him. After all, he was a busy doctor, right? After having a child, I often found myself resenting these tasks and I started making my husband aware of it. He responded by stating he was a grown man and not to treat him like a child. OK . . . music to my ears. Fast-forward a couple of weeks when dear husband comes home and, with a huge pout on his face, announces that I didn't pack him enough lunch, that he'd had a long day and was starving by two p.m. As if I was supposed to inquire with him about his surgical caseload prior to each day and dole out the appropriate amount of calories. Is there NOT a cafeteria at the hospital? Every hospital I've been to has a cafeteria. A few days later he followed up with a request to "cut his meats to a chewable size" because there are no knives in the doctors' lounge. Was I hearing him right? I would need to cut his meat? OK, that was it, game over. I went on strike and informed him my services were a luxury, and if he didn't want to be treated like a child, he needn't act like one. These days, he's in charge of packaging the leftovers for his lunch, and for the most part, he states how delicious my leftovers are . . . with occasional constructive feedback.

—Leigh

YOU (BOTH) CAN DO THIS

We want you to take on this "working mom" and "working dad" thing together. However, setting yourself up for success is going to require some work.

One, you need to take the time to figure out what each of you is going to do. Life gets a lot easier when you set up expectations on the front end. You'd never fail to do that at work, so why let it slip now?

Two, cut each other some slack. If you've been changing diapers for the last four months on maternity leave, chances are you've got it down and can do it with one hand while simultaneously taking a phone call. Give the man a break if it takes him a bit longer—he's trying! Same thing goes for you . . . Amy hasn't quite figured out the whole trash thing. Something about raccoons and how to properly put the trash can cover on occasionally slips her mind. And the last time it happened, Dwight was a saint and didn't curse her name while he cleaned up the mess.

Three, value the contributions that each of you make. If your husband is thinking of things like oil changes or maximizing your 401(k) while simultaneously minimizing your tax liability, GREAT. That stuff might never have been your priority. Recognize the fact that you both are working in the family's best interests, just in different ways.

Finally, everyone loves a little praise. The key to getting through this together is to take the time to pass on a little gratitude when someone goes the extra mile or just finds a way to get all of this stuff done. Who doesn't love to hear, "Thank you"?

Fried Eggs for Dinner and

Other Time-Saving Tips

Delusions

- All working moms assemble their to-do lists while sitting on the toilet.
- Nutritionally balanced meals will still be a top priority.
- I'll hit Costco, Target, the grocery store, and the dry cleaner's on Saturdays while my children are napping.
- No one will notice if I fold my laundry on the sidelines of the soccer game.
- Making/taking calls from the bathroom isn't rude if you run the water.

The fact that there are only twenty-four hours in a day sucks. We need about thirty to keep all of the balls in the air, live our fabulous lives, and get our beauty rest. No working mother wants to spend all of her free time doing all the requisite boring chores that must get done so that her household and family runs like a finely oiled machine. Now add to that the fact that you need time to yourself, and a bikini wax, and you can see why time always bites you in the ass. The daily race against the clock can make you sweat like a hooker on payday. We are living proof of that.

No phrase elicits such a joyful response from working moms as "time-saving tips." Well, maybe "vacation without kids," but that isn't happening, so why dream? The discussion and, more important, the sharing, of time-saving tips always gets both the creative and the competitive juices flowing. Who's got a good one and how much time can it really save? And please tell us you are not going to advise that we "plan ahead." We need something far more innovative than that, Captain Obvious.

The unfortunate reality of modern motherhood is we have very little time outside of work to accomplish a mountain of tasks—tasks that could easily be a full-time job unto themselves, thus the phrase "working inside the home," aka stay-at-home mom. And to top it all off, there is very little payoff when you actually finish the to-do list. It just needs to get done. Your kids don't know, or care for that matter, that you coordinated your refrigerator repair call over your lunch hour so they could still make the birthday party on Saturday. When's the last time you got a compliment for how thorough you were with the grocery shopping? Does "Honey, thanks for the razors" or "Mommy, I love these diapers" sound familiar? We didn't think so. Knowing how little appreciation you get for a Sunday afternoon run to Costco, just aim to get your errands done in the most efficient way possible. The only person who will appreciate your organizational prowess in this department is another working mom, so go tell one if you're looking for props.

How can you possibly get it all done? From our experience, you will have to start cutting corners in the hopes of saving five minutes here and twenty minutes there, and accept that good results—not great—are good enough. When we went back to work after having children, we didn't realize how little time we'd have, and we just naively thought we would pick up where we left off—work, dinner, TV, sex, no problem. What we could have used is some collective wisdom from our friends—some good tried-and-true time-saving tips that would become the new order. Now that we are in possession of this life-changing information, we must share it. We'd be cruel not to.

Trust Us, Ladies—We Know How to Land Our Butts in the Butter, and Now You Will, Too!

How will you manage? What's the key to shaving off thirty seconds from your morning routine in an effort to bank it for the big payoff (e.g., *The Bachelor*)? Prioritize and let go of control and perfection. Then, with a little hustle, these endless errands and to-do's will work themselves out. Now let's break it down into the main time-saving categories: Work, Looking Good, Home, and Meals.

TIME-SAVING TIPS FOR WORK

- **Get a personal assistant (aka, the dreaded PDA).** As in a BlackBerry, iPhone, Palm Pre, whatever! Stop whining about not wanting to look at e-mail at night or the fact that work should pay for it. Nobody cares.

You Can Have Anything, but Please Don't Take My iPhone!

I have an iPhone and a Mobile Me account. I have my family's calendar and my work calendar merged into one definitive calendar. Life is a rainbow—family is yellow, work is red, and my secret "me time" is blue. Everything is at my fingertips at all times and it keeps me sane. I sync both my personal and work e-mail accounts to one device for convenience. Plus, I have all of my contacts in one place. The applications for the iPhone are endless and not only will they help you but they can entertain your kids in a pinch if necessary (Chimps Ahoy, Powerboat, Dizzy Bee, Topple, Scoops, Nuts!).

I don't have an opinion about which one you get, just that you get one. Unless you have a financial hardship, stop talking because I don't want to hear your excuses. I've never met someone who regretted it—only wished they had done it sooner. I don't know about you, but after having children something happened to my memory (as in, I don't have one anymore), so I don't mind the fact that I get a chime and a pop-up reminder that I need to be somewhere or do something. Especially since administrative assistants are a thing of the past.

And it gives me the freedom to make it to doctors' appointments, parent-teacher conferences, and the like. I have a great boss, and we just have an unspoken agreement. She knows I check my iPhone all the time. If she needs me she'll call or e-mail. Regardless, I'm always on top of my business. So if I have to leave at four p.m. on occasion to go to the dentist, she knows it's OK because work isn't going to slip. When I leave the office, I change my device to chime when e-mail comes in. That way I know I have new incoming e-mail and if something is urgent, I can deal with it right away. Flexibility goes both ways and I don't mind. The sooner I'm aware of an issue, the sooner I can address it.

—Leigh

- **CAYG, Clean as you go!** Touch e-mail once. Don't read it, get overwhelmed by the contents, and then mark it as unread. Do one of the four following things: reply, file, delete, or flag for follow-up. Cleaning your in-box at the end of each week is a big waste of time. Not being able to send e-mail because your in-box is too full is a productivity killer. Must we constantly remind you to stop screwing yourself?

- **Combat meeting madness.** Attend only those meetings that are vital to your role and to which you have something significant to contribute. If you are invited to a meeting where everyone is just going to read a PowerPoint presentation, skip it if it won't get you fired. Based on the fact that you bought this book, we assume you can read. Form a partnership with a trusted colleague and take turns sitting in on weekly meetings and share the information. Think of time as your most precious resource—it is—and use it accordingly.

Let's Wrap This Up

I have an almost unnatural need for meetings with agendas. I need to know exactly what I'm expected to accomplish in any given meeting. Whether that just be sitting like a bump on a log listening, trying to come to a decision, or figuring out how to best get my e-mail answered while appearing to pay attention, I need to know what's supposed to get done. Otherwise, it's a big waste of time. And as soon as the objective is reached, in my humble opinion, the meeting is over. I'm not sure if anyone I've ever worked with has ever noticed, but if there's a chance to end a meeting ten minutes early, I'm doing it. And I'm going to use those ten minutes to do something else. Like prepare for the next meeting, call to see if I can reserve a spot for the birthday party, or actually respond, thoughtfully, to a few e-mails. It's the dirty secret of your Outlook calendar. You really only have the choice of a thirty-minute meeting or a sixty-minute meeting. And when is the last time you had a meeting that magically ended on the half hour?

No minute goes unused. Ever.

—Amy

- **Lunch time is no longer for lunch.** This was a biggie, because no one loves a lunch boondoggle more than we do, but leisurely lunches are a big waste of time. Going out to lunch takes a minimum of forty-five minutes, and often more if it's business. If you're not working your ass off to get yourself out the door at a decent hour in order to see the kids, use your lunch hour to take care of personal business or run some errands. Keep a cooler in your trunk and do the grocery shopping. We can get in and out of Trader Joe's in thirty minutes. On the weekend with kids and the long lines, it can be absolutely painful, and who needs the stress of getting flipped off in the parking lot and trying to explain that one to the kids? Do not forget lunchtime equals five hours per week of productivity. Don't waste it shooting the breeze at P.F. Chang's.
- **Delegate.** Don't be a martyr or lament that you used to be able to do everything. Call it a professional development opportunity, offload that time-sucking report pronto, and never look back. Be honest. You were too much of a control freak pre-children. Survival requires that you let go.
- **Say no!** Although it feels heartless, cut out the informational interviews, helping that friend of a friend of a friend, and all other professional networking compulsivity until you have your feet on the ground (i.e., until the youngest is at least two years old and you're not tearing up over the pile of laundry anymore). Seriously, ask yourself this question: is it more important for you to relax and watch *American Idol* or meet with a friend of a friend of a friend?

TIME-SAVING TIPS FOR LOOKING GOOD

- **Try a chic ponytail.** And by "chic," we mean low, neat, and tidy with a black elastic. Little girls' colored rubber bands with pink balls and flowers are not acceptable. Nor is it ever OK to come to work with wet hair. Get a grip!

- **Dress it up.** Wear dresses. It's the wardrobe equivalent of a one-pot wonder for dinner. You pick one thing and, voilà, you are ready with no time wasted trying to coordinate tops and sweaters. At best, add a few accessories and you are out the door.

- **Shower at night.** After you get your brood off to bed, take YOUR shower at night. If you can wake up without the blast of hot water on your face, you'll save yourself twenty minutes and go to bed feeling squeaky-clean. The added bonus is that there's very little chance of interruption and you get a real ten-to-fifteen-minute shower. Ahhhhhhhhhhhhhh.

TIME-SAVING TIPS AT HOME

What keeps you from the grocery shopping, the Costco runs, and all of that jazz? Work. Damn work is always getting in the way of errands. If your job is anything like ours, you are expected to put in at least a solid eight hours a day, and likely end up working a nine-to-ten-hour day, working over lunch, and checking e-mail at night. This schedule leaves very little usable time in the morning or the evening. So what can you do to get all of your household chores done and not sacrifice the weekend doing it?

Own the Morning or the Night— Whatever, Just Own It

We are in two different camps on this quagmire. Leigh is up at the butt-crack of dawn, and Amy loves going to bed without the dreaded to-do list. So regardless of where you fall, it can work. You just have to find the scenario that works for you.

Declare morning or night your time to get stuff done. We don't care if you are tired and need to get your sleep. Suck it up. You had a baby(ies) and survived, so you can indeed function with just a tad less sleep. These are the few times where you can be productive without having everyone interrupt you. Try it. Either set the alarm for five a.m., get out of bed, chug some coffee, and start busting some moves, or TiVo *American Idol* and force yourself to wait until you're done with your chores.

- **Plan the laundry.** Start it in the evening, flip and fold in the morning, or vice versa. Amy's too nervous to have the dryer running while at work, but Leigh says burn the house down if it means that the laundry is done when she gets home. Have a basket designated for each member of the family or each bedroom in the house. Fold the laundry and put it in the basket, and then make everyone responsible for putting his or hers away. OK, infants and toddlers are off the hook, but children over five are not. Do this frequently; too much laundry to put away equals a bad mood.

- **Do the dishes.** Unload your dishwasher (we pray you have a dishwasher, as many urban dwellers don't) and put away the pots and pans in the morning. When you get home from work, all you have to do is load it up with the dirty dishes from dinner. Who doesn't like coming home to a clean kitchen? The last thing you want to do when you get home is make dinner AND wash two nights' worth of dishes.

- **Make sure your children are set up for success.** Pack their lunches and make sure their backpacks or totes are ready for school and staged in the appropriate place. Have all paperwork inside (homework, permission slips, notes to the teacher). For older children, have them own this task so you can minimize the last-minute scrambling followed by the "I can't find my back-pack!"

- **Get the groceries.** It's a ghost town in the early morning or late at night, and what would usually take an hour can take thirty minutes. Typically your spouse is home, so the added bonus is that you can go alone, without any kids begging for SpongeBob macaroni and cheese, sugar cereal, or a balloon.

- **Do fifteen minutes of picking up.** Remember the fifteen-minute rule. Those fifteen minutes go a long way, and it's better than nothing.
- **Do fifteen minutes of family business.** Keep the family computer with Internet access in the hub of your house. Whenever the opportunity presents itself, jump on and take care of business. You can RSVP to birthday parties, pay a few bills online, e-mail your child's teacher . . . you get the picture. Basically deal with stuff. Anything that you can't finish at home, put into a personal folder that goes in your work bag daily. Handle it over lunch if you don't have other commitments. Don't let this stuff back up all week and then ruin your weekend. Again, you'll find that fifteen minutes a day goes a long way.

Procrastination is going to kill you, and if you read this and think, "Not gonna happen" (either early in the morning or late at night), then beware. You will always start each day that much further behind. If you are going to survive working motherhood, you are going to need to sacrifice a little bit of sleep to keep your sanity. We're sure you're asking, "When the hell am I supposed to sleep?" but it really isn't that bad. Try to recall all those sleepless nights before you delivered your child. Or those first few weeks after the baby's birth. Remember those hellacious days? You were being conditioned to live with little sleep for a reason, and working motherhood IS that reason. Stick to the plan, and you should be in bed no later than ten p.m. Seven hours of sleep per night is pretty good.

General TST (that's "Time-Saving Tips" for all of you too slow to pick up on the shortcuts!)

Beyond the morning or night routine, there are plenty of other opportunities to find yourself a few minutes to save. As we said, thirty seconds here and there equals a glass of wine in front of the TV. God bless wine. God bless TV.

- **Take an appointment/Make an appointment.** Every time you take an appointment—doctor, haircut, brow wax—make the next one, and save yourself the ten minutes of back-and-forth on the phone scheduling the next appointment. This goes for your and your children's appointments.
- **Fill prescriptions online.** Take the time once to set up an online account with your pharmacy and you'll rarely wait on line again. Don't forget to give the information to your spouse. Remember, you can't do it all!
- **Order EVERYTHING online.** Is that clear? Diapers, formula, groceries, prescriptions, children's snow gear, shoes. If you can't order it online, it's not worth having. Many online merchants have the order to you in less than two days (anyone who has ever bought shoes on Zappos.com can attest to that). Big deal if you spend $6.00 on shipping. Have you noticed the price of gas? It's worth it. Shift your thinking to opportunity cost and what you can do with your child(ren) now that you don't have to spend an hour looking for snow boots at Target.
- **Have dry cleaning delivered.** Set up the account and have it delivered to your house or office. In our case it's delivered to our office and automatically billed to our credit card for less than we would pay at our local dry cleaner. Can't beat it.
- **Establish a family calendar and use it.** Place a family calendar, bulletin board, and dry-erase board in your kitchen and use them. Keep the calendar current and keep all child-related papers pinned to the board. The dry-erase board can be used for to-do's, reminders to each other, and the grocery list. This command central keeps everyone in the family organized and informed. No more saying "I didn't know the kiddo had a soccer game on Tuesdays," and thus wasting time on the phone listening to all of those lame excuses.

VBMs (Very Busy Moms) Share Their Tips

• •

I don't bother running to two different stores for the best price. I've finally conceded that it is not worth it to run a block over to CVS to save eighty cents on diapers.

Jee, Mother of One, and TV Producer and Media Consultant

When you have child care, get as much done as you can. You can get twice as much done alone than when carting around your children.

Suzanne, Mother of One and Salesperson

Let the babysitter or nanny fold the laundry. Doing the wash takes no time . . . it's the f*cking folding that takes forever.

Pauline, Mother of Three and Librarian

Make sure your preteen daughter's clothes are picked out AND agreed upon the night before. This saves so much drama and time in the morning.

While your child is in the bathtub, get a container of wipes or a rag and start cleaning the sink and toilet while singing his or her favorite songs. You'll have a clean kid and a clean bathroom.

Michelle, Mother of Two and Research Project Director

Put some old music on that you haven't listened to in a long time, blast it, and grab a Swiffer! You will dance, move very quickly, get some exercise, and clean the house! Now that's multitasking.

Alex, Mother of Three, and Event and Marketing Director

I stopped sorting laundry—it's really just whites and everything else!

Denise, Mother of Two and Winemaker/Marketer

• •

WHEN 30-MINUTE MEALS ARE 25 MINUTES TOO LONG

This is an area where we've consistently struggled. Leigh and Amy were both raised by mothers who home-cooked everything. Leigh really appreciated the quality of her mom's food and the love she put into it. She's also eternally grateful because at least she learned how to cook—now she just needs the time. Amy has had a slightly different experience. She came from a family of foodies and has abandoned her roots. She can't remember the last time she cooked a traditional meal because it just isn't practical and no one really appreciates it at this stage in her family life. ("Mommy, we want mac and cheese from the microwave!") Yes, we're guilting ourselves into trying to cook the perfect meal. But if you are going to consistently navigate this essential duty, you are going to need to simplify your cooking for the work/school week.

Why Be Julia Child When Nobody Cares?

My father was perfecting tarte tatin long before the world heard of the Food Network. My mother made us muffins or scones with homemade lemon curd or pancakes from scratch EVERY morning. I grew up with a tremendous appreciation for food and the expectation that I would slave over elaborate meals and everyone would melt in a puddle of thanks for my efforts. And then I married a vegetarian who doesn't like vegetables. And then I had two kids who will turn up their noses at homemade mac and cheese made with artisanal organic cheddar cheese, but devour hot dogs with carrot sticks and ranch dressing on the side.

So, after some really disappointing reactions to my meals, I quit. I now cook only superfast, easy meals where no one complains, and I don't sweat. It's the biggest time-saver I could possibly manage. Fried eggs, microwave burritos, quesadillas, you name it. I've gotten over my food snobbery and figure if they don't care about me slaving over meals, neither should I.

Maybe when they are old enough to appreciate tarte tatin, I'll get back on the horse.

—Amy

Tricks of the Trade

- **Invest in specialty cookware.** You need only two pieces: a panini maker and a slow cooker. These two workhorses can do the majority of your cooking during the week, from grilled cheeses and quesadillas to pot roast.
- **Stick to the plan.** Determine what your meal planning strategy is. Are you cooking at home five nights a week? Sounds like a nightmare to us. How about two nights cooking, two nights leftovers, and one night restaurant or takeout? Whatever you decide, map it out and stick to the plan. You don't need to reinvent it weekly.
- **Cook once—eat twice.** When you cook, double the recipe and freeze half of it, carefully labeling your plastic storage containers so you know what it is after it has frozen. Then, when you've had a hectic day and you don't feel like that perky Rachael Ray—OK, we never feel like her—you can have a great home-cooked meal with almost no effort.
- **Take it SLOW.** Want dinner ready the minute you walk through the door? Spend fifteen minutes in the morning throwing a few ingredients into your slow cooker. That really is all the time it takes. When you get home, instead of making dinner

you can have a glass of wine, enjoy the aroma of the meal, and just spend time with your kids. Cleanup is a breeze because it is a one-pot wonder!

- **KISS (keep it simple, stupid).** Save the fancy cooking and new recipes for the weekend, when everyone can appreciate them. The work and school week are intense. Just get everyone fed in the most efficient manner possible. Taking on too much in the kitchen during the week will backfire and will only leave you frustrated. We guarantee it.

- **Dress it up and call it dinner.** Use ready-made foods and, if you must, embellish upon them a little bit and call them your own. As long as something's decent, why should you feel obligated to make it from scratch?

Following is a list of staples and convenience foods that are great to have for busy modern families. We can assure you if you have these items in your kitchen, you'll always be able to whip up a meal in twenty minutes or less. We must warn you that we worship at the altar of Trader Joe's and Costco, and we own big ole freezers. If you happen to live somewhere where you don't have these stores, that sucks! All is not lost though—chances are you'll have a Sam's Club or BJ's or something similar, fingers crossed. Please forgive us if you're anti-chain-store hippies. And of course, if you are feeling flush, there is always Whole Foods.

Kitchen Wisdom from Moms Formerly Known as Cooks

• •

Friday night = takeout night. My restaurant is closed for business on Friday nights.

                                    Miki, Mother of One and Recruiter

*Keep soup in your fridge. If you make a big pot on Sunday, not only will
you feel like Mrs. Cleaver, but it also makes for easy dinners that week.*

Gabrey, Mother of Two, and Business Owner and Creative Director

*I love to make big pots of pasta and portion them out in Ziploc bags
for the next few lunches and dinners. Just add different sauces (butter,
olive oil, pesto, Parmesan cheese, or red sauce) to jazz it up.*

Nada, Mother of Three, and Author and Small Business Consultant

*I can't live without Trader Joe's mini-pizzas, taquitos, and French
toast. Once you plop the kids in chairs (any chairs) and pour them
glasses of milk, dinner is only sixty seconds away.*

Amy, Mother to Three and Research Analyst

*Those little bowls that have lids that prevent spills have been great to
do cereal in the car on the run without spilling everywhere. But sometimes my boys beg for "breakfast at the table"—that's one of my more
frequent mommy-guilt moments.*

Laura, Mother of Two and Director of Manufacturing

• •

Ideas for Your Pantry

Staples	Convenience Foods
Fresh fruit (things that won't rot in five days or less)	Curly's Smokehouse Gold Pulled Pork (Costco)
Milk	Pork Gyoza (Trader Joe's)
Deli meat (turkey, ham)	Barilla's Cheese & Spinach Tortellini
Sandwich bread	Ready-made pizza dough (Trader Joe's)
Various cheeses (slices, shredded)	Annie's Organic Shells & Real Aged Cheddar (most grocery stores)
Dried pasta	Fra'Mani Savory Meatloaf (Costco)
Jars of spaghetti sauce	Turkey meatballs (Trader Joe's)

Staples	Convenience Foods
Flour tortillas	Hamburger Helper Beef Pasta
Instant mashed potatoes	Knorr's Rice Sides Cheddar Broccoli
Individual applesauces	Store-bought rotisserie chicken
Mozzarella string cheese	Ling Ling Potstickers (Costco)
Go-Gurt, Activia, Danimals yogurts	Chicken chow mein (Trader Joe's)
Hummus	Green Giant Pasta Broccoli, Carrots, Sugar Snap Peas & Garlic Sauce (grocery store)
Cereal	Tamales (Trader Joe's or Costco)
Eggs	Ready-made pot roast (Costco)
English muffins	Aidells Chicken & Apple Sausage
Cream cheese	Ready-made soup

Top Six Weeknight Dinners (in Five Minutes or Less!)

- Fried eggs on toast—if you're feeling fancy, fry the eggs up with deli ham.
- Quesadillas—if you have the time, serve with diced avocados, salsa, and sour cream.
- Microwave burritos—tortilla, refried beans, and cheese in the microwave for thirty seconds. Add diced avocado, sour cream, and salsa, and you're done.
- Anything on the panini machine—grilled cheese, grilled PB&J, grilled ham and cheese, tuna melt . . . the list goes on and on.
- Annie's Organic Shells & White Cheddar
- Any number of frozen prepared foods from Costco or Trader Joe's

Favorite Takeout Meals

- Rotisserie chicken from your local grocery store
- Burritos from the local taco stand (we've got a California bias on this one)
- Organic premade food from the local fancy grocery store, but only when we're feeling rich!
- Chinese—fried rice, chicken chow mein, potstickers
- Take 'n' bake pizza—fresh and ready in twenty minutes

If You're Feeling Fancy, Six Delicious Slow-Cooker Recipes

10-Minute Chicken Cacciatore

•

One whole chicken (or 3 lbs. individual breasts, thighs, and
   drumsticks)
One onion, minced
3 cloves garlic, minced
6–8 leaves fresh basil
2–3 tablespoons capers (if you don't have them, it's OK without)
½ cup black olives
1 red pepper, chopped
1 green pepper, chopped
One jar store-bought spaghetti sauce
½ cup water

Put everything in the slow cooker and set it on low temperature for 8 hours.

Serve it with pasta on the side or garlic bread.

Feeling ambitious? Grate some fresh Parmesan cheese over the top.

Chili

•

1 lb. ground beef (can substitute turkey if you like)
1 can kidney beans (dark or light), drained and rinsed
1 can pinto beans, drained and rinsed
1 can garbanzo beans, drained and rinsed
1 can stewed tomatoes
1 can (8 oz.) tomato sauce
2 cups water
1 onion, minced
1 red pepper, chopped
1 green pepper, chopped
1 Carroll Shelby's Chili Kit (can be found in all major grocery
    stores) or any other chili kit

Put it all in the slow cooker and set on low temperature for 8 hours.

Serve it with shredded cheese, sour cream, corn chips, and jalapeños if you like it spicy.

Lori's BBQ Pulled Pork Sandwiches

•

Pork tenderloin (approximately 2 lbs.)
2 bottles of your favorite BBQ sauce

Put it all in the slow cooker and set it on low temperature for 8 hours.

Serve it on hamburger buns with store-bought cole slaw on the side.

Dina's Mexican Chicken or Pork

●

6 boneless chicken breasts, or 3 lbs. boneless pork shoulder
2–3 cups of your favorite Mexican salsa
1 envelope taco seasoning

Put the ingredients in the slow cooker, making sure that all the chicken is covered with salsa and taco seasoning mix. If not, just add a little more salsa. Set the cooker on low temperature for 8 hours.

Once meat is done, pull it apart and use it in burritos, tacos, nachos, or quesadilla, or on top of a salad.

Aaron's Ass-Kicking Short Ribs

●

3 lbs. beef short ribs
1 jar sauerkraut, including juice
1 handful black peppercorns
1 yellow onion, quartered
4 dried bay leaves
1 can of beer (or more if needed to cover the meat)

Put all the ingredients in the slow cooker and cook on low temperature for 6 to 8 hours. Mmmmmm, tasty.

Jeanette's Italian Beef

•

2 jars Mezzetta peperoncini (do not throw away the juice in
*   the jar)*
3 to 4 lb. beef round-eye roast, with a bone if possible (adds some
*   flavor)*
1 can beef broth
1 can water

Cut the stems off the peperoncini and slice them in half. Reserve the juice.

Place the roast in the slow cooker. Cut in a few pieces if necessary. Pour peperoncini on top, along with their juice, the beef broth, and the water.

Cook on low temperature for 8 hours. When meat is done, pull it apart and serve on submarine sandwich bun. Mmmmm, mmmmm.

Children's Lunches (the Bane of Our Existence)

Pick one thing from each category and call it lunch!

Main	Vegetable	Fruit	Snack	Drink
Turkey and cheese sandwich	Green beans	Banana	Yogurt (Danimals, Go-Gurt)	Water, milk, or apple juice
Tortilla roll-up (cream cheese and ham)	Carrots (cut if age-appropriate)	Apple	Edamame (steamed soy beans)	
Chicken apple sausage (cut if age-appropriate)	Kernel corn	Fruit roll-up	String cheese	
	Broccoli (steamed)	Orange		
	Cauliflower (steamed)	Strawberries	Mini-box of raisins	
Leftover rotisserie chicken	Peas	Blueberries	Applesauce	
	Sweet potatoes	Raspberries	Pre-pack of crackers	
Leftover pasta with butter or sauce	Squash (butternut or kabocha)	Blackberries	Pre-pack of hummus	
Chicken nuggets			Pudding	
Ham and cheese sandwich				
Ready-made meatballs				

Part V

We've Got Your Back

The Circle of Trust

Motherhood is great, isn't it? Such purpose, such fulfillment, such joy—so much self-doubt it is no wonder you're neurotic. Honestly, can you think of another time in your life when you have been forced to learn so much on the fly? Whether it is breastfeeding, sleep training, selecting schools, methods of discipline, or how to pack the perfect nutritiously balanced lunch, how is the modern mom supposed to know and do it all? Is there a source you can turn to for help? Someone who understands exactly what you are going through?

The answer is yes. You are going to need a rock-solid posse of other moms, and you are going to have to get comfortable asking for help and in turn giving help. This is a difficult concept for many type A women because we are convinced we can handle it all. We could pre-kids, right? But creating a tight circle of trust is the only way you are going to make it. We are not talking about your hubby, your mom and dad, or your best girlfriend who lives across the country. We are talking about your mommy friends, the ones who are in your day-to-day life and are in a position to help you. Who's in your posse? If the answer is no one, heaven help you; it's time for you to climb out from under that rock and start socializing. Your long-term survival depends on it.

Why You Need the Circle of Trust

- You cannot do this alone—and neither can the other moms.
- It feels good, and it creates a sense of community (kumbaya, my Lord, kumbaya).
- If you're going to teach your kids anything, don't you think helping others is a good lesson?

What Is a Circle of Trust?

A circle of trust—"COT" from here on out, because we're working moms and we do not have time to type "circle of trust" a gazillion times—is a group of women whom you can *trust* to help you out in a bind. In our case, three to five mommy friends whom we can call at the drop of a hat and who will come running; problem solved! Members of the COT not only will save your ass in a pinch, but also are known to listen to your whining, keep your secrets, and give you honest feedback when asked. When you're spiraling down into the loop of doom or you're having heart palpitations because you're not going to make it to day care in time, these ladies will pull you out.

There can be two COTs: one at work and one at home. Both are going to save your ass and you're going to save theirs. Before you go and start stalking other moms to make your own COT, be forewarned. There are rules of engagement. This is a relationship that is reciprocal, nonjudgmental, and guilt-free. As a result, there are some definite boundaries, and you've got to pick your posse carefully. No one needs a psycho in their COT.

The Rules of Engagement

- No money, bribes, or presents exchange hands. You heed the call because it's the right thing to do.
- Don't judge, even though it's tempting.
- Never talk smack about a mom in need. It's bad karma and tomorrow you might be that mom.
- Never dodge the call of a mom in need. Again, it's the karma.
- Never use their words or their situation against them. This is applicable mostly at work.
- Offer advice only when asked. People don't care what you think unless they ask.
- Don't abuse the COT. Ask for help when you really need it, but it's not an errand-running service.

Abhorrent Violations of the COT

- Cell stalking. Calling all the time to check in and chat. This isn't high school. Calm it down a bit. If you call, for God's sake leave a message. Seeing nine missed calls will make your friend's heart skip a beat.
- Asking for favors, like picking up diapers, bottled water, a few bottles of wine, and some tampons at Costco. It's not a shopping service and your constant forgetfulness will get on everyone's nerves.
- Mooching things with monetary value. What we call "alligator arm syndrome": when your arms resemble those of an alligator and can't seem to reach into your pocket to get your wallet! This is rude. None of us are rich—that's one of the reasons we are working! No gators allowed in the COT!
- Flirting with other women's husbands. Yuck.

- Bad-mouthing another mom's kid. Enough said. We don't care if the kid has "issues"; you NEVER talk smack about a COT offspring. It's grounds for immediate expulsion.
- Always being on the receiving end of the favors. You know who you are.

YOUR HOME-LIFE COT

You probably met these ladies through your kids' school. They've got kids the same age, they probably work, too—maybe not, but in most cases they do—and they know exactly what you're going through. You see them constantly and they know your kids better than the out-of-state grandparents. Your relationship with these women, although formed recently, goes deep. They know things about you that lots of your old friends don't, simply because they see you daily and can tell when you've hit a rough patch. It goes without saying that you frequently save one another's asses.

Saving Your Ass at Home Includes

- Picking up or dropping off a child from school when you're late or stuck in traffic
- Giving rides to practice or activities when you can't
- Taking a kid for an overnight when your marriage has hit the skids
- Relieving you when you're puking your lungs out
- Helping with an emergency (stitches, flat tire, CEO rampage)
- Running to the aid of a new mother who's at her wit's end (what's a nipple shield?)

- Watching out for your kid at school (bullying, day-care neglect, etc.)
- Field trip duty (watching out that your kid doesn't eat poop at the petting zoo!)
- Providing a sounding board for parenting issues (yeah, we have doubts, too!)
- Giving pep talks
- Birthday party tag-teaming (sharing duty when both kids are invited to the same party)
- Drop-off play dates when age-appropriate
- Kid exchanges (saves tons of $$$ on babysitting)
- Pinch-hitting if you are traveling (We know your husband is mostly capable, but sometimes it's nice to have a security blanket.)
- Watching your back (e.g., the boss is on a rampage, or you just heard that her nanny is about to be poached)

Drugstore Drama

I had to stay home from work one day while my kids suffered through a horrific strep infection. One kid got it, then the other. It was one of those days. I shouldn't really have been gone from work as I was slammed, but I had no choice. To make matters worse I was also in the midst of trying to sell our house and in the middle of some crazy conversations with the real estate agent about a potential buyer. I was shuttling between the doctor's office and the pharmacy to get the infections under control, and on and on and on.

It all came to a head at the pharmacy. The kids hadn't napped and were incredibly fried and cranky, the pharmacy was going through some IT conversion/corporate merger and there were frustrated people EVERYWHERE, and the realtor was calling with questions. In the middle of all this, I saw one of my mommy friends and she instantly could tell I was going through hell. How do I know? Because she asked, "Are you OK?" with an empathetic look on her face.

Five minutes later, I got them all buckled in and the phone rang. It was Leigh. All she said was, "I've got your wallet and I'll meet you at your house." I hadn't even left the parking lot and certainly hadn't noticed that I didn't have my wallet, and the mommy circle of trust had in less than no time recovered my wallet, put the phone tree in action to find me, and set up a rendezvous. How cool is that? That seriously saved my ass. All I needed that day was to lose my wallet and I would have had to have been institutionalized.

—Amy

Building Your At-Home COT

We had two different approaches to how we were going to cultivate our individual support systems. Amy was lucky enough to have family close by, so she took the slow road and let her network evolve naturally over time. By the time her first son was a year old, she had two or three women whom she could lean on and to whom she graciously returned the favor. Leigh, on the other hand, didn't have the luxury of time. She had no family nearby, and her best girlfriend lived in Chicago. So she was über-motivated to find support. She went at it like it was sorority rush. She lingered at day care, collected e-mails, and initiated a moms' night out to get the ball rolling. All in all, we both got the job done, and while it's still hard for us to ask for help (what do you mean, we can't do it all?), we know that we could call any one of the ladies in our network and relief would be on the way.

We don't care how you go about it, but you must have some support. It really does take a village to raise a child, and the sooner you embrace that notion the better off you will be. Be forewarned, if you're not willing to reciprocate, go back to the rock from which you crawled. It's not a one-way street.

- Be a ringleader and initiate a moms' night out. This can be as simple as composing an e-mail and sending it out to the few working moms you know. Ask them to forward it to one or two of their friends and agree on a time and place for a "get to know you" mixer.
- Volunteer to be the roster mom at day care or school. Collect the personal information for each family and compile it into a class roster. Now you are instantly indispensable.
- Show up for soccer practice or swimming lessons early. This is a great opportunity to meet other moms and form a carpool.
- Seek out other families who have children of a similar age; it will be easier for you to help each other out since you'll have all of the age-appropriate gear.
- Be selective; just because they have kids and a pulse doesn't mean they should be in the COT. Seek out people you are comfortable around.
- Whenever possible, reciprocate a good deed to another mom in need.

How Can You Tell If Someone Belongs in the COT?

There are those interlopers—people you think are in the COT until they burst out with some obnoxious, judgmental comment that sends you into a spiral of doubt for the next week or two. Or they think they're doing you a favor by telling you that your kid eats his own boogers, when of course you know that and you've been trying to get him to stop for the last eighteen months. How can you sort out the good from the bad? Ask yourself a few questions when interviewing your COT.

Situation	In the COT	NOT in the COT
You run into school and realize you forgot your kid's lunch at home.	Laughs at you, says she did the same thing last week, and offers to split her kid's bologna sandwich. Now your kid has lunch and you won't be an hour late to work.	Looks on in horror and says, "Well, I guess you could get some premade food at the grocery store around the corner. But that's so unhealthy."
Your kid climbs the net around the gorilla cage on the zoo field trip.	Helps you climb the fence to get him and laughs while you all dodge the flying poo.	Gasps in horror, mutters something about ADD, and calls security.
You screech into the parking lot at school at the last possible second.	Leaves you her cell phone number and says, "Call me next time you're stuck and I'll wait with the kids." Follows up the next day with an e-mail so you know she means it.	Looks at her watch, then sneers and peels out of the parking lot.
On your way out of school, your kid escapes your grasp and runs and hides because he thinks it's funny.	Yells, "I've got him" so you can breathe easier.	Shakes her head and simply says, "You've got your hands full!" No sh*t.
You flake out on moms' night because your boss just loaded on an extra project.	Completely understands. She was there last month. Fills you in on everything that went on, making you feel a part of things.	Is secretly pissed there's an empty seat at the table. Somehow this makes her look bad since she was the organizer.

Situation	In the COT	NOT in the COT
You mention you've just discovered your kid has some sort of learning or social issue.	Gets it and offers to help any way she can. Confesses her kid has been in speech for a year and still can't say the word "doggy."	Inside, she believes you've messed up. In fact she says she's been concerned for some time.
You tell jokes at your own expense or talk about how you've totally gone haywire that day.	Laughs with you and admits she's been dancing on the edge lately herself.	Doesn't laugh. Looks horrified. Huge red flag. How can you survive this without laughing?
You confide that you just aren't doing that well and are crying and sleeping a lot more than usual.	Listens intently and, when you are finished, tells you that you are not alone, that she too went through a funk, got some happy pills, and now is back in the groove.	Looks at you like you are a social misfit and tells you she thinks Tom Cruise is a hero and that postpartum depression can be cured with a few jumping jacks and chants.

Raising children is the hardest job we've ever had, and unless you're the nanny, it's unpaid. We really didn't anticipate how important it would be to get involved and engaged in the community. Now we know, and it has been worth every ounce of effort we have put into it. We've met amazing women along the way and have been saved by them more times than we can count. On the flip side, we've helped others a lot ourselves. We can tell you it feels really good to be helpful and to have the honor of being inside another woman's COT (and, by the way, we're on a sales conference next week and could really use someone to pick up our kids).

• •

We have a "walk pool" in our neighborhood. Four parents rotate days of the week when we walk eight to ten neighborhood kids to school. The walk is a highlight of my week—the kids love it, the neighbors smile as they drive by, and it makes me reconnect with what is most important: our community. It also makes me feel better knowing that there are other parents who have an eye out for my kids (this will become more important as they reach middle and high school) and enables me to build a relationship with neighborhood kids.

Liz, Mother of Two and Environmental Consultant

• •

Stay-at-Home Moms—Not the Enemy

Who says SAHMs are the enemy? That kind of thinking is so yesterday. Why must it be us against them? Leigh's best friend is the biggest ass-kicking stay-at-home mom ever. Why would she ever malign her? Can we all just admit that we don't make the same choices or aren't in the same financial situation and move on? Once you reconcile that notion, you can see what an incredible pillar of support we can all be to each other.

Inherently SAHMs have a little more flexibility with their time and might be in a good position to help you out on occasion. Just make sure you can reciprocate because that is how the COT works. SAHMs are not your personal slaves, and just because they aren't working outside the home doesn't mean that they are available to drive your child all over hell and back. That makes you a mooch and will only lead to you being the subject of every mid-morning PTA coffee klatch from this point forward. Remember, all moms need help, so perhaps you can barter something such as child care or rides or something else that would help them out.

YOUR WORK-LIFE COT

Work is a whole different setting that requires its own COT. After you return from maternity leave, life is just different. You have a whole new set of problems and concerns, and you have to be careful whom you talk to around the office. Not everyone is out to do you a favor—some sharks, believe it or not, are out to do you in. Confide in the wrong person and rumors will surface that you have your head in mommy land or are not very focused. Either of those scenarios does not bode well for you professionally. In order to navigate the office politics, you are going to need to distinguish friend from frenemy. Who in the office is worthy of being in your COT? Think about this carefully and use your best judgment to select a few colleagues whom you can trust when the going gets tough.

Saving Your Ass at Work Includes

- Running interference for you when you're running late
- Filling you in on the meeting you totally forgot
- Telling you when you're regularly looking like the dog's breakfast
- Giving you a heads-up when the boss starts to question your work
- Turning over her office as a safe place to cry when you lose it
- Providing a sounding board when you're struggling. ("Is it okay that my career is going nowhere because I need to leave every day at five p.m.?")
- Handing over a scarf when you're about to go into a big meeting, and you just realized you have spit-up on your blouse.

Situation	In the COT	NOT in the COT
You're late to the 9:00 a.m. sales briefing.	Provides cover. Makes VAGUE statement about you running a few minutes late because of an urgent work matter.	Gives WAY too much information on your morning routine; blabs that after you drop your kids off at school, you arrive closer to 9:30 a.m. on a regular basis.

Situation	In the COT	NOT in the COT
While riding in the office elevator, she overhears a conversation among leadership about a business matter that will implicate you and your team directly.	She marches right into your office and gives you a heads-up about the conversation she overheard. The rest is up to you.	Says nothing, thus making you look dumb in front of your boss and team.
You return to work after being out two days with a sick kid.	Asks you how your kid is doing first; then asks how she can help you get caught up on two days' worth of work.	Passive-aggressively asks where your portion of the presentation is.

Definitely NOT in the Circle of Trust

- Your boss
- Human resources
- Your department colleague who not so secretly wants your job
- The office gossip
- Anyone who reports to you
- Anyone who might use the info against you (and that could be quite a few people!)

If you are anything like us, chances are you are going to have some bad days at work. Perhaps your kid is going through a nasty bout of separation anxiety or your performance lately just stinks and you question whether you are doing the right thing by working. It's on those days that you just want to quit, pick up the kids, and go live off the grid. This is the perfect opportunity to lean on a trusted colleague. Often all it takes is a ten-minute conversation to realize that you are not alone, and it puts your problem in perspective and puts you back on track. But imagine if you didn't have that sounding board? Your sadness could turn into a spiraling loop of doubt, and you'd end up walking around scared of your own shadow. Not what you need. Worse yet, you could wind up walking into your boss's office a blubbering mess and blabbing about all of your personal problems. Then you'd have a real problem: your boss would think you were nuts and slowly begin to write you off.

● ●

Suddenly those women whom I didn't understand and snubbed for jetting out the door at five became the women whom I admired. I was worried they wouldn't accept me and that they knew my pre-mom secret thoughts (that they were lazy slackers). Once that baby came, it was as though I had sudden status in their secret society!

Michelle, Mother of Two and Developer

● ●

GO FORTH AND SPREAD THE GOOD DEEDS

Given that we spend more waking time at work than we do at home, it's no surprise that our colleagues can tell when we are a little off. Many times they are the first to notice. But now, with this many women watching your back, you've got no excuse for losing it (in public).

Taking Care of You: More Than the Three S's (Shower, Sh*t, and Shave)

Delusions

- I can clear my head if I just run to the grocery store by myself.
- Locking myself in the bathroom qualifies as "me time."
- Since I work, all my free time should be spent with my child(ren).
- I can't afford a spa day; I've got college to pay for.
- I'm sure my husband will surprise me with a _____ if I just drop enough hints.
- I can't justify exercise; I'm six loads behind on the laundry.

Has it finally dawned on you that no one, and by that we mean no one, is going to take care of you but you? If you are lucky, maybe you'll get a little love from your mom and the housekeeper, but don't hold your breath. Unless you're under the age of eighteen, it's probably time to give your mom a break. And the housekeeper is paid to look after you, and we can assure you if you didn't pay her, the nice treatment would stop. Sure, your husband might send you flowers every once in a while or call to tell you that there's a traffic hazard ahead—cute but not exactly the fix you were seeking. And your kids will draw you something sweet when the teacher asks. But taking care of you goes beyond the casual moments of appreciation— this is about the full-scale and constant war on keeping you from getting too out of whack.

We hate to load more responsibility on you—God knows you've got enough—but it's time to rejigger your priorities. You need to stop folding the laundry, stop all the insane errands, pull your head out of the oven, and start carving out a few moments of time for you. We know that things are going to slip. This time isn't just going to magically appear; it's going to require some sacrifice. You'll have to walk out of the house, even when you see piles of laundry, and somehow be OK with it.

We're not suggesting you spend weeks at a time vacationing with your girlfriends. Or take every Sunday off to spend hours at the spa, although that sounds about equal to a golf game, if anyone is keeping score. We simply want you to take the time to go for a walk, go to the gym, or read a few magazine articles without anyone interrupting you. If that sounds like too much to ask, you've got issues that must be addressed immediately.

Do You Know How Important a Pedicure Is?

Imagine how lovely it would be to have a break—a moment of true relaxation, a multi-minute span of silence, a moment without children wrapped around your leg—that is all about you. You may never have realized it before when you took it for granted, but that is exactly what a pedicure is.

By taking some time for yourself here and there, you are setting an example for your kids. Do you want them to believe—long past the point that it's either endearing or excusable—that the world completely revolves around them? Hell no! That everyone will, just like their moms, drop everything to ensure they make it to three birthday parties consecutively scheduled on a Sunday afternoon, despite the fact that Mommy has to catch the red-eye to New York that night? Or fast-forward a few years. If you've got a daughter, do you really want to train her to be a martyr? To teach her that she should always come third, fourth, or fifth to the kids, the husband, work, and the household chores? And on the flip side, if you've got a boy, do you want him to think that he should marry some spineless girl who would actually volunteer to be a perpetual doormat? We think you are smart enough to know the answer.

Want yet one more reason? It actually makes life worse for everyone if you don't get out of the house and get what you need. Sh*t rolls downhill, and if you're in perpetual Debbie Downer mode, the rest of the household will soon adopt your toxic persona. Now you're a mean mommy, the kids are trying to kill each other, and your husband is whining about his lame job and lack of a sex life to anyone who will listen. Ugh. Do everyone a favor and get out of the house.

Why Are You Doing This to Yourself?

Getting some time for ourselves is not an obvious choice for most of us. When all of our friends are telling us that they're secretly looking forward to their dental appointments just to get a few minutes to themselves, there is a collective issue. So why don't we try to prioritize time for ourselves?

If we actually carve out a few moments, someone—and we're not sure who exactly—is going to accuse of us of being bad moms. Carol Brady didn't go for walks to escape for a few minutes, and she didn't even have a job that kept her away from the kids. And we're not sure we can remember our moms taking time for themselves. So how could we? It's gotten to the point where we've imagined horrible scenarios if we spend just one night a month going out to dinner with girlfriends. The minute the front door closes behind us, all the neighborhood moms will start critiquing our mothering skills, followed by Child Protective Services screeching up with an ambulance and a few police cars in tow. Not likely. Chances are the guilt and bad mommy feelings are all our own, and we just need to get over it. Do you remember us talking about guilt? Time to get over it and go enjoy yourself just a little.

We believe that our kids deserve all of our free time. Yes, our kids deserve our unwavering love. And they've got it—even when they take a black Sharpie to Mommy's new sofa. But just because we headed back to our college reunion without them doesn't mean that we don't love them. Or if we go for a run on Saturday morning instead of sitting and watching *Little Einsteins*, it doesn't mean that we're about to give them up to the state. They don't need ALL of our free time. When we talk about escaping for a few moments, we're not talking about taking a few months off. We just want a few solid hours every once in a while to stop thinking about everyone else's needs and potty habits and desperately try to remember our own middle names.

There's simply too much to do. How could we leave the house when there's the largest pile of laundry you've ever seen by the washing machine and a week's worth of lunches needing to get packed? Have you noticed yet that the to-do list is perpetual and ever-expanding? That despite your level of organization the to-do list is never done? Time to put it down and relax. You're a working mom and one of the most efficient creatures on the planet. You will figure this out—even if it means skipping the laundry, offloading responsibility onto your husband or a paid professional, or picking up the groceries on your way home from a girls' weekend.

It makes us look selfish. A good mother puts herself last—after kids, husband, work, chores, etc. Whoever came up with this messed-up logic is a bad person, because this means that a good mother is guaranteed to be the family whipping post for the rest of her life. This we know to be true. We may be hard-wired to nurture, but we've got to turn that instinct on ourselves first so we have the energy and stamina to nurture those who truly need our services.

THAT'S WHAT YOU CALL A GOOD TIME?

It should be obvious by now that the definition of time to yourself is not what it once was. Regular nights out, laughing with friends over nice food and enough wine that you're in a stupor the following day . . . Last-minute weekend getaways to Napa, the Hamptons, Cape Cod, Vegas, wherever . . . All-day bike rides or hikes that exhaust you to the point of immobility . . . Shopping for hours and hours for the perfect pair of shoes or lipstick or something equally unimportant . . . Watching the latest blockbuster movie on opening night. It all sounds wonderful and extravagant and if you can pull even one of these things off, more power to you. But once we had kids, we had to assign a totally different definition to time to ourselves. The angst of finding a babysitter or depleting the college savings account to have time to ourselves messes with our heads and our ability to relax. God, it sucks. Why can't we be self-centered like we used to be without all the mulling it over?

What does it look like now? Warning, if you don't yet have kids and are considering having some soon, please avert your eyes as you will likely lose all will to procreate.

Our New Definition of Time to Ourselves
- Take the long way home. Purposefully take the back roads or get stuck in traffic so you can finish that cell-phone call with your girlfriend. Or simply enjoy the silence of a car all to yourself.
- Hang out in the driveway/down the street to relax, regroup, and breathe before you actually go in the door.
- Stop, drop, and drink—unwind at the bar of P.F. Chang's, the Cheesecake Factory, or some equally respectable suburban chain, while hubby cuts the kids' steaks.
- Get fifteen to thirty minutes of exercise—even if it's your sad-sack run around the block each week, at least it gets you out . . . alone.

- Take a trip to Starbucks prior to the grocery shopping.
- Get a haircut. It's a necessity but we've now somehow turned it into some sort of over-the-top luxury. Ooooh, someone shampooing your hair and rubbing your scalp, followed by—you guessed it—a haircut. Big deal, right? To a working mom, a two-hour haircut is akin to an all-day spa trip. You're alone, and someone is actually paying attention to you.
- Convince the kids and hubby to leave the house and then sit on the couch reading *People* magazine, *Us Weekly,* and *InTouch* all in one sitting. OMG, who knew that Britney was dating her agent and that Lisa Rinna did too much Restylane filler? What, Nicole Richie is pregnant?
- Lock the door while you take a shower. Now you can actually shave without your kids staring at your private parts for minutes on end.
- Tell the kids you've got to go poo-poo, and hide in the bathroom with a glass of wine and your cell phone.
- Claim, "We're out of _____," and head out for a long trip to the store to pick up whatever it is that you claimed you needed.

When Running Errands (Alone) Just Won't Cut It

Ladies, you don't need to tell us that it's not enough to sneak a furtive trip to the grocery store or lock yourself in for bath time. It sounds pathetic—a reality, but pathetic nonetheless. Sometimes you need to leave the screaming kids behind, trade your husband for sexual favors, and do the total reboot. It doesn't have to be anything fancy— just enough to reconfigure the molecules in the brain.

- **Girls' weekend.** Get away with your girlfriends—who are guaranteed not to ask you to help them find their keys or sunglasses or wallet or to beg for sugary cereal—and just relax. Make sure you are all on the same page (i.e., no one is pregnant, no one is nursing, and you can just cut loose and yuck it up). No point in jumping through the hoops of scheduling a girls' weekend if you're going to spend the whole time listening to someone else complain about their hemorrhoids. That's what baby showers are for.

- **A vacation by yourself.** The pre-kids us would never have thought this sounded fun. A vacation by yourself? What a waste of time. Well, the new us, the post-kids us, would love to spend a few days on our own—just relaxing by the pool, scheduling a few beauty appointments, even talking on the phone with friends. How great does that sound? And your chance of doing any of that with kids, or even your husband, is little to no chance in hell. Try it; what's the worst that could happen? Seriously, we've even considered checking in to the local dive hotel just for a night of peace.

- **Something new (that has regularly scheduled times).** When all other attempts to find time to yourself fail, it's time to push the issue. Schedule a weekly class or something that costs money and force yourself to get out of the house and separate yourself from the daily grind. And if you've paid good money for it, who is going to argue that you shouldn't go? If your husband isn't fully onboard, get him on board. Tell him you are going to therapy or have a work project or something.

All of these are likely going to require money. Which is why you need a slush fund. Call it the working mommy support fund—$20 a week and soon you've got some mad money. You work for a living, right? Last time you checked, you were indeed collecting a paycheck, so we recommend tithing a little to your mad money account. Just think, start with $20 a week, and in a year that will net you over a thousand dollars. Now with a little cash on hand, don't tell us you can't find a little fun and regroup. Ideally we'd love it if your husband was onboard, but if he's not, we say what he doesn't know won't hurt him. In the end he's going to benefit.

The "Big Getaway" for the Old You and the New You...

	Pre-Kids	Post-Kids
A Night Out		
Frequency	At least three nights a week	One time per month with friends (if you're lucky!) Once a week with spouse (again, if you're lucky and rich!)
Destination	Fancy restaurants, dives—doesn't matter if it's a five-minute walk or a three-hour drive	Someplace close by and superfast where parking isn't a challenge. For God's sake, we are paying a sitter to look for parking!
Duration	Marathon meals, complete with predinner cocktails, appetizers, desserts, after-dinner drinks, etc. (typically requires a "recovery" period the next day)	Really hurried meals since the babysitter has the meter running at $ per hour Not that much alcohol since you've got eight a.m. soccer practice to get to and a toddler who gets up with the birds
Participants	Usually spouse, friends, or some combination thereof Conversations about movies, pop culture, work, gossip, etc.	Friends or spouse, and rarely a combination (like you guys have time to hang out with mutual friends!) Conversations about kids, babysitters, schools, lack of sleep, and other peoples' parenting skills
A Weekend Getaway		
Frequency	Maybe once a quarter—more frequently if ski or beach houses are involved	Once a year—typically around anniversaries or birthdays

	Pre-Kids	Post-Kids
Destination	Beaches, mountains, Vegas, wine country—you name it	Someplace within driving distance and with no two-night minimum—everything costs double when you are paying a sitter
Duration	The full weekend—from Friday at 4:59 p.m. all the way to Sunday at 11:59 p.m.	One night—and make it home in time to see the kids when they wake up from nap
Retail Therapy		
Frequency	Whenever you feel the whim and for whatever speaks to you	When your girlfriends are telling you that it is no longer possible to wear that blouse without damaging your career prospects
Destination	Any shop you want to see! Doesn't matter the price or the merchandise—you've got plenty of time to browse.	Online—and if that doesn't work, a prearranged trip to the mall for which you had to trade a golf day with your husband
Duration	If it takes you all day to find the perfect shade of eye shadow, then so be it.	How quickly can you negotiate a parking space, wind your way around the racks, and commandeer a dressing room? Two-hour trip, tops.
Exercise		
Frequency	Almost every day Supplemented by weekend hikes, bike rides, etc.	Whenever you find the time—i.e., never
Destination	The fancy gym, the trailhead five miles away, etc.	Around the block, or if you are Leigh, you call "natural movement" exercise. Natural movement includes walking from the parking lot to the store or walking around your house. See . . . you're exercising.

	Pre-Kids	Post-Kids
Duration	As long as you could manage to keep moving! Weekend jaunts could take all day	Twenty minutes before you keel over, get distracted by housework, or the kids start screaming for more Cinnamon Toast Crunch
Beauty Routine		
Frequency	Weekly pedicures and manicures Monthly massages and facials (because we thought we needed to relax . . . ha!) Quarterly trips to the hair salon for a cut, color, and blowout	Pedicures only when the paint starts chipping (badly) and the heels are literally cracking open Facials, massages, wraps are all things of the past—we're on basic maintenance mode now. A 15-minute neck rub while getting your pedicure is the best you can hope for. Facials—try the St. Ives apricot scrub at Walgreens. Hair treatments only when the roots are excessively dark or gray. Skip the blowout—you've got to go grocery shopping and the meter is running.
Destination	Spas with fuzzy bathrobes or the fancy salon in the city	Local corner dive nail shop and hair salon that's open late on Thursday nights—who cares about the actual cut
Duration	Could take all day—but, boy, did you deserve it	You skip the leg massage at the nail salon because it takes too long

CARVING OUT THE TIME FOR YOURSELF (AKA "THE BARTER SYSTEM MAKES ITS WAY INTO YOUR HOME ECONOMY")

So how in the world do you actually find time to do all of this relaxing and rebooting? We're not going to lie to you. It's going to take trading favors with friends, your parents, and most especially your spouse. It might take some money for babysitters. It's also going to take a few creative stories. Don't let the money or the morality get in your way. This is all to save you mental angst, and it's cheaper than therapy or divorce.

Yes, it would be nice to believe that you and your spouse would suddenly just volunteer some free time to the other out of the goodness of your hearts. But however much you love each other and want to be nice, sometimes life gets too busy and even you forget that your husband would probably LOVE a few hours on his own to regroup. And we know from experience that until your spouse sees your head spin off your shoulders for the fourth time, he wholeheartedly believes that everything is fine on the home front. So it's established: unless you ask for time, you're probably not going to get it. And neither is your husband. You must rely on the barter system to survive. You ask for an hour and then you give an hour back. We're absolutely sure that you wouldn't just trade a boys' weekend in Vegas for nothing. You're no fool!

Table of Measurements and Equivalents

Activity	Free Time Equivalent
Bike rides/hikes/runs/other sports excursions	Simple hour for hour calculation (i.e., two-hour bike ride = two hours of free time)
Book club, poker night, bridge club, investment group, etc.	Three hours
Boondoggles (overnight trips to visit friends, etc.)	One for one equivalent

Activity	Free Time Equivalent
Business dinners of questionable importance	Four hours (after all, there is liquor and good food involved)
Cover-to-cover reading of *Vanity Fair*/magazine of your choice	Three hours
Golf game	Six hours
Mani/pedi	One hour
Spa trip (massage/facial, etc.)	Two hours
TV "events" (Oscars/Super Bowl/ weekend golf tournament)	Trade event for event, or chalk up the hours and trade for your choice
Uninterrupted time while "working from home"	One for one equivalent
Voluntary professional projects	One for one equivalent

Are They "Lies" If They Save You from Certain Insanity?

We want to provide you with a handy-dandy go-to list of excuses to buy you some time. OK, yes, technically, these are lies. Or, if you're feeling generous, omissions of fact rather than bald-faced lies. But apparently we're not the only ones who stretch the truth a bit to carve out a few minutes for ourselves. At least one of these has to sound familiar to even the most honest mom out there. Of course, in a perfect world, you wouldn't need these. Everything would be totally on the up-and-up and honesty the best policy, and so on. But here's the deal: sometimes it's a lot easier to simply say that grocery shopping took a lot longer than you expected, so that you could have the time to sit with your iced coffee for ten minutes before diving headfirst into the weekly shopping list. You need regular time to yourself alone. Not work, not date night, but time to yourself to remember who the hell you were before these aliens swooped in and stole your former identity.

"Excuses" to Get Some Free Time

- **Grocery shopping:** It's a good hour-long excuse and will buy you ten minutes on either end of the trip. If you're using it for more devious purposes, just remember to bring the groceries back home.

- **Work "emergencies":** How can anyone argue with that? It's a work emergency! Your paycheck depends on you taking care of this issue.

- **Friend in need:** No details necessary. Just race to the rescue of your friend(s) who wants to chat over an afternoon glass of Sauvignon Blanc.

- **Daddy's turn to put you to sleep:** It can also be Daddy's turn to give the kids a bath, read to the kids, etc. Buys you just enough time to read a section of the paper or catch up on all your TiVo'd shows. Ahhhh.

- **Doctor's appointment/dental emergency:** Tricky, since there needs to be some evidence of pain prior to the appointment or repair after the fact. Desperate times call for desperate measures, and when in need, sometimes you just have to cross your fingers and hope that you won't be found out.

- **Long lines:** When asked, "Where were you?" this excuse works brilliantly. "The lines were so long! It took forever!" Then get an exhausted look on your face, sit down, and say you need a few minutes to recover. Brilliant!

GUILT BOMBS AND OTHER HAZARDS OF FINDING FREE TIME

You know how busy you are and how valuable the five-minute period that you've desperately carved out for yourself actually is. No one else really gets that. So if someone starts to lob some guilt bombs your way, you've got to ignore them. They either haven't figured out a way to find time for themselves and they're jealous or they are truly nuts and they want you to be just as miserable as they are. No reason to pay attention to them either way. With confidence, you can say any of the following—we've got your back.

- "Yes, we did go on vacation for a week—without the kids. We all had a fabulous time, and my husband and I had the best sex of our lives. Can't do that with the kids sleeping on a pullout couch!"
- "Yes, I did go on a date midweek with my husband. Date night is our only time to have actual conversations that aren't constantly interrupted with 'She pinched me! Can I watch another *Arthur*?' Or, 'I'm hungry. Can you make me spaghetti and meatballs?'"
- "Uh-huh. That's my second glass of wine." Deliver this line with a smile on your face as if you're daring them to say one more thing about your penchant for wine.
- "Yes, I did get a massage/facial/etc. I saved my money and I went for it, and, boy, was it relaxing. Lord knows I deserve it."
- "Yep. The babysitter comes two nights a week. That way we've got a guaranteed date night, and I can goof off one night a week without relying on my husband to make it home in time. What I spend on the sitter I now save in therapy. You should try it."
- "Every Tuesday night I go out with my friends. In exchange, I trade my husband a new sexual position every Saturday night. Men are suckers for that kind of guaranteed action."
- "Yes, work gets out early on Fridays, but I still pick up the kids at the regular time. They love day care."

IT'S ALL UP TO YOU

We've done all we can. Given you the rationale, given you the ideas, and given you the excuses you need to get the hell out of the rut you're in and try to put yourself in a permanent good mood, or as close to it as you can set. But it's up to you to do it. No one knows as well as you when you've got to catch a break. There will be no magic mommy fairy who floats down and lets you know that it's OK to linger at the bookstore a bit longer than it takes to buy your kid's friend a birthday present.

Consider this a priority—just as much as making sure that your kids are well cared for, you and your husband are happy, and you've got enough money in the bank to pay one month's mortgage when it all comes crashing down. You deserve it. If no one else knows that, we do. We've got your back.

Yes, It's Hard, but We're Not About to Change It

No one said this was going to be easy. They also never really said exactly how hard it would be, but no matter. If you were to ask us if we'd ever trade it all in, we'd say "NO!" Sure, it would be nice to work less and be paid more, but that's kind of like saying it would be nice to eat gallons of ice cream a day and look like a supermodel.

Would we trade in the "mommy" part of being working moms? Oh, hell no. There is no way. As hard as this is, it's the most joy we've ever experienced. A single smile from our kids or watching a simple accomplishment, like peeing without touching one's penis or recognizing the difference between an S and a 5, is enough to fill our hearts. And would we trade in our spouses for better models or at least ones who come home at a predictable hour? No, no, no, no, no! They are pretty great guys and outstanding dads. Besides, who else would tolerate our loony behavior and whacked-out senses of humor?

You've read the book, and you know that there is no other way for us to finish but with a completely incomplete and inadequate chart of why there is overwhelming joy in our lives because we are WORKING MOMS!

Amy's List of the Joys of Being a Working Mom, with Two Amazing Kids and a Super-adorable, Loving, Smart, and Funny Spouse	Leigh's List of the Joys of Being a Working Mom, with One BRILLIANT Kid and an Accepting, Funny, Super-talented, Sometimes Grouchy but Always Lovable Spouse
Instead of saying, "I love you, too," my youngest says, "I love you and love you and love you."	Hearing my son ask, "Do you want to hold hands, Mommy? I love holding hands cuz you're my best fwend!"
I am in awe when I look out the window into our yard and see my two boys laughing with each other.	When I say, "I love you," my son responds with "I love you sooo much it hurts!"
My oldest son defines a good time as hanging out with me and snuggling. How many more months/weeks/days/minutes will he still feel that way?	Overhearing my husband brag about me to his friends; totally unnecessary but it really drives home the point that he's proud of me.
Dwight can make me laugh when I'm at my most stressed and miserable.	Feeling like I belong in two clubs, the mommy club and the professional club.
Dwight reminds me to see the glass half full, the silver lining, and the bright side of life.	When I make a mistake, hearing my son say, "It's OK, Mommy, everyone makes mistakes . . . even mommies."
Every morning Dwight makes my coffee, and he puts the laundry away.	Working with lots of smart and engaging people. I LOVE learning, and my career has allowed me to learn every day for the last nineteen years.
Dwight can drive my family through horrific traffic in Boston and emerge needing only a beer and a few minutes to himself. No one else could do that.	My job is so different and challenging every day. Ninety-five percent of the time I love the challenge, The other 5 percent can be really tough, but it forces me to grow.
My job is fun and challenging—nine times out of ten. What more can you ask for?	My husband's sage advice: There are benefits to being married to someone who has lived a little longer on this planet. He simply has more experience and knows how and when to talk me off the ledge.

Acknowledgments

A huge thank you to Danielle Svetcov, our agent, without whom this book would never have happened. She coached, encouraged, and cajoled us through this process, and her never-wavering faith and incredibly calm demeanor were just what these two rookies needed. We were amazed at all of the ladies who told us their stories—all very funny and honest and, at times, heart-wrenching. It's not easy to put it out there (trust us), and so for your faith in our project we thank you. Reading your stories reaffirmed our commitment to making sure that they were *shared*. And a huge thank you to all of the stressed-out working moms who read the book in its early stages, gave us feedback, and helped us improve it (Jill, Jen, Kelly, Kelly, and Kelly, Julie, Mary Catherine, Meredith, Stephanie, Jenny, Stef, and Cath—superheroes all). Finally, to Wellington's Wine Bar for giving us safe haven, free Wi-Fi, killer wine, and a comfy place to cuss and discuss. Our butts have worn holes in that leather couch.

Thank you to our bosses, Katherine and Tricia. Your support, encouragement, and understanding were invaluable and just what we needed when we got hit with lice, the flu, ear infections, and field trips—all in the same month. And to all the women we work with who paved the way before us . . . you made us realize it was possible. There are so many we can't name them all, but we would especially like to acknowledge Laura for her support of working mothers. And to our colleagues Abby, Aaron, Aaron, and Jill, thanks for covering your share of maternity leaves. You made us look good and suffered tremendously.

To Lauren, who recognized that working moms need practical tips, a good laugh, and the confidence that they are not alone. We hate to say that you had the Crazy Eyes, but we suspect that you knew *exactly* what we were talking about.

The fact that I'm writing the acknowledgments is a good sign. It means we are so close to the finish line that I can taste it. I have to start by thanking my husband, Jack, for insisting that I seize this opportunity even though he knew it would affect him greatly. I would not have done it without his blessing, and I certainly couldn't have done it without his support. Thank you, Jack, for following through on your promise to help me so that I could do this, and for your patience; I know there were moments when I was driving you absolutely crazy with my schedule, moods, and disappearing acts. I also know it was hard—and I had a few Crazy Eyes relapses—but fortunately you talked me away from the ledge in a way only you can do. Thanks also to my son, Jack Jack, who truly is my favorite little dude. Without you I wouldn't be in this "mom club," and life would be so dull. I love you more than Indian food, and that's some kind of love. Someday you will grow up and read this, and I want you to know that even though I went through some rough patches, I never once, not once, wished life were any other way (OK, I did buy a few lottery tickets that first year). To my mom, whom I lost six years ago, thank you for encouraging me and making me believe in myself. I miss you every day.

Now to my ladies. Thank you, all of you, you know who you are, for encouraging me and for listening and for the constant progress checks. It's because of you that I kept going, even though there were many times I wanted to quit. But being the people pleaser that I am, I didn't want to let you down; so here's to Lori, Patti, Katie, Jen C., Susan M., Nada, Susan C., Jane, Steph N., Jen M., Michele, Christine, Emily R., Jenny O., Carla K., Gabrey, Amy K., Jee, and Emma. Last, to Amy, "Thank you" seems insufficient, but I gotta start somewhere. Thank you for being goal-oriented. Thank you for dreaming that this could be possible, because I'm not so sure I would've thought it up. Thank you and your parents for putting you through those good schools so I could benefit from your formatting skills on the computer and for those incredible outlines. *Gawd*, where would I be without those outlines? They are magic—I can do anything with an Amy outline. Thanks for being patient when I ran into that nasty jag of writer's block. I hope I made up for it with some of my organizational prowess. Thank you for being such an incredible friend and for loving Sauvignon Blanc as much as I do. I'm convinced it sparked some creativity. And finally, thanks for your wisdom and advice. You've never steered me wrong.

—Leigh

Okay, I'll admit it: Working a full-time job, being a mom to two crazy boys, *and* writing this book was *hard*. Then add all the curveballs that life throws, and it's a wonder that I didn't get Crazy Eyes yet again. I would not have been able to write this book without Dwight. He is an amazing, supportive husband, and he helped me get it to the finish line, despite the craziness that takes over both our lives and the fact that he doesn't think he comes out smelling like a rose. In my humble opinion, he is one of the best human beings on the planet. Without his love, kindness, and patience, I would not have had the guts to write. He thinks I can do things that I'm fairly certain I would never have had the courage to try without him cheering me on. He makes me a better person. And if our children turn out anything like him, we will be blessed. My kids are a constant source of inspiration and amazement and the recipients of fierce, unconditional love. They will be reading soon . . . and when they do, I want them to know that I wouldn't change a thing about our life. And that they should really try to refrain from using four-letter words. . . . Thank you to my parents and sister, who help my kids, and who love them, and who offer invaluable weekly babysitting, the occasional toilet installation service, and amazing free meals. We are so fortunate to live only one freeway exit away, and I appreciate your help. To the "wenches": Remember the night that I was completely exhausted and overcome with Crazy Eyes and we went out to dinner and I ended up fainting and you picked me up off the ground? And the entire restaurant thought I was drunk (even though I hadn't had anything to drink)? Good times! Thank you for dusting me off and helping me through. It's easy to find the humor in life with you as friends. Who else would you call but a wench when you've locked yourself in the closet to escape your own screaming children? How did I get lucky enough to make such terrific friends and to have them since kindergarten? Finally, to Leigh, I could not imagine a better person with whom to work on this project. You got me to write like I talk, to say what I mean, and to believe that we could pull this off. Without you, at the very least, the book would have been half the length and most likely in outline form . . . It certainly wouldn't have been as much fun. I never knew that one of the benefits of being a working mom was the chance to make a truly great friend.

—Amy

Resources

Babysitters

Your best bet might be Craigslist or referrals from your mom friends.
www.sittercity.com (Check availability in your area.)

Books

Breastfeeding

Colburn-Smith, Cate, and Andrea Serrette. *The Milk Memos: How Real Moms Learned to Mix Business with Babies—and How You Can, Too.* New York: Tarcher/Penguin, 2007.

Huggins, Kathleen. *The Nursing Mother's Companion.* Boston: Harvard Common Press, 1999.

Pryor, Gale, and Kathleen Huggins. *Nursing Mother, Working Mother: The Essential Guide to Breastfeeding Your Baby Before and After You Return to Work,* rev. ed. Boston: Harvard Common Press, 2007.

Child Rearing (Sleep, Health, and Everything Else)

Ezzo, Gary, and Robert Buckman. *On Becoming Baby Wise: Giving Your Infant the Gift of Nighttime Sleep,* 4th ed. Sisters, Ore.: Parent-Wise Solutions, 2006.

Hogg, Tracy, with Melinda Blau. *Secrets of the Baby Whisperer: How to Calm, Connect, and Communicate with Your Baby.* New York: Ballantine, 2001.

Karp, Harvey. *The Happiest Baby on the Block: The New Way to Calm Crying and Help Your Newborn Baby Sleep Longer.* New York: Bantam, 2002.

Shelov, Steven P., et al., eds. *Caring for Your Baby and Young Child: Birth to Age 5,* 5th ed. Elk Grove Village, Ill.: The American Academy of Pediatrics, 2009.

Spock, Dr. Benjamim. *Dr. Spock's Baby and Child Care,* 8th ed., updated by Robert Needleman. New York: Pocket Books, 2004.

Cooking

Barnard, Melanie. *Essentials of Slow Cooking: Recipes and Techniques for Delicious Slow-Cooked Meals* (Williams-Sonoma). Birmingham, Ala.: Oxmoor House, 2008.

Kolpas, Norman. *Food Made Fast: Slow Cooker* (Williams-Sonoma). Birmingham, Ala.: Oxmoor House, 2006.

Funny Reads

Armstrong, Heather B. *It Sucked and Then I Cried: How I Had a Baby, a Breakdown, and a Much Needed Margarita*. New York: Simon Spotlight Entertainment, 2009.

Ashworth, Trisha, and Amy Nobile. *Dirty Little Secrets from Otherwise Perfect Moms*. San Francisco: Chronicle Books, 2004.

Ashworth, Trisha, and Amy Nobile. *I Was a Really Good Mom Before I Had Kids: Reinventing Modern Motherhood*. San Francisco: Chronicle Books, 2007.

Mellor, Christie. *The Three Martini Playdate: A Practical Guide to Happy Parenting*. San Francisco: Chronicle Books, 2004.

Wilder-Taylor, Stefanie. *Sippy Cups Are Not for Chardonnay, and Other Things I Had to Learn as a New Mom*. New York: Simon Spotlight Entertainment, 2004.

Pregnancy

Iovine, Vicki. *The Girlfriends' Guide to Pregnancy*. New York: Pocket Books, 2007.

Kropp, Tori. *The Joy of Pregnancy: The Complete, Candid, and Reassuring Companion for Parents-to-Be*. Boston: Harvard Common Press, 2008.

Murkoff, Heidi, and Sharon Mazel. *What to Expect When You're Expecting*, 4th ed. New York: Workman, 2008.

Serious Reads

Ashworth, Trisha, and Amy Nobile. *I'd Trade My Husband for a Housekeeper: Loving Your Marriage After the Baby Carriage*. San Francisco: Chronicle Books, 2009.

Hochschild, Arlie Russell, and Anne Machung. *The Second Shift*. New York: Penguin, 2003.

Meers, Sharon, and Joanna Stober. *Getting to 50/50: How Working Couples Can Have It All by Sharing It All*. New York: Bantam, 2009.

Shipman, Claire, and Katty Kay. *Womenomics: Write Your Own Rules for Success*. New York: HarperCollins, 2009.

Waldman, Ayelet. *Bad Mother: A Chronicle of Maternal Crimes, Minor Calamities, and Occasional Moments of Grace*. New York: Doubleday, 2009.

Breastfeeding Paraphernalia

Breast Pumps, Supplies, Bras, and Hands-Free Gizmos and Gadgets

www.amazon.com

www.ameda.com

www.babiesrus.com

www.barenecessities.com (bras)

www.breastpumpdeals.com

www.breastpumpsdirect.com

www.glamourmom.com (Leigh's favorite nursing camisole!)

www.medelabreastfeedingus.com

www.mommygear.com (bras)

www.motherhood.com (bras)

Child-Care Resources

Tips to Selecting Quality Day Care

www.babycenter.com/0_how-to-find-good-daycare_5924.bc

www.thenewparentsguide.com/choosing-a-daycare-center.htm

www.nyc.gov/html/doh/html/dc/dctips.shtml (specific to New York, but we love
their chart of questions to ask)

www.wikihow.com/Find-Excellent-Day-Care

Au Pair Information and Agencies

www.aupaircare.com

www.aupairinamerica.com

www.aupairusa.org

Nanny Information (all things related to finding and employing a nanny)

www.nanny.org/

Nanny Contracts

www.4nannytaxes.com (10 tips for writing a nanny contract)

www.4nannytaxes.com/forms/workagreement-livein.pdf (live-in nanny contract)

www.4nannytaxes.com/forms/workagreement-liveout.pdf (live-out nanny contract)

www.babycenter.com/0_printable-childcare-contract_5940.bc

www.sitterservice.com (search sample nanny contract)

Nanny Payroll Services

www.breedlove-online.com
www.gtm.com
www.nannychex.com
www.nannypayroll.com

Cooking Websites
www.allrecipes.com (great iPhone application!)
www.epicurious.com (great because you punch in the ingredients you have, and it
    will kick out a recipe based on what you have!)
www.foodnetwork.com
www.simplyrecipes.com
www.slowandsimple.com (great slow cooker recipes)
www.williams-sonoma.com (go to the recipe section)

**Housecleaning Services (your best bet might be Craigslist or a referral, but
here are some national services)**
www.merrymaids.com
www.servicemagic.com

Internet Resources for All Things a Mother Would Need
www.amazon.com (search in listmania for great lists)
www.babycenter.com
www.mommytrackd.com
www.whattoexpect.com

The Law and Pregnancy

ADA (Americans with Disabilities Act)

www.ada.gov

Employment Law

www.eeoc.gov/types/pregnancy.html
www.workplacefairness.org/pregnancy

FMLA (Family Medical Leave Act)

www.dol.gov/esa/whd/fmla

Leave Resources

www.parents.com/pregnancy/my-life/maternity-paternity-leave/maternity-leave-
by-state/

www.parents.com/pregnancy/my-life/maternity-paternity-leave/maternity-leave-
rights/

Magazines / Websites

Fit Pregnancy: www.fitpregnancy.com

Parenting: www.parenting.com

Parents: www.parents.com

Pregnancy: www.pregnancymagazine.com

Working Mother: www.workingmother.com

Maternity Clothes

www.babygap.com

www.bellydancematernity.com

www.destinationmaternity.com

www.doulashop.com (belly band)

www.duematernity.com

www.expectingcomfort.com (belly band)

www.japaneseweekend.com

www.momsthewordmaternity.com

www.oldnavy.com

Online Family Calendar

www.cozi.com (free—just create an account)

www.google.com (free—just create an account)

Through a Mobile Me Account on Apple (Amy and Leigh use this option. Must pay
annual subscription fee of approximately $99.)

Online Grocery

www.freshdirect.com (New York metro area)

www.harristeeter.com (for states in the Southeast)

www.mashable.com/2008/06/05/online-grocery-shopping/ (a terrific article with
a long list of online grocery stores for home delivery all around the country)

www.netgrocer.com

www.peapod.com (to eleven major metropolitan areas)

www.safeway.com (where there's a Safeway)

Online Shopping Resources (or where we spend our online dollars)

www.amazon.com

www.babiesrus.com

www.cvs.com

www.diapers.com

www.drugstore.com

www.oldnavy.com

www.riteaid.com

www.target.com

www.walgreens.com

Personal Assistants

www.asksunday.com

www.getfriday.com

Price Comparison Websites (find the best price online for anything!)

www.bizrate.com

www.pricegrabber.com

www.shopzilla.com

Travel Tips

Voice over Internet (stay connected with your family while traveling)

www.skype.com (create an account and it's free)

www.tripit.com (organize and share your travel plans online)

Index